AF688760

"Legal Issues in Japanese Real Estate Investment manages to distill a broad range of technical legal sources, judicial and public policy interpretations, market customs, recent trends and the author's practical execution experience into a clear, readable and comprehensive guide to real estate transactions in Japan. I am certain this volume will become an indispensable resource to Japan market practitioners of all experience levels."
Thomas Silecchia
Managing Partner, Merchant Capital K.K.

"This is the most comprehensive book in English I have read explaining the Japanese legal framework for real estate investments with particular focus on issues important to foreign investors."
Alexander Jampel
Partner, Baker & McKenzie, Tokyo, Japan
Member, Baker & McKenzie Asia Pacific Structured Real Estate
Steering Committee

"This book is an important contribution to the internationalization of the real estate market in Japan. Most of the content has never made it into English before and this should help international investors get more active in Japan."
Seth Sulkin
President and CEO, Pacifica Capital K.K.

"An excellent overview of some of the key topics in Japan real estate investment."
Theodore Seltzer
Partner, Morrison & Foerster LLP

Legal Issues in Japanese Real Estate Investment

Jeff Wynkoop

Legal Issues in Japanese Real Estate Investment

Copyright © 2012 by Jeff Wynkoop

All rights reserved. No portion of this book may be reproduced, stored in a retrieval system, or transmitted in any form or by any means -- electronic, mechanical, photocopy, recording, scanning, or other -- without the prior written permission of the publisher. Published by SCW Publishing, Costa Mesa, California. ISBN 978-0-9882174-0-9.

Printed in the United States of America

Table of Contents

Preface

My goal in writing this book is to provide an introduction to legal issues in Japanese real estate as well as to make a small contribution to the existing body of knowledge about Japan in English. Japan can be daunting to the uninitiated, and in the past I have found there were very few good English resource materials about Japanese real estate. Nevertheless, it is not meant to contain an exhaustive explanation of every subject, and can only supplement the numerous Japanese language materials already on the market.

The original concept for this work was to put together a short explanation of twenty topics of potential interest to foreign investors. I have tried to pick topics which are distinctive to Japan, and the subjects range from specific laws to investment vehicles to more regulatory topics. There are many other subjects which could be discussed, and I found in the course of working on the manuscript that some subjects required a much more thorough explanation than others, which accounts for the varying length of the chapters.

The contents are intended not only for foreign real estate professionals and investors, but also for those engaged in the study of comparative law. The chapters have thus been written to be broad in scope, and there may be some sections too elementary for certain readers, and some sections too academic or technical for others. It is difficult to put a reference book together that is suitable for all readers in every situation, regardless of their varying legal backgrounds, real estate knowledge, investment experience, and degrees of familiarity with Japan.

Commercial real estate transactions in Japan resemble transactions in many other parts of the world. In most cases, deals are thoroughly documented by attorneys representing each of the parties, and purchasers (or their representatives) carry out sometimes lengthy due diligence procedures. Japan is a civil law country (in contrast to the common law systems in the United States or the United Kingdom), and the legal rules which apply to specific situations are derived chiefly from written legal codes enacted by the national legislature. In addition, Japan has a unitary system of government, meaning the national laws concerning real estate generally apply throughout the entire country, although local and municipal ordinances also play a role.

This book can only supply a starting point, and the contents are not intended to be relied on nor used as legal advice with respect to any issues arising in any specific situation. However, the explanations can assist in acquiring an initial understanding of the various subjects, to be followed up with specific guidance from Japanese legal professionals. I hope that this work can play a small part in moving the international understanding of Japanese real estate issues forward.

I would also like to thank Alex Jampel for his valuable comments on the final draft.

Jeff Wynkoop
November 2012

Disclaimer

This book is intended to be used as a reference resource only. Although the author has made every effort to ensure the accuracy and completeness of the information presented, Japanese legal rules and customs may substantially differ from the contents hereof in any given case. The contents are not intended to be relied on nor construed to be advice with respect to any dispute or legal issue. In addition, the laws and customs concerning Japanese real estate transactions change over time, and in the future the matters explained herein may be subject to substantial revision. Any opinions expressed herein are the author's alone, and the author shall not be liable for any fees, losses or damages arising from any use of the contents hereof. All rights reserved. ©2012

1 The Real Estate Transactions Law

I. Application of the Real Estate Transactions Law

The purpose of the **Real Estate Transactions Law** ("RETL") is to regulate individuals and entities *engaged in the business of real estate transactions* in Japan. One way it does this is by generally requiring such parties to apply for and receive an RETL license prior to beginning business. There are, however, various exceptions to application of the law, and certain trust banks and financial institutions are exempted from the licensing requirements as well. Whether an RETL license is required prior to engaging in real estate transactions in Japan can best be understood by analyzing the relevant legal meanings of 'engaged in the business,' 'real estate,' and 'transactions.'

To be **Engaged in the Business** of real estate transactions as defined under RETL case law, one must have "the intention to carry out continuous and recurring transactions in land and/or buildings with multiple and indeterminate parties." Accordingly, based on this definition companies are normally permitted to sell land or buildings to their own employees without an RETL license, since a company's employees are not legally considered to be 'indeterminate parties.' Further, a company or person who wishes to sell a parcel of land or building in a one-time transaction does not need to obtain a prior RETL license. However, if an entity wishes to sell multiple parcels of land or buildings to multiple and indeterminate third parties, either alone or through a real estate agent or intermediary, not only the agent or intermediary, but also the transacting entity must have an RETL license. The RETL does not specify whether the 'business' of real estate transactions must be for profit, although there is case law which generally indicates that a profit motive should be present.

The definition of **Real Estate** under the RETL refers to land and/or buildings and excludes roads, rivers, parks and any land where residential, commercial or industrial use is prohibited. Typically any land where a building is or may be legally located falls under the definition, and registration of ownership in the relevant legal register is not material. In addition, not only transactions involving a building in its entirety, but also transactions with respect to specific sections of a building (such as a condominium) are considered to be transactions in 'real estate.'

Transactions are defined under the RETL as the act of buying, selling or exchanging buildings or land on one's own account, or acting as an agent or intermediary for buying, selling, exchanging or *leasing* land or buildings for third parties. It is important to note the exception here that the leasing of land or buildings on one's own account, as opposed to acting as an intermediary or agent in leasing another's property, is not considered to be a 'transaction' under the law. As a result, if an owner wishes to lease out (as opposed to sell) multiple parcels of land or buildings to third parties through a real estate agent, only the real estate agent is required to have an RETL license.

II. Setting up a Licensed Business under the Real Estate Transactions Law

There are five basic steps for setting up a licensed real estate transactions business under the RETL. These five steps are: (1) **Setting up an Office** in compliance with the RETL regulations, (2) **Applying for an RETL License**, (3) **Receiving the License**, (4) **Depositing Indemnity Money** (*eigyou hoshoukin*) with the relevant **Government Depository** (*kyoutakujo*) or **Joining the RETL Guarantor Association** (*takuchi tatemono torihikigyou hoshou kyoukai*), and (5) **Sending Written Notice** (with receipts attached) **to the RETL Licensing Authority** evidencing the business has joined the RETL guarantor association or deposited the appropriate amount with the relevant government depository. Legally, an RETL business may only begin engaging in real estate transactions after all of the above steps have been completed, and the entire process usually takes less than three months.

To apply for an RETL license, an individual or company must first set up an office in compliance with the RETL to have a valid address from which to submit the license application. To set up an RETL office, an individual or company must, among other requirements, (1) display "in a place easy for the public to see" an official **Real Estate Company Sign** (*hyoushiki*) under Art. 50 of the RETL, listing the contents required pursuant to applicable ministerial ordinance, (2) display "in a place easy for the public to see" an **Indication of Fees** within the specified legal limit under Art. 46, Paragraph 4 of the RETL, (3) set up and maintain a **Transaction Book** (*choubo*), which is a written register of the basic details of each real estate transaction (date, parties, addresses, size of property, fees received, etc.) for each fiscal year under Art.49 of the RETL, to be stored for at least five years from the end of the relevant fiscal year, (4) set up and maintain a **Register of Employees** (*juugyouin meibo*) under Art. 48, Paragraph 3 of the RETL, with an indication of whether each employee is a certified Real Estate Transaction Manager or not, to be stored for at least ten years since the last entry, and (5) employ the requisite number of certified Real Estate Transaction Managers for each office in accordance with Art. 15 of the RETL. The **Ministry of Land, Infrastructure, Transport, and Tourism** ("MLIT") has established these rules in order to set forth a minimum legal framework that can easily be complied with not only by large multinational corporations but also by individual RETL business operators. Please note that the above office requirements apply to the main office and every branch of an RETL-licensed company engaging in the real estate transactions business (branches not engaging in the RETL business are exempt, but if a branch is engaged, then the company's main office must also comply).

Next, the RETL license applicant must submit the license application to the competent licensing authority. The competent licensing authority is the prefecture where the RETL office is located, or in the event two or more RETL offices located in two different prefectures are being set up, the licensing authority is the MLIT by way of the prefecture where the main office is located. It generally takes one to two months to receive an RETL license after filing an application, and usually before the license is sent out, a person from the local chapter of either the **Real Estate Transactions Business Association** (*takuchi tatemono torihikigyou kyoukai*) or the **All Japan Real Estate Federation** (*zennihon fudousan kyoukai*) will visit the RETL office. RETL licenses expire every five years, although in the usual case they can be renewed.

One of the most important requirements for receiving (and maintaining) an RETL license is the general rule that per office one out of every five full-time employees engaged in the RETL business must be a certified Real Estate Transaction Manager (*takuchi tatemono torihiki shuninsha* or '*takken*'). Thus if an individual would like to apply for an RETL license, the individual should either be a certified Real Estate Transaction Manager or hire at least one certified Real Estate Transaction Manager as a full-time employee. Further, as the individual's business grows and the owner wants to hire more employees, the one-to-five ratio for Real Estate Transaction Managers to regular employees must be maintained (two out of every ten employees, three out of every 11 employees, and so on).

If an RETL-licensed company comes to have less than the one-to-five ratio after receiving the license, under Art. 15, Paragraph 3 of the RETL, the company must take corrective action within 14 days (*e.g.*, hire the requisite number of certified Real Estate Transaction Managers). After 14 days, if there are no new hires, the company should cease operations until the ratio is met, or the company will be in breach of the RETL. Breach of this rule can result in a monetary fine (Art. 82, RETL), a suspension of the RETL license (Art. 65, Paragraph 2, RETL), *and* a loss of the ability to renew the RETL license at expiration for a period of time (Art. 5, Paragraph 3-2, RETL).

There are many other rules which apply to RETL business operators to supplement the above requirements. For example, licensed real estate companies may not lend out their corporate name to other companies to allow them to engage in real estate transactions under the borrowed name (*meigigashi no kinshi*, Art. 13, RETL), *ask* for fees in excess of the maximum amounts allowed under the RETL (whether actually received or not, Art. 47, Paragraph 2, RETL), or engage in deceptive advertising practices (Art. 32, RETL). Moreover, under Art. 9 of the RETL, RETL business operators must send a written notification to their licensing authority within 30 days of the following amendments: (1) a change in corporate name, (2) a change in name or location of an RETL office, (3) a change in name of company director or responsible manager as designated by ministerial ordinance, or (4) a change in name of any RETL office's certified Real Estate Transaction Managers.

III. What is a certified Real Estate Transaction Manager?

A certified Real Estate Transaction Manager is a real estate professional who prepares and provides oral explanations and written disclosure materials (such as the **Explanation of Important Matters** document described in the next Chapter) for parties to Japanese real estate transactions. In practice, they also usually provide services similar to real estate agents found in other countries around the world. Please note that one does not have to be a certified Real Estate Transaction Manager in order to work in Japan as a real estate agent (*i.e.*, to assist customers in finding suitable properties or tenants/buyers), provided the agent works for an RETL-licensed company.

In order to become a *certified* Real Estate Transaction Manager, a person must (1) pass a minimum competency exam covering the legal, tax and regulatory rules for buying, selling, exchanging, and leasing land or buildings in Japan, (2) register with the local government after accumulating a minimum of two years of experience working in the real estate industry or after completing additional coursework and an additional exam deemed equivalent to obtaining two years of experience in Japanese real estate transactions, and (3) complete all additional registration procedures and receive an official Real Estate Transaction Manager certificate. The Institute for Promoting Real Estate Transactions in Japan (*fudousan tekisei torihiki suishin kikou*) reports that as of March 31st, 2012, there were 899,958 registered Real Estate Transaction Managers in Japan. (A *registered* Real Estate Transaction Manager has completed step 1 and 2 above only. The reason the number of registered (not certified) Real Estate Transaction Managers is tracked is registration is valid for life, but the certification must be periodically renewed. Sometimes Real Estate Transaction Managers keep their certification status inactive, for example, if they are not working at an RETL-licensed company for a period of time.) Further, the Institute reports as of March 31st, 2012, there were 123,979 RETL license holders (103,802 businesses and 20,177 licensed individuals). (The procedure for becoming an RETL license holder is explained in Section II above.)

IV. What roles do Real Estate Transaction Managers perform?

In addition to acting as real estate agents, Real Estate Transaction Managers perform a type of statutory consumer protection role in Japanese real estate transactions. As a general rule, under Japanese law there are three acts only Real Estate Transaction Managers are authorized to carry out for RETL-licensed companies: (1) the required *pre-contract oral* explanation called the explanation of important matters (*juuyou jikou setsumei*, also known as the '*juusetsu*'), (2) the required *pre-contract written* explanation of important matters (described in the next Chapter), and (3) the required *post-contract written* explanation. To protect tenants, buyers and parties to a property exchange, **Article 35** of the RETL requires RETL-license holders have a certified Real Estate Transaction Manager provide a pre-contract oral explanation of specific matters concerning the transaction property, with a written explanation of such matters stamped by a certified Real Estate Transaction Manager. In addition, in accordance with **Article 37** of the RETL, RETL-license holders are generally required to provide to both the purchaser and seller (or landlord and tenant or each exchange party) a post-contract written explanation of certain contract details in the executed real estate transaction contract, with the written Article 37 explanation stamped by a certified Real Estate Transaction Manager.

Real Estate Transaction Managers also typically perform a variety of services other than providing the oral and written explanations described above. They help buyers and sellers connect by recording relevant data and searching for potential transaction partners in the **Real Estate Information Network System** (REINS). (REINS is the Japanese multiple listing service and there are separate databases for the four main regions of Japan: Eastern, Central, Kinki, and Western Japan.) They also research property registration records and compile a list of existing legal and regulatory issues in the course of drafting the explanation of important matters. Perhaps owing to the relatively small number of Japanese lawyers, for smaller deals Real Estate Transaction Managers sometimes prepare first drafts of leases or purchase and sale agreements modeled on sample agreements published by the MLIT, and also provide basic guidance to clients with respect to various legal, tax and regulatory issues.

V. Consequences for Violating the RETL

As can be expected, the legal penalties for violating the RETL vary with the severity of the type of breach. For example, the penalty for operating a real estate transactions business without a license is up to three years incarceration and/or a JPY three million fine, while the fine for operating an office without the required number of Real Estate Transaction Managers is not more than JPY one million. It is also possible for a company's license to be revoked or suspended for a material breach of the RETL (although normally not for more than one year), in which case the company may not renew its license for five years from the date of revocation (or suspension in the event of a 'material' reason for the suspension).

It is important for RETL-license holders to avoid breaches of the RETL which can trigger a fine or incarceration. One reason for this is that an RETL license must be renewed once every five years, and if a prison sentence or fine is levied for an RETL violation, the license holder is not allowed to renew its license for five years from the date of the fine (or end of the prison sentence) (Art. 5, Paragraph 3-2, RETL). Accordingly, a finable breach of the RETL can have severe ramifications for a company wishing to conduct a real estate transactions business in Japan.

2 The Explanation of Important Matters

The **Explanation of Important Matters** (*juuyou jikou setsumeisho* or "Explanation") is a disclosure document legally required under **Article 35** of the **Real Estate Transactions Law** ("RETL"). It is to be issued by businesses licensed under the RETL to purchasers, tenants, or both parties in a property exchange ("Purchaser, etc.") every time the business sells or exchanges land or buildings on its own account, or acts as an agent or intermediary in the sale, leasing or exchange of land or buildings for a third party. Under the RETL, the Explanation must be stamped by a certified **Real Estate Transaction Manager** (*takuchi tatemono torihiki shuninsha* or '*takken*') employed by the RETL-licensed business and delivered *prior* to the execution of any binding transaction agreements. In addition, a certified Real Estate Transaction Manager from the business must verbally explain the contents of the Explanation to the prospective Purchaser, etc. *prior* to the execution of any such agreements. In practice, the Explanation is usually prepared concurrently with the relevant transaction documents, and the entire Explanation with attachments can range anywhere from 20 to 200 pages.

The purpose of the Explanation is to provide all material information necessary for the Purchaser, etc. to make an informed decision regarding whether to conclude a binding agreement for the subject property. The RETL requires this advance disclosure of all material risks with the goal of reducing the number of disputes arising from real estate deals. This is very different from countries where *caveat emptor* ("let the buyer beware") is the basic philosophy, since in these countries Purchasers, etc. (and their advisors) have the primary responsibility for researching all legal and financial risks. In Japan, the burden is on the seller (or the landlord or both parties to a property exchange), as well as the RETL business operator, to disclose and not misrepresent any material facts which could impact the decision of the prospective Purchaser, etc.

Art. 35 and Art. 47 of the RETL specifically require the disclosure of all information which could materially influence a Purchaser's etc. decision, and Art. 35 contains a list of minimum matters which must be disclosed when they may be material to a transaction. The Art. 35 list is not exhaustive however, and the law makes clear that there should be written and verbal disclosure of all relevant facts and risks prior to the conclusion of any binding agreements. Please note that the Explanation must be provided to all potential Purchasers, etc., regardless of whether the relevant Purchaser, etc. is a certified Real Estate Transaction Manager or an RETL-licensed business operator. In the event an RETL business operator fails to provide the Explanation in accordance with the law, it may have its license temporarily suspended or revoked (Art. 65, Art. 66, RETL). In the worst case scenario, where material risks are intentionally concealed or misrepresented, fines and criminal penalties may be imposed on the responsible parties (*e.g.*, up to one year incarceration under Art. 80 of the RETL).

A Real Estate Transaction Manager compiles information for the Explanation based on various laws and regulations applicable to the property, a review of any prior Explanations, and an inspection of the most up-to-date legal records concerning the property such as the publicly available land register, building register, fixed asset (property) tax records (for additional proof of ownership), etc. The Explanation is prepared with many attachments to provide a full disclosure of the potential risks. However, the appropriate attachments and contents of the Explanation differ depending on the type of transaction.

The contents of an Explanation can vary in at least five different ways depending on the transaction: (1) a sale of property, (2) a lease of property, (3) an exchange of properties, (4) a sale of property subject to the **Law on Sectional Ownership etc. of Buildings** (*tatemono no kubun shoyuutou ni kansuru houritsu*, "Sectional Ownership Law"), and (5) a lease of property subject to the Sectional Ownership Law. The contents of the Explanation also vary depending on whether the subject real property transaction concerns land only, a building only, or both land and buildings. Typical attachments for an Explanation for a land and building purchase transaction include up-to-date copies of the building register and the land register, a map of surrounding owners and private lot boundaries, a copy of the relevant **Official Map** (*kouzu*, the publicly available map kept at the local Legal Affairs Bureau specifying the legal boundary lines for all registered parcels of land and the location of buildings on each parcel), a detailed map showing the location of all pipes, plumbing, and wiring (*e.g.*, water, gas, waste, electricity, etc.), a survey map, and any agreements with surrounding owners regarding property boundaries or boundary objects (fences, trees, etc.).

The first section of an Explanation is by and large the same regardless of the type of transaction. This section lists the registered owner of the property and indicates details regarding any registered legal interests such as superficies, mortgages, leasehold interests, etc., as well as information regarding utilities for the property. Next, there are sections explaining the relevant contractual provisions regarding termination or rescission, details regarding any liquidated damages clauses, any termination penalties or similar damage clauses, and details regarding how any deposit money will be handled (*e.g.*, whether an escrow-like service is being used for custody of any deposits). (Depending on the amount, an escrow-like arrangement may be required if an RETL business operator is selling a property it owns and receives a deposit in advance as explained at the end of Section I of Chapter 13.)

After the first section, each Explanation takes on a particular, individual form. There is a long explanation of any legal restrictions or conditions on use of the property (or development of the land) under any applicable laws and regulations such as the City Planning Law, the Building Standards Law, the National Land Use Planning Act, etc. For purchase transactions, there are usually explanations such as whether there is any latent defect liability insurance (or any other such measures taken by the seller), any asbestos or soil pollution issues with the property, information regarding private roads (if any, including information regarding any public roads in development in the event of a land deal), whether the building has been subject to an inspection for earthquake resistance, and measures to be undertaken if financing doesn't come through to close the deal. For leases, the Explanation contains matters such as the term of the lease, renewal conditions, whether the lease is a traditional or fixed-term lease, the name and address of the property manager (if any), the handling of deposits, and any offset of deposit amounts for repairs, etc. at the termination or expiration of the lease.

Explanations regarding properties subject to the Sectional Ownership Law are a little different because they must include information regarding the contents of the homeowners' association ("HOA") bylaws and any material HOA resolutions. For example, the Explanation should indicate matters such as any impact from the bylaws on the use of common areas, site rights, voting rights, any plans for remodeling or renovation (including current cash reserves), any restrictions on the use of exclusive areas, any HOA fees, property management fees, or any other potential payment obligations, etc. It is also important for the Explanation to disclose any drafts or potential plans for future amendments to the HOA bylaws which could materially affect the rights of owners or tenants in the building.

3 The Registration of Rights in Real Estate

I. Introduction

Although in some countries land and buildings are considered to be one asset, in Japan they are separate assets, and there are separate registers for each parcel of land (*tochi toukibo*) and for each building (*tatemono toukibo*). There is also a specialized register for units of a building owned pursuant to the **Law on Sectional Ownership etc. of Buildings** (*tatemono no kubun shoyuutou ni kansuru houritsu*). Each register is maintained and managed at the local **Legal Affairs Bureau** (*houmukyoku*) with jurisdiction over the relevant property, and there are fifty Legal Affairs Bureaus covering all regions of Japan.

The verification of existing rights and registration of new rights in the relevant land or building register is an important part of any Japanese real estate transaction. This is because prior registered rights (such as a mortgage or a leasehold interest) generally remain effective even after registration of a change of ownership. Since registration is deemed to give constructive notice to all subsequent owners that a property is subject to the rights indicated in the register, registration in Japan is said to follow a **Public Notice** system.

The public can obtain a certified copy of any land or building register at a minimal cost, and an online service in Japanese can be found at http://www1.touki.or.jp/gateway.html. This broad availability promotes transparency with respect to ownership and existing encumbrances for those wishing to purchase Japanese real estate. Inspecting the contents of a land or building register is also a useful way of getting an in-depth understanding of each property, since the registers generally contain a history of all former owners, mortgagees, etc.

Legal registers for property have two main parts: the **Heading Section** (*hyoudaibu*) and the **Rights Section** (*kenribu*). The rights section is further broken up into two sections, one section for the **Registration of Ownership** (*kouku*), and one section for the **Registration of Rights Other than Ownership** (*otsuku*), such as a mortgage. For properties where there are no registered rights other than ownership, the relevant register contains only a heading section and a section concerning ownership rights (there is no section for the registration of rights other than ownership).

II. The Heading Section (*hyoudaibu*) of Land and Building Registers

The purpose of the heading section (*hyoudaibu*) is to create a record of the property for identification purposes, and thus contains information such as the type of land or building, name of owner, address, type of structure, floor space, etc. In the event a new building is constructed on a parcel of land, the general rule is that the owner of the new building must apply to record identifying data in the heading section within one month of completion of construction, otherwise the owner can be fined up to JPY100,000. In addition to being used for identification purposes, the information recorded in the heading section is also used for assessing fixed asset tax liabilities. (There are separate fixed asset (property) taxes for land and buildings assessed as of January 1st each year payable quarterly in April, July, December, and February of the following year.)

After recording information in the heading section, there is no requirement for the owner of a newly constructed building to make a **First Ownership Registration** (*shoyuuken hozon touki*) in the rights section (*kenribu*), since for identification purposes the name of the owner is already listed in the heading section. In addition, generally the only person allowed to cause a first ownership registration in the rights section is the person listed in the heading section. Occasionally an owner will wait until a transfer of ownership is planned to have his or her name entered into the rights section, since the first ownership registration is subject to a tax equal to 0.4% of the value of the building (reduced to 0.15% for residential properties). However, if the owner listed in the heading section is not registered in the rights section, the owner cannot cause the registration of a mortgage, cause the registration of a change in ownership in the event of sale, or legally assert ownership of the building over any third parties.

III. The Act of Registration

There are many different types of registrations, such as the **Registration of a Right** (*settei touki*), **Transfer of a Registered Right** (*iten touki*), **Variation of a Registered Right** (*henkou touki,* for example due to a name change of the beneficiary, etc.), **Correction of a Registered Right** (*kousei touki,* where there is a discrepancy between the registered right and the actual situation due to mistake, inadvertent omission, etc.), **Removal of a Registered Right** (*masshou touki,* for example in the event a building is destroyed), **Setting of a Note Registration** (*fuki touki,* a type of registration used to provide notice regarding a registration), and **Setting of a Provisional Registration** (*kari touki*). The basic legal rule is that the priority of rights to a property is determined by the date of registration, and registered rights prevail over unregistered rights. Generally, only property rights (*bukken*) may be entered in a land or building register (the main exceptions are leasehold interests (*chinshakuken*) and rights to repurchase (*kaimodoshiken*), which are personal rights or *saiken*). In the past there was a requirement that both parties affected by a registration (*e.g.*, the buyer and the seller) or their representatives had to be physically present at the Legal Affairs Bureau for a valid registration, but this requirement has been abolished.

Under Japanese law, the general rule is that both of the affected parties (*e.g.*, the buyer and seller) must *agree* to an act of registration (*kyoudou shinsei shugi*). Usually the parties indicate their agreement by each giving a judicial scrivener a written power of attorney to carry out the registration. The main exceptions to this joint rule for registration of ownership are: (1) an application for the first ownership registration (*shoyuuken hozon touki*) in the rights section (*kenribu*), (2) a registration carried out pursuant to a final legal decision which orders such registration, (3) a registration due to a person inheriting a property, or (4) in the event either a variation registration (*henkou touki*) or correction registration (*kousei touki*) is necessary.

Judicial scriveners (*shihou shoshi*) are the main professionals in charge of carrying out registrations for individuals and non-government entities. A judicial scrivener is a licensed professional who is an expert in registration matters and is authorized under Japanese law to make an application to effect a change of ownership, etc. on a land or building register, and to make registrations on a company's corporate register. In practice, judicial scrivners are not unlike paralegals licensed to take care of real estate registration matters in some jurisdictions. Since property registers are maintained locally, judicial scriveners used to have to travel physically to the local Legal Affairs Bureau to make an application. However, since July 2008 an online registration system has been implemented, so in the usual case it is possible to complete application procedures online (in addition to physical application). Also, please note that the Japanese words for 'legal affairs bureau' (*houmukyoku*) and 'registration office' (*toukijo*) are often used interchangeably to indicate the name of the government office where registration takes place (in certain regions in Japan, the Legal Affairs Bureau is called the 'Registration Office').

The traditional process of selling a property and registering a change of ownership and new mortgage is relatively simple. Once the buyer has confirmed the contents of a recent copy of the relevant property register, the seller and the buyer each draft and sign a power of attorney authorizing a judicial scrivener to register the new owner and set the mortgage in accordance with their instructions. Along with the power of attorney, the seller gives the judicial scrivener a copy of the relevant transaction documents (to evidence the transaction and provide basic information for the registration), documents for personal identification (such as a certificate of registered seal (*inkan shoumeisho*) issued within the last three months), and the **Confidential Identification Number** (*toukishikibetsu jouhou no bangou*) card or the **Title Deed** (*kenrisho*, also known as the *toukizumisho*, which is traditionally the document required to be submitted to cause a change in registration at the Legal Affairs Bureau).

On the closing date, the judicial scrivener calls the buyer and seller (and a representative of the mortgagee) to let them know that all the necessary documents for registration are at hand, and the buyer calls the buyer's bank (or mortgagee) to make a wire transfer of the purchase price. Subsequently the seller calls the seller's bank to verify the seller's account has received the purchase price, and upon confirmation immediately calls the judicial scrivener to cause the judicial scrivener to submit the documents necessary for registration of the new owner and the mortgage. Once the registration of change of ownership is complete and the new owner is designated with title on the land or building register, the new owner receives a new confidential identification number (*shikibetsu jouhou no bangou*) card from the local Legal Affairs Bureau (and the mortgagee a certified copy of the building or land register with the newly registered mortgage). If requested, the purchaser may also apply for and receive a **Document of Completion of Registration** (*touki kanryoushou*) issued by the local Legal Affairs Bureau.

Possession of the title deed (*kenrisho*) used to be one of the hallmarks of ownership in Japan, because without this document generally no change in a land or building register could take place. However, in connection with the ongoing computerization and modernization of the Japanese real estate registration system, new owners now receive a card with a confidential identification number (*touki shikibetsu jouhou no bangou*, similar to a credit card number) in lieu of the title deed. The confidential identification number on the card is used just like the old title deed, and no new title deeds are currently being issued. Nevertheless, the title deed system is still effective for properties which haven't yet been subject to a registration of change in ownership. Accordingly, both the title deed system and the confidential identification number system will continue to exist in parallel until a time in the future when the title deed system is phased out.

IV. Provisional Registrations (*kari touki*)

A **Provisional Registration** (*kari touki*) is a type of registration used in either section of the rights section to reserve priority of a right. Generally it may be used when information which must be submitted to complete a valid registration is not yet available. It may also be used in order to reserve the priority of a disputed claim (for instance, when a party wishes to reserve the priority of its claim of ownership). When the information becomes available or the dispute is resolved favorably, the provisional registration may be replaced by a definitive registration (*hontouki*), *e.g.*, registration of transfer of ownership (*shoyuuken iten touki*), with the right recorded as a definitive registration taking effect as of the time of the provisional registration on the property register.

A provisional registration does not restrict an owner from transferring ownership or making a new registration of rights on the building or land register. It merely provides notice of a claim which could become a valid right with priority in the future. Accordingly, purchasers registered after a provisional registration for change of ownership may lose title in the future depending on resolution of the provisional registration. A provisional registration can be useful when, for example, a purchaser has completed an acquisition but for some reason the seller will not cooperate with the purchaser to transfer title, or when a purchase and sale agreement is executed but will only become effective at a future date (and the purchaser wants to preserve the priority of its right in the relevant land or building register). A provisional registration of transfer of ownership can also be used to secure a loan for a lender (*i.e.*, the lender may be given in advance a written agreement and custody of all necessary documents (powers of attorney, etc.) to effect a definitive registration of change of ownership if the loan isn't repaid).

V. Registration in the Ownership Section (*kouku*) of the Rights Section (*kenribu*)

The rights section (*kenribu*) is divided into two sections, the **Section for Registration of Ownership** (*kouku*) and the *otsuku* section for registration of all other rights. The most frequent entries in the ownership section are the first ownership registration (*shoyuuken hozon touki)* and the registration of a change in ownership (*shoyuuken iten touki*), although other potential registrations include, for example, an attachment of the property by government entity, an entrustment of the property, and a right to repurchase (*kaimodoshiken*). A right to repurchase is registered as a note registration (*fuki touki*) (which is a type of registration used to provide notice regarding a registration, in this case, that a registration of change in ownership is subject to a right to repurchase). If the repurchase is carried out in the future, title is registered in place of the original change of ownership which contained the note registration.

Although registration of ownership in the rights section (*kouku*) is not legally required (unlike registration in the heading section), as a rule purchasers require registration of a change of ownership (*shoyuuken iten touki*) to reserve the priority of their interest and be able to assert their ownership over third parties. In general, the first person permitted to apply for registration of ownership (*shoyuuken hozon touki*) in the rights section of a property register (*kouku*) must be the same person recorded in the heading section (*hyoudaibu*). This rule applies except where (1) the person or entity applying for registration has inherited the property, (2) the person applying for registration has obtained title through a court decision which has been finalized (for example, a completed foreclosure proceeding), or (3) the person or entity applying for registration has obtained title through an expropriation (*shuuyou*) proceeding. The purpose of this rule is to promote the creation of a clear chain of ownership back to the initial recording of property information in the heading section (*hyoudaibu*).

VI. Registration in the 'Other than Ownership' Section (*otsuku*) of the Rights Section

Under Art. 3 of the **Real Estate Registration Law** (*fudousan toukihou*), there are eight basic rights to property which may be registered in the **Section for Registrations 'Other than Ownership'** (*otsuku*): **Superficies** (*chijouken*), **Mortgages** (*teitouken*), **Easements** (*chiekiken*), **Pledges** (*shichiken*), **Farming Rights** (*eikosakuken*), **Liens** or **Preferential Rights** (*sakidori tokken*), **Leasehold Interests** (*chinshakuken*), and **Mining Rights** (*saisekiken*). There are, however, other important rights pertaining to property which do not need to be registered or cannot be registered, such as possessory rights (*sen'yuuken*), rights of common (*iriaiken*), rights of retention (*ryuuchiken*), and quasi-leasing or use rights (*shiyou shakuchiken*). In practice, the most common interests registered in this section are mortgages (*teitouken*) and revolving credit mortgages (*neteitouken*), superficies (*chijouken*), easements (*chiekiken*), and leasehold interests (*chinshakuken*). Pledges (*shichiken*) are also very important because they are the security interest most commonly used with respect to financial instruments such as trust beneficiary interests. Nevertheless, pledges are usually not used with respect to unentrusted real estate, and thus real estate pledges (*fudousan shichiken*) not normally found in land or building registers.

Mortgages and easements are familiar to those who live in common law jurisdictions, whereas **Superficies** (*chijouken*) are usually not. A superficies is a property right (*bukken*) generally created by contract permitting the holder of the superficies to use land for the ownership of something on such land (typically to build and own a building). Payment of rent may or may not be required in the superficies agreement, and is not obligatory under the **Japanese Civil Code** ("JCC").

A superficies allows its holder (and successors or transferees) to assert rights to the land against the original landowner without being registered. However, a superficies must be registered in order to be able to be claimed against a third-party purchaser of the encumbered land. Holders of superficies enjoy most of the rights typically associated with ownership, provided the holder complies with the objective of the property right indicated in the superficies agreement. In addition, in the event a landowner refuses to cooperate with the holder to cause registration of the superficies in the land register, the holder may institute a legal action against the landowner to cause such registration by the landowner (or the authorities).

Interestingly, a superficies in Japan can be set not only on the surface of land but also underneath or above ground (for example, to build and own a subway or to plant and own trees). In practice, landowners prefer to create leasehold interests (*chinshakuken*) instead of superficies since generally leasehold interests confer a lesser degree of legal rights. For example, a superficies is freely transferable but a leasehold interest may not be transferred without the consent of the landowner. Consequently, a superficies formed by contract is relatively rare in Japan.

However, there is an interesting situation which can occur in the event land and a building on the land are owned by the same person, but through foreclosure on a mortgage (on either the land or the building), become property of two separate owners. Provided the mortgage on the land was created after the building was constructed, the owner of the building would receive a **Legal Superficies** (*houtei chijouken*) to use the land by operation of Japanese law (Art. 388, JCC). Any land rents to be paid would be decided by a court upon request by the parties. Also, it should be noted that ownership of the building does not have to be registered for the building owner to receive a legal superficies.

The situation would be different if the building were constructed after the mortgage on the land was registered, provided the owner did not have the consent of the land mortgagee to construct the building. In this case, if the mortgage on the land were foreclosed on, the mortgagee would have the legal right to cause both the land and the building to be sold in auction (Art. 389, JCC). Nevertheless, the mortgagee would only have a priority right to repayment from proceeds from the sale of the land.

VII. The Trust Register (*shintaku mokuroku*)

At the time a property is entrusted to a trust bank, a separate **Trust Register** (*shintaku mokuroku*) is drafted and recorded as an appendix to the relevant property register. The main contents of the trust register are taken from the trust agreement entered into by the trust bank and the beneficiary, and its purpose is to provide public notice of the important contents of the trust agreement. Registration of the trust register creates a priority interest for the trust over all third parties, and compliance with the contents of the trust register is obligatory. In the event a trust agreement is amended, the trust register must also be amended accordingly and re-registered in order for the amended part to be effective vis-à-vis third parties.

Please note that except for the mandatory provisions of the Trust Law and the other Japanese laws applicable to trusts, in general the provisions of the trust register and the trust agreement are controlling between the beneficiary and the trust bank. In October 2011, it became possible to receive copies of trust registers in electronic form from each Legal Affairs Bureau. In addition, on January 30th, 2012, the Ministry of Justice enabled the online registration of all trust registers for entrusted properties in Japan at http://www.moj.go.jp/MINJI/minji72.html.

4 The Transfer of Rights

Under the **Japanese Civil Code** ("JCC"), the transfer of ownership in a property (*shoyuuken iten*) occurs at the time a buyer and a seller declare their intention (*ishi hyouji*) to execute a transaction. That is, the general rule is that a transfer of ownership occurs at the time a contract is signed, before delivery occurs and irrespective of whether the transfer has been recorded in the land or building register or any payments made. Nevertheless, the parties usually change this legal rule by agreeing that ownership in a property will transfer based on the completion of certain conditions, *e.g.*, at the time payment in full is received. Further, the right to collect rent transfers to the buyer upon actual delivery of the property, not from the time of transfer of ownership, under Art. 575, Paragraph 1 of the JCC. However, the risk of loss (*kiken futan*) in a property is borne by the buyer from the time of contract (Art. 534, JCC), not the time of delivery, unless the parties agree otherwise.

There are generally two types of rights concerning property which may be relevant in Japanese real estate transactions, **Property Rights** (*bukken*) and **Personal Rights** (*saiken*). Under Japanese law, a *property right* (*bukken*) is the absolute right a person or entity has over an asset to the exclusion of all others (such as ownership of a building), whereas a *personal right* (*saiken*) is the right a person or entity has to demand another person or entity to perform some act (for example, the right to demand an owner to lease out a building or the right to demand repayment of a loan). (In US law, there is a similar legal distinction in that a mortgage is a type of *in rem* right (a right in property) used to secure a note, which evidences an *in personam* right (a personal right), the right of a lender to demand repayment of a loan.) Most of this Chapter concerns the most common transfer in real estate transactions, the transfer of a property right (*bukken*) from a seller to a buyer, and thus generally applies not only to a transfer of ownership, but also to a transfer of all other property rights such as the transfer of a mortgage (*teitouken iten*) to a new lender.

I. The Significance of Registration

In Japan, the transfer of ownership in a property from a seller to a buyer is valid between the parties without any registration of the transfer, and there is no explicit legal requirement to register a change of ownership. However, Art. 177 of the JCC provides the general rule that in the event of a change in a property right (*bukken*) such as the right of ownership, the change of property right must be registered in order to be effective with respect to third parties. This means that in principle purchasers must be recorded in the land or building register to assert their rights to a property over the rights of any third parties.

A dispute regarding ownership of a property can arise, for instance, when an unscrupulous seller sells the same property to two different parties (*nijuu baibai*). Without a system for registration, it could be unclear which of the two buyers should be the legitimate owner of the property. The basic legal rule is that the party who has its ownership interest recorded in the building or land register first in time prevails (*i.e.*, Japan is a 'race only' jurisdiction). Further, registered interests prevail over unregistered interests. Please note, however, that based on Japanese case law, even without being legally registered, valid purchasers may assert their rights to a property over third parties who have no legitimate right or interest in the property.

In the double sale (*nijuu baibai*) scenario described above, the buyer who does not effectively receive the property right (*bukken*) may still have a personal right (*saiken*) with respect to the seller, *i.e.*, the right to demand delivery of the property, and non-performance will normally give the thwarted buyer a right to sue the seller for damages. Interestingly, it is also possible for a person to enter into a valid contract to sell another person's land to a third party, even if the seller has no current legal right to the other person's land. In the case of non-performance (where the seller cannot deliver title), normally the third-party buyer would be able to sue the seller based on a breach of the buyer's personal right (*saiken*) to demand delivery.

Another good example of these rules is the situation where a seller dies after selling a property to a third party. In this case, the buyer may generally assert ownership over the deceased owner's heirs even without registration. However, if the owner's heirs have already sold the property, in general the first buyer to register in time (either the buyer from the deceased or the buyer from the heirs) will prevail.

As one may gather from the discussion above, issues with respect to ownership and the priority of ownership in Japanese property law are divided between the right of a buyer to claim title over a seller and the right of a buyer to claim title to the exclusion of all third parties. An unregistered buyer can thus receive a property right (*bukken*) from a seller and have the full right to own and use the subject property, only to lose these rights to a registered subsequent purchaser. This holds even if the subsequent purchaser knows of the earlier transaction in the same property, provided the subsequent purchaser didn't commit any fraudulent or violent acts preventing the earlier unregistered purchaser from registering the transfer of ownership. In addition, if a legitimate buyer purchases a property from a seller who has purchased the property from an earlier seller, in the usual case the buyer would be able to claim ownership over both the first and second seller through the chain of contractual obligations, regardless of whether or not either transfer of title were registered.

II. The Transfer of Rights Other than Ownership

Since mortgages are property rights (*bukken*) under Japanese law, a similar analysis applies to the sale of mortgaged land. If a mortgaged parcel of land is sold prior to the mortgage being registered, after the sale the mortgage will be cut off from the land. That is, the unregistered mortgagee may not assert any rights over the land vis-à-vis the subsequent purchaser (although the mortgagee would generally still have a personal right with respect to the mortgagor in the form of the previously secured loan*)*. However, if a loan (a personal right or *saiken*) secured by a registered mortgage is transferred to a third party, by operation of Japanese law, the property right (*bukken*) will follow the related personal right (meaning the third party will generally be allowed to enforce the mortgage in the event the borrower fails to repay the transferred loan), regardless of whether the mortgagee's name has been changed in the land or building register.

Application of the analysis is a little different with respect to leasehold interests (*chinshakuken*) however. This is because under Japanese law, a leasehold interest is a type of personal right (*i.e.*, a right to cause someone to lease out a property), not a property right. Thus, unlike a transfer of a mortgage (a property right or *bukken*), in order to validly transfer a leasehold interest to a third party, as a general rule a tenant needs to get the building owner's prior consent.

In the converse, however, the **Law on Leasing Land and Buildings** (*shakuchi shakuyahou*) provides special protection for tenants of buildings sold to third parties. Although the general rule under the JCC is that a tenant cannot enforce the terms of a lease against a subsequent buyer unless the leasehold interest is registered, pursuant to the Law on Leasing Land and Buildings, a tenant with an unregistered leasehold interest may enforce the interest against a subsequent buyer provided that the tenant is actually occupying and using the building (and provided sale of the building didn't arise from a prior mortgage right). In this way, Japanese law protects tenants' rights to a greater extent than the rights of unregistered mortgagees (who lose their rights if mortgaged land is transferred). One reason unregistered leasehold interests are protected in this way is that it is often difficult for tenants to get owners to cooperate to register leasehold interests, and there is a legal rule that both affected parties have to jointly agree to register a right on a property register.

There are also other ways tenants are specially protected under Japanese law. If a building owner sells a leased property, the general legal rule is that at expiration of the lease, the tenant may automatically enforce its right to receive repayment of any security deposits directly with respect to the new owner. In addition, if a person owns a registered building on a leased parcel of land, the owner of the building may enforce its leasehold interest against any third-party purchaser of the land (except if sale of the land arises from a prior mortgage right).

III. The Quasi-Adverse Possession (*shutoku jikou*) Exception

Notwithstanding the above, there are exceptions to the rule that a registered ownership interest prevails over an unregistered ownership interest. For example, in Japan there is a legal rule which in practice is similar to the common law rule called 'adverse possession.' Under this rule, if there is a person openly and continuously occupying and using a property, and the rightful owner does not ask the person to leave, after the passage of a certain amount of time (either ten or 20 years depending on the facts of the situation), the occupier will become the rightful owner of the property. Accordingly, an occupier can attain rightful ownership of a property over a registered owner due to the owner *sleeping* on his or her rights.

Moreover, in the scenario where there is a third-party purchaser, if the conditions for this quasi-adverse possession rule have already been satisfied by the occupier (including the requisite number of years), and the property is sold to a third party, the person (either the purchaser or the occupier) who first in time registers their interest after the sale will be allowed to assert ownership. However, if the conditions are only partially satisfied, the situation is different. In this case, if all legal conditions are met by the occupier at the time of sale except for the necessary number of years, and subsequent to the sale the occupier continues with unfettered possession for the remaining number of years necessary to assert a quasi-adverse possession claim, the occupier will generally be allowed to assert ownership over the new owner as well, regardless of registration.

In sum, if the new owner is validly registered upon completion of the transaction, and immediately begins occupying and using the property in its entirety, the new owner will be able to cut off any potential quasi-adverse possession claims. For the avoidance of doubt, in the usual case purchasers (and lenders) physically inspect properties to confirm there are no occupiers prior to completing a real estate transaction. It is also advisable to confirm that there are no tenants prior to purchase in order to prevent the purchaser from having to take ownership subject to a prior leasehold interest as explained in Section II above.

IV. Other Exceptions to Registration

There are other circumstances where a buyer of real estate in good faith may not have legitimate title even after completing registration, for example, in the unusual situation where the seller's registration of ownership was obtained by fraud or use of intimidation (*e.g.*, in the event the seller was registered as the owner by stealing or forging the necessary identification documents, sales contract, etc. for registration). In this case, the legitimate owner will generally be allowed to assert its ownership over the fraudulent party and all subsequent buyers of the property, since in principle a seller without legitimate title cannot convey ownership. Moreover based on this reasoning, there is a rule that a person who breaches a legal duty and thereby becomes the registered owner of a property (for example, a dishonest judicial scrivener (*shihou shoshi*) registering a property in his or her own name) may not legitimately assert or convey such registered rights.

These above exceptional situations (fraudulent registration, registration through intimidation, and registration through breach of a legal duty) constitute legal risks for buyers who wholly rely on the contents of the land and building registers and the name on the title deed (*kenrisho,* the document used to effect a change of registration on a land or building register, which is currently being replaced with a confidential identification number (*touki shikibetsu jouhou no bangou*) card as explained in Chapter 3 on the Registration of Rights). Nevertheless, in Japan the above exceptional circumstances are considered to constitute an acceptable level of risk for many buyers and lenders, provided the seller is of reputable character and the title deed and the land and building registers are in order. Please note, however, that there are other risks as well (such as a seller who has not paid all due and payable fixed asset (property) taxes, boundary disputes with neighbors, unregistered buildings or buildings under construction, etc.), and as a general rule it is advisable to have professionals carry out an on-site and legal due diligence prior to committing to a significant property purchase.

V. Relying on the Contents of Land and Building Registers

Generally buyers in Japan are not entitled to wholly rely on the contents of land and building registers, although this doesn't mean that the contents of the registers are frequently wrong. In certain other legal jurisdictions with a registration system (for example Australia), purchasers are said to be allowed to *rely* on the register. *Reliance* in this case means that the government guarantees the validity of title as reflected in the registers (and owners have a right to redress from the government if the register is inaccurate). In other jurisdictions such as the United States, lawyers research the historical chain of title to issue an opinion regarding ownership and/or purchasers use private companies to obtain title insurance to mitigate this risk. (In the US, the recording system does not conclusively determine who has title to real property, the courts do.)

In Japan, there is no system of public or private title insurance, and the government does not guarantee the accuracy of the registers or that the legitimate owner of a property is listed on the relevant register. However, if the official in charge of entering a registration makes a mistake in the registration process, damaged parties may apply for compensation under the **National Redress Law** (*kokka baishouhou*). Also, in the event of a dispute between two parties, the burden of proof is on the party arguing for the invalidity of the registration entry. In general, registration creates a presumption of validity of ownership (and the presumption of validity of other registered property rights), and if a seller is registered with title on the relevant legal register, and is in possession of the property and the title deed (*kenrisho*) or confidential identification number (*touki shikibetsu jouhou no bangou*) card, typically there will be no problem with the validity of title transferred by the seller (provided there are no problems found in the on-site and legal due diligence reports, etc.)

VI. Basic Issues for Transferring Real Estate Loans

When a real estate loan (which is a *saiken* or personal right to demand payment) is transferred, the transferee (the purchaser of the loan) may want to have all rights under the loan agreement perfected against both the underlying borrower and all third parties. The transfer should be perfected against the underlying borrower in the event the transferee would like to be allowed to demand repayment directly from the borrower (rather than use the original lender to service the loan). The transfer should be perfected against all third parties because the original lender could transfer the loan to a third party even after the initial transfer (similar to the double sale scenario described in Section I above).

If the loan were transferred to a third party after the initial transfer, and the third party were to perfect its right to the loan first, generally the third party would prevail over the first transferee. Further, if the original lender were to file for bankruptcy after an unperfected transfer, depending on the circumstances it may be possible for the bankruptcy trustee to prevail over the unperfected transferee. Please note that even if a loan agreement were to contain a restriction on transfer, as a basic rule the transfer would still be valid under Japanese law, provided the transferee had no knowledge of the restriction prior to transfer.

In order to perfect the transfer of a loan against a borrower under Art. 467 of the JCC, either the original lender or the transferee must obtain the borrower's consent to the transfer, or the original lender must send a notice of the transfer to the borrower. To perfect the transfer against third parties however, the written consent or notice should be notarized with a notary date stamp (*kakutei hizuke*). When the loans of many borrowers are to be transferred, sending notices or receiving consents and obtaining notarizations can be very time-consuming and expensive, and it may be confusing for borrowers if they receive a notice that their loan has been transferred but the original lender is still to service the debt.

Therefore in 1998, the **Special Law regarding Transfer of Claims** (*saikenjouto tokureihou*) was enacted to create a new way for a loan transfer to be perfected against third parties. Under this law, a loan transfer can be perfected against all third party claims through registration of the transfer in a special register for the assignment of receivables maintained at an office of the Legal Affairs Bureau. Please note, however, that this method of perfection is ineffective against the underlying borrower(s).

In the event the original lender (who oftentimes functions as the loan servicer) develops financial problems, it may nonetheless become advisable for a transferee registered under the Special Law regarding Transfer of Claims to perfect the loan transfer directly with respect to the underlying borrowers. This is so that the transferee could directly demand repayment from the borrowers under Japanese law. In order to perfect the loan transfer against the borrowers in this case, the original lender should send a notice to the borrowers with a copy of the registration certificate issued by the relevant Legal Affairs Bureau, or either the original lender or transferee should receive individual consents from the underlying borrowers.

5 Japanese Trust Banks

Trust Banks (*shintaku ginkou*) are financial institutions licensed and regulated by the Japanese **Financial Services Agency** (*kin'yuuchou*), and they are mainly governed by the **Trust Law**, the **Trust Business Law**, and the **Law on Concurrent Operation of Trust Businesses by Financial Institutions**. Their main real estate business is to accept the entrustment of land and/or buildings (*i.e.*, the delivery of legal ownership), and to hold and manage such properties for the benefit of the trust's beneficiaries. Trust banks (and trust companies) play an important role in the Japanese real estate industry because of the large number of properties which are entrusted (according to the Japanese Association for Real Estate Securitization, in 2011 entrusted properties made up 85% of the value of all real estate held by private real estate funds in Japan). Please note that the Trust Business Law was significantly amended in 2004, and currently almost any type of asset in Japan may be entrusted, not just real property.

Upon the entrustment of a property, in the usual case the trust bank issues to the entrustor (*tousho juekisha* or the "initial beneficiary") a certificate evidencing the **Trust Beneficiary Interest** (*juekiken* or "TBI"). In turn, the trust bank holds (and oftentimes manages) the entrusted property on behalf of the beneficiary in order to earn trust fees. The TBI certificate, a 2nd tier financial instrument under the **Financial Instruments and Exchange Law** ("FIEL"), is issued to document ownership of the beneficial rights in the entrusted real estate. These rights are mainly derived from the above Japanese trust laws and the trust agreement entered into by the trust bank and the initial beneficiary. Broadly speaking, trust beneficiaries in Japan enjoy a bundle of rights which are similar to the rights of equitable owners in common law jurisdictions such as the United States.

The trust bank is registered as the legal owner of the entrusted property pursuant to a **Trust Register** (*shintaku mokuroku*) for the property, and the entrustor is registered as the beneficiary of the trust. The trust bank is obligated to follow the reasonable directions of the beneficiary and act in the beneficiary's best interest at all times based on a legal duty of loyalty (*chuujitsu gimu*). Trust banks also have a duty to act with the diligence of a good manager (*zenkan-chuui gimu*) in the performance of their services, and a duty not to comingle entrusted assets (*bunbetsu gimu*) with their own assets or other entrusted assets. The beneficiary has a legal right to sell the TBI to third parties, or even dissolve the trust, in which case the beneficiary would be directly registered on the relevant land or building register as the legal owner, and recover full ownership of the previously entrusted property.

There are many reasons why trust banks are used so frequently in real estate transactions in Japan. One of the most important is that real estate investments in TBIs are not subject to the **Real Estate Syndication Law** ("RESL"). (Please see Chapter 17 for a discussion of the RESL.) This law, which on its face applies to certain collective investment schemes involving passive investors in real estate and real estate managers actively operating such real estate, came into effect in the early 1990s after the collapse of the Japanese real estate bubble. In short, the law requires real estate managers to obtain a separate RESL license if they would like to arrange and manage certain types of real estate investment schemes which were popular during the Japanese bubble years. Nevertheless, transactions in TBIs have been regulated under the FIEL since 2007, and as a result of the new legal regulations, there has been a tendency for some investors to move away from using TBIs (when possible and depending on the investment structure).

Another important reason for the use of trust banks is the relative convenience of transferring a TBI when compared to transferring title for unentrusted properties. Since trust banks hold legal ownership of entrusted properties, usually they enter into contracts with various service providers such as master lessees, property managers, building managers, etc. directly for the benefit of the trust beneficiaries. When a TBI is transferred, it is thus generally unnecessary to change any of the existing contracts pertaining to management, maintenance, etc. of the entrusted property, since only the TBI holder changes.

There are often compelling tax reasons to use a trust bank structure. When ownership of *unentrusted* real estate is transferred, there is a real estate acquisition tax levied which can be as much as 3% of the appraisal value for land and 4% for buildings. Further, there is a stamp duty on the acquisition agreement which varies with the value of the property and can be as much as JPY600,000, and a change of ownership registration tax which can total 1.5% for land and 2% for buildings. However, when a TBI is transferred from seller to buyer, there is no real estate acquisition tax levied, the stamp tax costs JPY200, and the registration tax for a change of registration is JPY1000. Further, there is no real estate acquisition tax levied when a property is initially entrusted (although there is when the trust is dissolved if there is a different TBI holder than the initial beneficiary), and the registration tax for a new trust is greatly reduced as well. Consequently, in practice real estate properties are usually entrusted when the total expected cost of the trust bank's fees is less than the total of all costs and taxes to be incurred if the property were to be transferred directly from seller to buyer without being entrusted.

Because trust banks hold and manage so many properties, over time they have been able to build up considerable experience and knowledge in most asset classes and locations around Japan. For this reason, trust banks oftentimes are used by beneficiaries to market and act as intermediaries for transactions of entrusted properties. The network of buyers and sellers that Japanese trust banks have at their disposal is indeed impressive, and very much helps enhance liquidity in the Japanese real estate market.

Trust banks also serve a variety of important roles in real estate investment schemes. When a property is entrusted, trust banks can issue multiple TBIs with varying seniorities, creating a senior-subordinate payment structure of any rents to be passed through to beneficiaries arising from the entrusted property. In the event the TBIs are sold by the original entrustor, and the entrustor subsequently files for bankruptcy, generally any new TBI purchasers are shielded against claims from the entrustor's creditors (and the bankruptcy trustee) that the entrusted property should be part of the bankruptcy estate of the entrustor. This is provided, however, that the amounts paid for the TBIs were reasonable and certain other legal and regulatory requirements have been satisfied. Further, entrusted assets are typically not regarded as being part of the trust bank's own assets for the purpose of Japanese bankruptcy laws, meaning they are generally considered to be safe from creditors' claims in case of the trust bank's bankruptcy.

The use of trust banks fosters dependability and transparency in real estate transactions in Japan. Trust banks are required by law to issue periodically to each of their beneficiaries an accurate and complete trust report, with a detailed accounting of all cash flow in and out of the trust account. When properties are initially entrusted, and subsequently when TBIs are transferred, the subject property also undergoes a rigorous inspection process by the trust bank to ensure that it does not have serious legal or compliance issues (such as building code violations). This vetting process can be rather strict however, and in the end not all properties may be accepted for entrustment without substantial changes.

6 The Law on Measures against Soil Pollution

The **Law on Measures against Soil Pollution** (*dojou osen taisakuhou,* "Soil Pollution Law") first came into effect on February 15th, 2003 and was amended effective April 1st, 2010. Its purpose is "to establish countermeasures for protecting the public health from soil pollution by (1) setting forth procedures for discovering soil that may be polluted with certain hazardous materials, and (2) instituting safeguards for protecting the general public from being harmed by such pollution, etc." From February 2003 to March 2009, there were approximately 341 soil pollution districts designated throughout Japan. This unexpectedly high number was a factor in the 2010 legal revisions to expand testing and increase measures to counteract the spread of soil pollution.

The Soil Pollution Law gives the prefectural governor the power to cause a landowner (or designated third party) to investigate soil for contamination and report on the results if it is believed the soil may contain pollution at levels harmful to public health. In addition, the Soil Pollution Law requires all owners of facilities using certain hazardous materials (such as cleaning companies, tanneries, and pesticide manufacturers) to have a designated third party carry out a soil inspection at the time the facilities are closed. Under the 2010 legal amendments, there is also a new rule mandating anyone developing at least 3000 square meters of land to notify the prefectural governor at least 30 days prior to beginning development. After notification, if the authorities decide there is reason to believe the site contains a prohibited level of soil pollution, they may demand the land be tested for contamination as well.

Depending on the results of the initial soil inspection, the competent authorities may demand an additional inspection (*chousa meirei*). If the presence of certain hazardous materials above the legal limits is confirmed, the area may be designated one of two types of **Soil Pollution Districts** (*dojou osen kuiki*). There are 25 types of hazardous materials specified under the law, and inspection results are generally made available to the public (along with drawings indicating where soil pollution was found, a map of the site and surrounding area, and a map of the area to be remedied). To protect public health, owners of soil pollution districts can be required to carry out remedial actions (*e.g.*, excavation activities, etc.) and may be restricted in their use of the property. The authorities may also demand compensation in the event they are forced to remove the soil or carry out remedial measures to prevent the pollution from spreading.

I. The 2010 Legal Amendments

Under the 2010 changes, in addition to the mandatory testing of sites at least 3000 square meters in area prior to development, soil pollution districts are now divided into two categories. The first type, called **Districts Requiring Remedial Action** (*yousochi kuiki*) under Art. 6 of the Soil Pollution Law, are districts where certain remedial actions (such as soil removal, enclosure, etc.) are necessary due to a present danger to human health. The second type, **Pre-Development Notification Districts** (*keishitsu henkouji youtodokede kuiki*) under Art. 11 of the law, pose no current danger, but any development of the land may cause contamination of local groundwater, etc. As a result, there is a pre-development notification requirement for these districts, which gives the authorities the opportunity to demand a change to the relevant development plan in a timely manner. It should be noted that officials may retract either soil pollution district designation if the problem is rectified.

Pursuant to the 2010 amendments, there are new standards for transporting polluted soil, and a new permit system for the business of treating polluted soil as well. Furthermore, in most cases a notification to the prefectural governor is now required prior to transporting soil containing hazardous materials. The purpose of this notification is to allow the authorities to more effectively track and restrict such soil from being moved around the country.

II. Soil Pollution in Real Estate Transactions

If a parcel of land is designated as one of the two types of soil pollution districts, the seller must disclose this fact to the buyer in the **Explanation of Important Matters** (*juuyou jikou setsumeisho*, explained in Chapter 2 of this book) prior to entering into a binding purchase and sale agreement. However, even if the land is not so designated, in general sellers are still obliged to disclose any material facts which may be relevant to determining whether the soil is contaminated. Also, if the parcel of land is a designated soil pollution district, the seller must disclose the consequences of such designation, such as any use restrictions, sale restrictions, etc. In any event, it may be advisable for buyers to include a condition precedent in their purchase and sale agreements that there is no soil pollution above the legal limits at the subject property.

One of the objectives of the Soil Pollution Law is to make soil inspections and soil contamination reporting a regular part of real estate transactions in Japan. In addition, one of the intended effects of the law is to spur developers to carry out a soil inspection at an early stage in the development process, otherwise they may incur unexpected time delays and extra costs after a project has been started. Even a nearly completed building may be ordered to be demolished if certain levels of soil pollution are found at a development site.

Nevertheless, one unintended result of the regulations is that suspected areas may be completely avoided by developers, meaning the areas will not be subject to any soil testing or remedial measures (and thus not meet the law's objective of promoting the discovery of contaminated land throughout Japan). Also, testing may be considered undesirable by landowners where there is a risk of third-party damage claims and lower appraisal amounts. It should also be noted that there are certain localities in Japan with soil pollution rules stricter than those of the national government, so depending on the circumstances it may be worthwhile to speak with a local expert prior to executing a real estate acquisition in certain parts of the country.

III. Soil Inspections

As part of the due diligence process in commercial real estate transactions in Japan, it is common for buyers to request sellers to carry out a soil inspection and include the results in an engineering report on the property. Procedures for the inspection are typically derived from the **Phase I Environmental Site Assessment Process**, E1527 established by the American Society for Testing and Materials ("ASTM"). Phase 1 testing in Japan first began in the late 1990s as a result of the growth in Japanese real estate securitization, and since 2002, soil inspection results have been included as part of the Japanese standards for real estate appraisals. In 2007, the Building and Equipment Long-life Cycle Association ("BELCA") and the Japan Building Owners and Managers Association drafted well-known standards based on the above ASTM rules in the **Guidelines for Engineering Reports for Real Estate Investment and Transactions in Japan** (*fudousan toushi/torihiki ni okeru enjiniaringu repooto sakusei ni kansuru gaidorain*).

The ASTM rules describe a 3-phase process for verifying soil pollution risk in private real estate transactions. **Phase 1** consists of actions such as (1) checking any existing public information about the land, including any change of use in the past, the types of prior businesses located on the land, and any administrative inspection data, (2) carrying out a physical inspection of the site such as investigating any cracks in buildings and observing any water or streams on the land, and (3) talking with the landowner and any business operators at the site, including speaking with local administrative authorities as needed. Please note, however, that Phase 1 does not involve any sampling or chemical testing of soil. At the conclusion of Phase 1, a report is drafted which specifies the likelihood of any **Recognized Environmental Conditions** ("RECs") at the site, and if the likelihood is low, then there is no need to proceed to Phase 2.

In the event there are RECs discovered in the Phase 1 inspection, the buyer will usually request **Phase 2** testing. Phase 2 involves actual chemical or gas testing of the soil, including boring holes, testing groundwater, and taking samples at various locations on the site. If soil contamination is found, then **Phase 3** is requested, which entails carrying out remedial measures (if possible) or building an enclosure around the contaminated soil, assessing the necessity of monitoring the site, and drafting a report on the likely causes of the pollution and potential effects on the water supply, etc. At this point, the landowner should also notify the prefectural governor of the existence of the pollution in accordance with Art. 14 of the Soil Pollution Law.

7 An Overview of the Building Standards Law

I. Introduction

The purpose of the **Building Standards Law** ("BSL," *kenchiku kijunhou*) is to establish minimum requirements applicable to the construction and use of buildings and land in Japan. Whereas the **City Planning Law** (*toshi keikakuhou*) sets forth rules for creating a 'blueprint' for the development of **Urban Planning Areas** (*toshi keikaku kuiki*), establishing a legal basis and procedural rules for designating the zones or districts which may be located in such areas, numerous other laws such as the BSL, the Landscape Law (*keikanhou*), the Road Law (*dourohou*), and the Urban Parks Law (*toshi kouenhou*) augment this blueprint by instituting detailed regulations applicable to such zones or districts. In this way, the BSL supplements the rules of the City Planning Law, and along with various local ordinances and other laws, creates a legal framework for regulating the construction and use of buildings and land in Japan.

The BSL establishes both **Basic Regulations** (*tantai kitei*, found in Chapter Two of the law) and **Collective Regulations** (*shuudan kitei*, found in Chapter Three). The basic regulations apply to all buildings and parcels of land throughout Japan, and regulate general health and safety matters such as minimum ventilation, lighting, utilities, the quality of construction materials, and construction requirements for fire evacuation. The focus of the collective regulations, on the other hand, is on how a structure affects a certain municipality as a whole, and thus generally these regulations apply only in urban planning areas and quasi-urban planning areas (*jun toshi keikaku kuiki*) as designated by prefectural or national government authorities. The purpose of the collective regulations is to indicate standards and restrictions on building use, height, total floor area, etc. which pertain to specific use zones or districts designated in Japanese metropolitan areas. Please note that the matters covered in the collective regulations make up a majority of the Explanation of Important Matters described in Chapter 2 of this book.

The following is a brief description of some of the most important collective regulations in the BSL.

II. Use Zones (BSL, Articles 48-51)

Urban Planning Areas (*toshi keikaku kuiki*) are usually divided into **Urbanization Areas** (*shigaika kuiki,* areas where urbanization is to be promoted) and **Non-Urbanization Areas** (*shigaika chousei kuiki,* areas intended to be used mainly for agriculture or preserving the environment and where in principle no construction is allowed) in accordance with the City Planning Law. In turn, urbanization areas are configured mainly into **Use Zones** (*youto chiiki*) and **Adjunct Use Districts** (*hojoteki chiiki chiku*). There are different types of adjunct use districts, and certain adjunct use districts may only be established in use zones while others may be established anywhere in urban planning areas (other than non-urbanization areas). Adjunct use districts are primarily employed to adjust or supplement the regulations of the different use zones.

There are twelve types of use zones which may be used to plan and design an urban blueprint under the City Planning Law: three types of industrial zones, two types of commercial zones, and seven types of residential zones. One way the BSL regulates these zones is by listing the types of uses for buildings or facilities (including size categories) which may be located in each of the twelve zones without special license. For example, generally libraries may be located in any of the use zones other than exclusive industrial zones *(kougyou sen'you chiiki*), and stores larger than 500 square meters in area are not allowed in the first three residential zones (which tend to have the most zoning restrictions). In addition, please note that the designated local administrative authorities (*tokutei gyouseichou*) may permit a non-conforming building in any of the twelve zones.

As a general rule, adjunct use districts either amend (increase or decrease) the restrictions of the twelve use zones, or they establish special, separate districts with specific building standards as needed. Examples of adjunct use districts include 'high utilization districts' (*koudo riyou chiku*), which set, among others, a maximum and minimum floor area ratio ("FAR") and a maximum building-to-land ratio in a certain use zone, and 'special city districts' (*tokutei gaiku*), which may be designated in any part of an urban planning area (other than a non-urbanization area), and are used to relax restrictions like FAR rules, building-to-land ratio rules, and restrictions on maximum height. A good example of a special city district (*tokutei gaiku*) is the famous skyscraper district in Tokyo's Shinjuku ward.

III. Fire Prevention Districts (BSL, Articles 61-67)

Because Japan is such a densely populated country, with a high percentage of its population living in crowded urban centers, there are adjunct use districts called **Fire Prevention Districts** (*bouka chiiki*) and **Semi-Fire Prevention Districts** (*jun bouka chiiki*) which may be established anywhere in urban planning areas (other than non-urbanization areas). Their objective is to regulate the design and construction of all buildings in these districts to prevent a fire from quickly spreading across the entire city. In addition, there are certain buildings in urban planning areas (schools, hospitals, theaters, department stores, warehouses, etc.) which, regardless of their location, must meet the requirements of **Fire-Resistant Buildings** (*taika kenchikubutsu*).

The BSL requires all buildings constructed in fire prevention districts to qualify as either a fire-resistant building or a semi-fire resistant building. Roughly speaking, a fire-resistant building has a core structure that will likely resist the temperatures of a regular fire, without extensive burning or major damage (for instance, any buildings in a fire prevention district may not be made exclusively of wood). If a specific district or use zone is designated as a semi-fire prevention district, any buildings which are taller than four stories, or with a total area of more than 1,500 square meters, must qualify as a fire-resistant building. There are also many design rules and rules regarding materials used for walls, sign boards, etc. in fire prevention and semi-fire prevention districts.

IV. Floor Area Ratios and Building-to-Land Ratios (BSL, Articles 52-53)

The size and height of buildings are regulated by the BSL establishing maximum acceptable **Floor Area Ratios** (*yousekiritsu*) and **Building-to-Land Ratios** (*kenpeiritsu*), which can vary based on factors such as which use zone the property is in, whether the property is located on a corner lot, and whether the building qualifies as a fire-resistant building. The FAR regulations function to limit population density in a certain neighborhood by limiting the total amount of floor space (height and area) for any building constructed on a certain parcel of land. This not only protects access to sunlight for surrounding buildings, but also prevents roads in the vicinity from becoming overcrowded. The building-to-land ratio, on the other hand, limits the percentage of a parcel of land that may be covered by a building (area only). This regulation serves to make it harder for fires to spread in the city and restricts buildings from completely obstructing light and the flow of air at the street level, thereby helping to maintain a more livable urban environment.

V. Roads and Adjacent Land (BSL, Articles 42-44)

The connection between roads and specific parcels of land is very important for those wishing to build on such land. This is because in principle buildings may only be built on parcels of land which border at least two meters of a **Road** as defined under the BSL. The BSL designates a 'road' as generally all thoroughfares complying with the Road Law (*dourohou*) definition, the City Planning Law definition, roads which existed prior to the BSL, or roads so designated by competent administrative agencies.

Under the BSL, as a general rule every road must be at least four meters wide (unless a local administrative agency has mandated it to be six meters wide). In the event a road is less than four (or six) meters wide for some legitimate reason (for example, because the road existed prior to the BSL), an owner of a parcel of land bordering the road who wishes to build on such land may not build on the area which is less than two meters (or three meters in the case of a six meter road) from the center line of the abutting road (this is called a **Setback**). The area of the setback is not included in FAR or building-to-land ratio calculations, and since the setback portion of land may not have any buildings, walls, etc. built on it, the existence of a setback can represent a significant use restriction for landowners.

VI. Height Restrictions (BSL, Articles 55-56-2)

There are many detailed height restrictions for buildings in Japan under the BSL. These height restrictions are generally a product of the densely populated nature of Japanese cities and are either (1) absolute height restrictions or (2) restrictions which require buildings to be built at a slope (*i.e.*, sloping inward away from the road) over a certain height (*e.g.*, over 20 meters). There are three types of **Sloping Restrictions**: (1) roadway sloping restrictions (*douro shasenseigen*), (2) neighboring land sloping restrictions (*rinchi shasenseigen*), and (3) north sloping restrictions (*hokubu shasenseigen*). These restrictions aim to preserve sunlight and the flow of air to surrounding buildings and roads, and in particular to allow sunlight (which shines from the south in Japan) to reach neighbors in buildings situated to the north. Please note that only buildings in the first two residential use zones, and buildings in the next two residential use zones not subject to the **Height Restrictions to Protect Access to Sunlight** (*hikage kisei* as described below), are subject to the north sloping restrictions.

The 'height restrictions to protect access to sunlight' complement the FAR and building-to-land ratio rules. Their main purpose is to protect relatively small buildings from being completely blocked out of direct sunlight by tall neighboring buildings. In addition, in the first two residential use zones, the maximum height of all buildings under the BSL is limited to either ten or twelve meters (as determined in the blueprint created under the City Planning Law). Further, all buildings in commercial use zones (*shougyou chiiki*), industrial use zones (*kougyou chiiki*), and exclusive industrial zones are exempt from the height restrictions to protect access to sunlight. The relevant legal rules are very detailed, however as a basic guide, only buildings in the first two residential use zones which have eaves over seven meters high or four or more stories, and buildings over ten meters high in the other use zones, are regulated by the height restrictions to protect access to sunlight.

8 The Building Certification Process and Acts of Development

I. The Building Certification Process

The purpose of the building certification process (*kenchiku kakunin seido*) is to confirm that buildings are designed and constructed in accordance with the requirements of the **Building Standards Law** ("BSL," *kenchiku kijunhou*) and other laws and ordinances concerning structures, building sites, and building equipment. The process, which can involve multiple inspections for legal compliance by either an authorized local public officer (*kenchiku shuji*) or, based on a 1998 BSL amendment, a private company authorized by the **Minister of Land, Infrastructure, Transport, and Tourism** ("MLIT") (or authorities in the relevant prefecture), generally entails two steps, a pre- and post-construction confirmation process. However, due to the limits of time and manpower, it is not practical for every type of construction project to be subject to the rigorous inspection process, and as a result there are various rules regarding whether the process is legally necessary based on location, size, type of construction, and/or intended use of the structure. In this context, project types include new buildings (*shinchiku*), additions (*zouchiku*), reconstructions (*kaichiku*, legally defined as the partial or total reconstruction of a building destroyed through disaster with substantially the same intended use, structure, location, floor number, and size), relocations (*iten*), renovations (*shuuzen*), remodelings (*moyougae*), and changes of use (*youto henkou*).

Under Art. 6 of the BSL, companies or subcontractors wishing to carry out certain construction projects (described in Section II below) are required to apply for and receive a **Construction Confirmation Certificate** (*kenchikukakuninzumisho*) prior to beginning construction. Receipt of a construction confirmation certificate for subject properties is also required prior to advertising a new property or concluding a purchase and sale agreement (not a lease) for a new property under Art. 33 and Art. 36 of the Real Estate Transactions Law. At this initial stage, the building certification process primarily focuses on an inspection of the design plans for the project. The responsible party must attach to the construction confirmation application various documents such as a summary of the project and drawings indicating, among other matters, the physical location of the future structure on the construction site.

After the construction confirmation certificate has been received and construction begun, an intermediate inspection may be necessary in cases where the building is deemed to contain a mechanism or structure which will be difficult to inspect (or rectify) after completion of the construction work (for instance, a reinforced steel frame on the bottom of the second floor of an apartment building to be over three stories high when completed). In these cases, the responsible party should apply for and receive an **Intermediate Inspection Approval Certificate** (*chuukan kensa goukakushou*) prior to continuing the construction. In addition, if there are material changes to the project after the construction confirmation certificate has been issued, the party should file and receive approval of a **Confirmation of Plan Change** (*keikaku henkoukakuninsho*).

Upon completion of the entire construction project, there is a final inspection process (*kanryou kensa*), and provided the structure is acceptable and constructed in accordance with the approved design plans, the competent authority (either the authorized local public officer or private company) will issue a **Completion of Building Inspection Certificate** (*kensazumisho*). There are also separate certification processes for each elevator of a building, other important building equipment (such as furnaces), and certain other structures on the building or building site such as signs and retaining walls (*kousakubutsu*). Additionally, after completion there are periodic building and fire prevention inspections for certain buildings depending on size, use, location, etc.

A construction company or owner may choose to use either the local authorized public officer or the authorized private company for the building certification process. The reason a private company option was introduced in 1998 was to help speed up the inspection process. However, one of the main differences between the two options is that there is no statutory maximum period for the private company to inspect design plans and issue the construction confirmation certificate, whereas the local public officer is generally obliged to inspect and respond to an application within either seven or 35 days (depending on the type of project). A list of the private companies authorized by the MLIT (or prefectural governor) to carry out the building certification process may be found in Japanese at http://www.icba.or.jp/index.htm.

II. Criteria for Receiving the Construction Confirmation Certificate

There are a variety of rules depending on the size, type of construction project, location, and intended use of the completed building which determine whether a construction confirmation certificate is legally required. For example, there is a location rule requiring a construction confirmation certificate for all new buildings in urban planning areas (*toshi keikaku kuiki)*, quasi-urban planning areas (*jun toshi keikaku kuiki*), and quasi-landscaping districts (*jun keikan chiku*), unless the new building site is in a location which has been specially excepted from the certificate (by either the prefectural governor or local mayor). A construction confirmation certificate is also necessary in such locations for an addition (provided it creates more than ten square meters of new floor space) or a relocation or reconstruction project (provided it involves more than ten square meters of floor space). This rule based on location, however, does not apply to large-scale renovations, large-scale remodelings, or change of use projects. (Legally, 'large scale' means affecting over 50% of the main structural part of a building.)

Another location rule concerns whether the new building, addition, relocation or reconstruction is in a fire prevention district (*bouka chiiki*) or a semi-fire prevention district (*jun bouka chiiki*). If the construction project is so located, the responsible party must receive a construction confirmation certificate prior to carrying out the project. Please note that under this rule, the size of the total floor area of the new building, addition, etc. is immaterial.

There are rules which overlap with the above location rules for buildings of specific uses over a certain size, regardless of their location (these buildings are legally designated as **Large Buildings**). For example, theaters, hospitals, schools, hotels, department stores, parking garages, warehouses, and other structures commonly used by the general public (and enumerated in the BSL) are generally subject to the building certification requirement, provided the floor area to be affected is over 100 square meters. Moreover, these buildings are subject to the certification process in the event of any new construction, any addition, relocation or reconstruction concerning more than ten square meters of floor space, or any size of large-scale remodeling, large-scale restoration, or change of use under Art. 87 of the BSL (provided that the new change of use is considered to be substantially different from the prior use). For example, a change of use from a large play theater to a large movie theater would normally be excepted from the requirement.

The above definition of 'large buildings' also includes: (1) wooden structures with at least three floors, over 500 square meters in total area, over thirteen meters high *or* over nine meters high from the ground to the structure's eaves, and (2) non-wooden structures with at least two floors *or* over 200 square meters in total area. For these 'large buildings,' a construction confirmation certificate is required for buildings to be newly constructed as well as any addition, relocation or reconstruction (concerning more than ten square meters of floor space), or any large-scale remodeling or restoration, regardless of location. However, there is no construction confirmation certificate requirement for the above buildings in the event of a change of use.

III. The Completion of Building Inspection Certificate (*kensazumisho*)

As explained above, at the end of the building certification process, the inspecting authority can issue a document called a 'completion of building inspection certificate' (*kensazumisho*, also commonly known as a *kenzumi*, which is similar to a certificate of occupancy in the United States). The *kenzumi* provides conclusive evidence that the structure complies with the BSL and all other applicable laws at the time of completion of the construction project, but unlike a construction confirmation certificate, receipt of a *kenzumi* is not legally required. However, as a general rule, Art. 7-6 of the BSL makes it *illegal* for the owner of a **Large Building** (as defined in Section II above) to use or allow a third party to use the new building, addition, reconstruction, etc. prior to receipt of a *kenzumi*.

Nevertheless, there are two circumstances in which the use of such buildings is allowed prior to receipt of a *kenzumi*. If such use is deemed to be for 'temporary use,' and is approved by the designated administrative authority (*tokutei gyouseichou*), the owner may begin using the completed construction. In the alternative, after seven days have elapsed from receipt of the **Notice of Completion of Construction** (*kouji kanryou todokede*) by the authorized local public officer or private company, the owner may begin using the property, provided that the authorized public officer or private company has not responded to the notice.

If there has been a response to the notice, it will usually either contain an issued *kenzumi*, a request for more information about a certain section of the property, or a notice that a *kenzumi* will not be issued for some reason. Also, if a *kenzumi* is received and subsequently lost (which can occur occasionally since it is a one page document and some properties change hands frequently), it may be possible to get the local administrative authority to issue a document called a *kenzumi shoumeisho* (or 'proof of *kenzumi*') based on the local construction confirmation register (*kenchiku kakunin daichou*). It should be noted however, that for a certain percentage of properties without a *kenzumi*, no *kenzumi* was ever issued due to an illegal addition, etc. after issuance of the construction confirmation certificate.

In addition to satisfying the legal requirement for using a 'large building,' there are other reasons why receiving a *kenzumi* at the time of completion of a construction project is desirable. For instance, usually a building without a *kenzumi* will not be accepted for entrustment by a trust bank, and it can be exceptionally difficult to receive bank financing for a property without a *kenzumi*. In addition, owners holding a *kenzumi* do not need to worry that their property may be deemed an **Illegal Building** (*ihan ken-chikubutsu*) under Art. 9 of the BSL. Although not common, pursuant to this article the local administrative authority may, at its discretion, demand that owners of illegal buildings demolish, remodel, or cease partial or full use of an illegal property.

It is possible for a building with a *kenzumi* to become a property which is considered to be a **Pre-Existing, Non-Conforming Structure** (*kizon futekikaku kenchikubutsu*) (unlike buildings with no *kenzumi*). A pre-existing, non-conforming structure is a building which complied with the BSL and other laws at the time of completion, but due to some subsequent legal change, would not be legal if newly constructed. For example, a building that was legal at the time of completion can be in a use zone (*youto chiiki*) that has been subject to legal amendment. Also, prior to 1968, Japanese buildings were regulated by height only, but presently the floor area ratio ('FAR') (*yousekiritsu*) rules apply. The height restrictions to protect access to sunlight (*hikage kisei*) were also only introduced in 1976.

Although building standards change over time, owners are obliged under law to comply with current legal standards to the extent possible. Nevertheless, as in the above examples, sometimes this is not reasonably feasible without severely infringing on individual rights of ownership. Rather than requiring the complete demolition of such pre-existing, non-conforming structures, in Japan they are usually grandfathered in and allowed to remain in use. However, if after completion, a pre-existing, non-conforming structure is substantially remodeled, renovated, etc., as a general rule the structure will have to be brought up to current legal standards in order for the owner to receive a new *kenzumi*.

There are other documents that are also significant for proving legal compliance such as the structural calculations documentation (*kouzou keisansho*). In 2005-2006, an architect working at Aneha Architectural Design Office was found to have been falsifying earthquake resistance data for construction companies building certain hotels and condominiums. The data was falsified in order to reduce construction costs by lessening the amount of concrete needed to be used in the construction projects. There were many people arrested in the scandal, and as a result of this illegal conduct, the BSL was amended in 2007 to require that a designated third party carry out an independent verification of the architectural design drawings (*ishou sekkeizu*), the structural design drawings (*kouzou sekkeizu*), and the structural calculations documentation (*kouzou keisansho*) for certain structures (such as for wooden buildings over 13 meters high or over nine meters high from the ground to the structure's eaves, steel frame buildings at least four stories high (but not exceeding 60 meters), and for reinforced concrete buildings over 20 meters high (but not exceeding 60 meters)). In addition, all apartment buildings higher than three floors were required to receive an **Intermediate Inspection Approval Certificate** (*chuukan kensa goukakushou*), and the legal penalties for architects falsifying earthquake resistance data were greatly increased as well.

IV. Acts of Development (*kaihatsu koui*)

Prior to beginning a building project, it is necessary to determine whether the construction project will be considered an **Act of Development** (*kaihatsu koui*) under the **City Planning Law** (*toshi keikakuhou*). In the event a project qualifies as an act of development, under Art. 29 of the City Planning Law, the developer must receive a permit from the prefectural governor (or in certain cases, the mayor) prior to beginning the project. Acts of development are regulated in **Urban Planning Areas** (*toshi keikaku kuiki*) so that the authorities may verify in advance that a construction project will be compatible with the urban blueprint designed under the City Planning Law, and outside of urban planning areas, in order to prevent any negative effects from overdevelopment.

An act of development is defined in Art. 4, Section 12 of the City Planning Law as "a change in the natural condition of a parcel of land mainly for the construction of a building or industrial facility." This change may include not just the construction of a new building, but also a renovation or addition. Although the regulations are fairly detailed, as a general rule any project in a designated **Urbanization Area** (*shigaika kuiki*) requiring the transformation of land that is at least 1000 square meters in area, and any project that is 3000 square meters or larger in a **Quasi-Urban Planning Area** (*jun toshi keikaku kuiki*), requires a prior act of development permit. In **Non-Urbanization Areas** (*shigaika chousei kuiki*), any project regardless of size requires a prior permit, and as a general rule the construction of a golf course, asphalt plant, or industrial facility *in any area* necessitates a permit.

There are however many exceptions to when an act of development permit is needed. For example, projects where there is considered to be no change to the natural condition of the land, or a change to the natural condition of the land without the intention of constructing a building or industrial facility (*e.g.*, for building a parking lot), do not generally necessitate an act of development permit. Further, there are exceptions for projects considered to be for the general public's benefit, for instance libraries, welfare centers, schools, etc., as well as for projects undertaken by a prefecture or other government entity. Interestingly, there is also a general exception for buildings erected for use in the agricultural, fishing or forestry industries regardless of size, unless the building is in an urbanization area (*shigaika kuiki*), in which case the developer needs a prior permit if at least 1000 square meters will be developed.

9 Building Standards for Earthquake Resistance

As became tragically evident in March 2011, Japan is a land of earthquakes and tsunamis. As a consequence, the Japanese government has improved building standards frequently over the last century to better protect its citizens from these disasters. In modern Japan, the most significant legal changes regulating the construction of new buildings for earthquake resistance occurred in 1981. Unfortunately, it is not economically viable for buildings to be constructed with 100% resistance to earthquakes of any magnitude, and the basic goal of the law is to prevent the significant loss of life and limb and severe damage which may render a building uninhabitable.

The revision of the **Building Standards Law** (*kenchiku kijunhou*) that was made effective from June 1st, 1981 was a reaction to the 1978 earthquake in Miyagi Prefecture. Under the prior law, construction companies were generally only obliged to construct a building so that in the event of an earthquake which *would definitely occur* during the life of a new building (assumed to occur once every several decades and measuring approximately 5 on the Japanese Earthquake Scale or 4.5-5.5 on the Richter Scale), damage from the earthquake would at most only result in minor cracks in its walls. The 1981 revision, however, added a further condition that in the event of an earthquake which *may possibly occur* during the life of a new building (assumed to occur once every several hundred years and measuring approximately 6 to 7 on the Japanese Earthquake Scale or 6.5-8.5 on the Richter Scale), the building would not be completely destroyed or collapse. (The Richter Scale and the Japanese

Earthquake Scale are disparate because they measure different things: the Richter Scale is a measure of total energy released, whereas the Japanese Earthquake Scale describes the degree of shaking at a location on the earth's crust.)

The revised Building Standards Law applies to all buildings which received a **Construction Confirmation Certificate** (*kenchiku kakunizumisho*) after May 31st, 1981. However, in the building certification process, a construction confirmation certificate is issued prior to the completion of construction, which means buildings with a construction confirmation certificate issued prior to May 31st, 1981, but with construction completed after that date, were grandfathered in and not subject to the revised law. Consequently, there are presently buildings in Japan which were completed in 1982 that are still only subject to the requirements of the prior law (completion of construction can easily take over seven months after the construction confirmation certificate is issued). Nevertheless, many of these buildings completed after 1981 have subsequently been subject to seismic retrofitting to make them more earthquake resistant.

According to a Japanese Ministry of Construction Report (a predecessor to the **Ministry of Land, Infrastructure, Transport, and Tourism**, "MLIT"), 29% of all buildings subject to the pre-June 1st, 1981 Building Standards Law and affected by the Great Hanshin Earthquake (which struck the Osaka area on January 17th, 1995 and measured approximately 6.8 on the Richter Scale or 7.3 on the Japanese Earthquake Scale) suffered major damage (including 14% that were considered completely destroyed or had collapsed). In comparison, only 8% of buildings subject to the revised law suffered major damage, with roughly 3% that were considered completely destroyed or had collapsed. This suggests that compliance with the newer 1981 building standards led to significantly less overall structural damage.

There are a variety of measures Japanese construction companies use to increase earthquake resistance for buildings. For example, some buildings have hollowed out walls which cover sliding metal plates designed to help dissipate motion. Top class skyscrapers frequently use even more advanced technology such as fluid-filled shock absorbers. Thick oil in the absorber is made to spill in the opposite direction of the building's sway. The Roppongi Hills Mori Tower, one of the tallest buildings in Japan at 781 feet, deployed this damper technology when it was finished in 2003.

Other earthquake resistance measures in buildings include special reinforcement materials in the sub-floors to prevent ceilings from caving in during an earthquake, special buffers in both the construction joints and weight-bearing pillars to absorb the shock waves from earthquakes, and emergency elevators with special elevator shafts to prevent smoke and fire and enable smooth evacuation during a disaster. Still, buildings over 20 stories tall (roughly over 61 meters or 200 feet) have a very long natural swaying period due to the length of their axis beams, which makes the upper floors especially susceptible to shaking. Technology to dampen this can only have a limited effect, and according to a recent survey by the Japan Building Owners and Managers Association, the average height of commercial buildings completed in Tokyo after 2006 is roughly 74.4 meters (about 244 feet).

Probable Maximum Loss ("PML") is the measure that is most often used to assess the potential risk of loss from an earthquake. It is also used as a criterion when applying for earthquake insurance. Although the exact definition of PML varies with the appraisal company, it is generally a measure of the percentage of economic damage (*i.e.*, the repair or replacement cost) to a building that would likely arise from a 'maximum credible earthquake' occurring during the useful life of the building (a **Maximum Credible Earthquake** is an earthquake that happens once every 475 years, meaning an earthquake that has roughly a ten percent chance of occurring in any 50-year period). For example, if a building has a PML of 15%, this means that the building would likely suffer damages equaling approximately fifteen percent of its total cost from the occurrence of a maximum credible earthquake. Generally in Japan, a PML of 15% or less is acceptable to most purchasers of individual buildings, and for bulk purchases or larger securitizations, a 'portfolio PML' of no more than 20%.

There are still many buildings in use throughout Japan which were built based on the pre-1981 Building Standards Law. Although some of these already satisfy the newer building standards based on their structural design, seismic retrofitting is a major issue for many owners. Balancing the costs of retrofitting versus the costs of demolishing and rebuilding is difficult, especially when the building is a condominium with many owners of differing means.

Recently the MLIT announced plans to require all buildings over 5000 square meters in area, and certain other buildings located on major emergency roads, to undergo an earthquake resistance examination beginning in 2015. Of the roughly 150,000 buildings in Japan at least 10,000 square meters in area, the MLIT estimates that roughly 40% have never been measured for earthquake resistance. The new legal amendments will propose a three-tier grading system, and for buildings with the lowest grade, seismic retrofitting will be mandatory. The MLIT is also proposing subsidies for owners in the event retrofitting is necessary, and fines for noncompliance.

10 Japanese Land Valuations and Real Estate Indices

I. Public Valuations of Land

An interesting characteristic of the Japanese real estate market is that there are regular land valuations published by the **Ministry of Land, Infrastructure, Transport, and Tourism** ("MLIT"), the **National Tax Office**, and each prefectural or local government. These valuations, although not indicative of the prices which would be agreed between buyers and sellers in the open market, can serve as a useful guide for buyers of regional real estate where land transactions are infrequent. In addition, it is common practice for Japanese real estate professionals to use the valuation for inheritance and gift tax (one of the 'roadside land values' explained below), plus a certain premium, to compute a fast, rough-and-ready estimate of market price for a given parcel of land.

It should be noted however, that all of these public valuations pertain to land values only, and there are no published government valuations of buildings. Further, the custom in Japan is that in land and building purchase transactions, the price of the land is assessed at a relatively high percentage of the total transaction when compared to transactions in other countries. In fact, for large commercial deals in major metropolitan areas, sometimes the land alone is assessed as over 80% of the total transaction value.

The MLIT issues the **Official Land Value** (*kouji chika*) one time a year measured on January 1st and usually announced in the middle of March. It is calculated by at least two licensed real estate appraisers valuing parcels of land based on a review of past transactions and an assessment of the highest potential cash flow from the land (regardless of any existing buildings). In 2011, there were roughly 26,000 parcels of urban land assessed for this valuation.

The subject parcels are chosen year to year by the **MLIT Land Appraisal Committee** (*tochi kantei i'inkai*), and the official land value has been published for properties in each of Japan's 47 prefectures since 1974. This valuation is used as a benchmark for Japanese real estate appraisers as well as for compensation for the expropriation of private land by government entities, and thus can be considered one of the most important public valuations of land. The reason the MLIT announces the official land value is to provide an "estimate of inherent land values" while attempting to take out the various speculative and subjective factors driving price between buyers and sellers, thereby "indicating an objective measure" for the general real estate market.

The **Standard Land Value** (*todoufuken chika chosa*, also known as the *kijun chika*) has been estimated one time a year since 1975 by each prefecture in accordance with the Enforcement Ordinance for the National Land Use Planning Act. The date of measure for the standard land value is July 1st, and it is generally announced in late September every year. Last year there were 22,264 separate parcels assessed, and the method of calculation is substantially similar to the method used for the official land value described above. However, the main differences between the standard land value and the official land value are (1) different parcels of land are measured (although there is some overlap), (2) the difference in date of measure (July 1st versus January 1st), (3) that the standard land value does not have to be estimated by more than one appraiser, (4) that the standard land value does not directly affect dealings with the general public (as opposed, for example, to expropriations based on the official land value), (5) that not only land in urban areas but also forested regions and resort areas are covered by the standard land value, and (6) that there are less total parcels of land measured for the standard land value.

The third main public valuation is carried out for taxation purposes. Since 1955, the National Tax Office has been publishing the **Valuation for Inheritance and Gift Tax** (*souzokuzei hyouka*) every year with January 1st as the date of measure. It is one of the two **Roadside Land Values** (*rosenka*), which are used for assessing taxes on land bordering major thoroughfares. The other roadside land value is the **Valuation for Fixed Asset Tax** (*koutei shisanzei hyouka*), which has been calculated by local government authorities once every three years since 1958. Although the date of measure is January 1st (like the official land value), roadside land values are announced every July 1st. The reason the results are published six months after measurement is the very large number of parcels subject to this valuation (approximately 410,000 in 2011). Each of the roadside land values is based on the applicable official land value when available; in general, the valuation for fixed asset tax is roughly 70% of the official land value, whereas the valuation for inheritance and gift tax is approximately 80%.

The **Chika LOOK Report** has been published quarterly by the MLIT since 2007 for the main wards of the three largest metropolitan areas (the Tokyo, Osaka and Nagoya areas). This public valuation of land takes into consideration a variety of factors such as price, current yield, number of transactions, general demand for investment real estate, and office, shop and apartment rent levels. Since it is released quarterly as opposed to one time per year, it can be used as a more up-to-date assessment of land values than any of the other public valuations of land.

II. Private Valuations of Land

The **Urban Land Price Index** (*shigaichi kakaku shisuu*) is an estimate of urban land values calculated by the Japan Real Estate Institute twice a year with March 31st and September 30th as the dates of measure. (For Japanese companies, the fiscal year traditionally ends at the close of business on March 31st.) It was first published in 1936 and as such is the oldest real estate valuation in Japan. In addition, there are the Mitsui Real Estate **Japanese Real Estate Statistics Report**, and the Nomura Real Estate **Urbannet** valuations, both of which focus on major urban areas. Although they cover fewer parcels of land in their estimates in comparison to the public land valuations, they are issued four times a year like the Chika LOOK Report.

III. Japanese Real Estate Indices

Real estate indices serve an important function for real estate investors because they provide an objective standard for assessing the performance of a specific asset and its asset manager. Markets necessarily fluctuate over time, making it hard for investors to know to what extent performance of an asset should be attributed to its manager, and to what extent performance is due to the market itself. Accordingly, having a broad-based real estate index or set of indices is vital to the creation of an efficient and transparent market for professional investors. In addition, real estate indices can be used for creating real estate derivative securities which are investment instruments with values varying with the performance of the subject real estate. This type of security is useful for investors who desire real estate exposure in their portfolios without owning any hard assets.

In Japan, recently there have been several interesting developments in the area of real estate indices. The **Association of Real Estate Securitization in Japan** ("ARES") is planning on publishing a new index called the **ARES Japan Fund Index** beginning in late 2012, and ten of the most prominent operators of private real estate funds in Japan (including Nomura Real Estate Asset Management, Mitsui Fudosan Investment Advisors, Sumitomo Mitsui Trust Real Estate Investment Management, Tokyu Land Capital Management, Mitsubishi Jisho Investment Advisors *et al*) will contribute data for this index based on approximately JPY two trillion (USD 2.5 billion at JPY80 per US dollar) of privately held Japanese real estate assets. At present, ARES publishes the **ARES J-REIT Property Index**, which first came online in April 2006 and covers all 35 currently listed J-REITs holding over JPY eight trillion (USD ten billion at JPY80 per US dollar) in Japanese real estate assets. However, there are also plans to combine the new ARES Japan Fund Index with the existing ARES J-REIT Property Index, and rename it the **ARES Japan Property Index**. If successful, the new ARES Japan Property Index will encompass approximately 40% of all real estate investment assets in Japan, including for the first time a number of privately securitized assets not traded on a public exchange.

Another important development in Japanese real estate indices concerns residential assets. In April 2011, the **Tokyo Stock Exchange** ("TSE") started the **TSE Residential Price Index**, which is based on changes in residential asset prices and modeled on the **S&P/Case-Shiller Home Price Index**. This index uses actual transaction prices for 470,000 deals involving existing residences in the greater Tokyo metropolitan area, beginning from June 1993 and compiled monthly. In addition to benefiting consumers, in the future this residential price index should provide a good yardstick for macroeconomic comparisons with other countries with similar indices such as the United States. In addition, the MLIT announced in August 2012 that it has started a two-year trial period for a country-wide residential real estate index based on the **Residential Property Price Indices Handbook** compiled in November 2011 with the assistance of the International Monetary Fund, the Bank for International Settlements, and other national and international organizations. When in full operation, this will be Japan's first public real estate index. The MLIT has also announced that it has plans to start a similar new public index for commercial real estate in Japan.

The ARES J-REIT Property Index is an **Average Price Index**, whereas the above-mentioned TSE Residential Price Index is a **Repeat Sales Index**. The other main type of real estate index is a **Hedonic Regression Index** such as the **IPD/Recruit Residential Price Index**. A repeat sales index is based on a historic sample of prices (at least two actual sale prices) for the subject properties, and an average price index is based on an aggregated average price of a certain measure (for example, price per square foot). The problem with this type of index is that an average price index isn't always the best measure for investors because it doesn't take into consideration how property prices have changed between two periods of time. Since properties sold in one period never coincide exactly with properties sold in another period, changes in price may be due to specific characteristics of the properties changing hands (*e.g.*, different average age of the buildings transacted), rather that any aggregate change in the market per se. That is, comparing different properties of varying locations with different construction dates and other building characteristics may not accurately reflect actual market conditions (*i.e.*, if prices go up from one period to the next, it may be because the average quality of the properties changing hands increased or the properties were in better locations, rather than due to any change in the market fundamentals themselves.)

The repeat sales index and the hedonic regression index were both developed to try to overcome this basic problem of comparing apples and oranges. The repeat sales index is based on groupings of individual properties which have been transacted a multiple number of times. This aggregation is used to control differences in price due to differing locations, attributes, etc. of properties. Since this type of index varies due to actual changes in prices paid by buyers for the same properties, performance of this index is comparable to the performance of stock indices (which change in price over time only due to changes in what buyers are willing to pay for the same securities).

The hedonic regression index takes another approach to solving the problem of not comparing like-for-like. Rather than tracking changes in price in the same properties (which may not occur for large intervals of time), a hedonic regression index is calculated by using a model of individual property and transaction characteristics (for instance location, age, size, building quality, etc.), and tracking the changes in these characteristics over time. In this way, a hedonic regression index is able to isolate outside factors which may affect price and distill any variance in price as due only to actual market changes, provided the characteristics used as constants in the model remain constant and are complete enough to provide a good assessment of price changes for each property.

Please find in the following chart a reference list of Japanese real estate indices with notes indicating whether they are compiled using a hedonic regression, average price, or repeat sales methodology.

Reference Chart of Japanese Real Estate Indices

		First Published	Data beginning from	Frequency
Residential Property Indices				
1	Tokyo Kantei Index	Oct-94	Jan-85	monthly
2	IPD/Recruit Index	Mar-01	Jan-86	monthly
3	At Home/Ken Corporation/JREI Index	Nov-01	yearly 1998	biannually
4	JRI/Eastern Japan REINS Index	May-02	Jan-95	monthly
5	Tokyo Stock Exchange Residential Price Index	Apr-11	Jun-93	monthly
6	MLITResidential RE Price Index (tentative)	Aug-12 (trial started)	Aug-08	monthly
Investment Real Estate Indices				
1	MUFJ Trust/CBRE Index	Nov-98	1970	annually
2	IPD Japan Index	Sep-04	2003	annually
3	ARES J-REITProperty Index	Apr-06	Jan-02	monthly
4	T-MAX Kawaguchi Index	Oct-10	May-02	monthly
5	Waseda/MFI/Nikkei BP Index (not official name)	Oct-11 (planned)	Dec-00	quarterly
6	NLI Research/Sanko Estate	Jan-11	Oct-11	quarterly
J-REIT Indices (Investment Unit Indices)				
1	Quick REIT Index	Jul-02	Sep-01	monthly
2	TSE J-REIT Index	Apr-03	Mar-03	real time
3	STBRI J-REIT Index	Oct-04	Sep-01	monthly
4	MFI J-REIT Style Index	2011 (planned)	Mar-03	monthly

Area Covered	Calculation Method	Type of Data
Tokyo, Osaka, Nagoya	moving average	Condo sale price (new properties from catalogue/existing properties from own research)
Tokyo, Osaka	hedonic regression	Condo sale price (existing condos based on advertised and actual price)
Tokyo	hedonic regression	Condo sale price (new and existing actual price, actual rent price and cap rate also considered)
Tokyo	hedonic regression	Condo sale price (existing condos and actual price based on Eastern Japan REINS data)
Tokyo	repeat sale	Condo sale price (existing condos and actual price based on Eastern Japan REINS data)
Japan	hedonic regression	Actual residence price (survey at registration or notified to MOJ or REINS)
13 Main cities	(own calculation method)	Virtual office revenue calculated from official price, construction unit price, and market rent level estimate
Japan	weighted average	Appraisal value from J-REIT properties, rent revenue. Also based on data from insurance companies
Japan	weighted average	Appraisal value from J-REIT properties, rent revenue. From 2010 also based on private fund data
Japan	weighted average	Current price of J-REIT properties. Properties also assessed individually based on current market
Japan	repeat sale	Actual office building prices. Also based on Nikkei real estate market information
3 main wards of Tokyo	hedonic regression	Actual rent prices for Chuo, Chiyoda and Minato wards (broken up by scale of building)
	weighted average	Distribution/non-distribution basis. First J-REIT Index using Quick terminal
	weighted average	Distribution/non-distribution basis. Data on property use from June 2010
	weighted average	Distribution/non-distribution basis. Residential J-REIT and office J-REIT indices also prepared
	weighted average	Distribution/non-distribution basis. Categorized by asset type and sponsor

11 Leasing in Japan

I. Introduction

Many of the legal rules and customs regarding the leasing of land and buildings in Japan developed during the periods of acute housing shortage from 1940-1950 and high economic growth from 1950-1990. In this latter period, there were three times of especially rapid price growth in land prices: the appreciation of industrial land prices in the early 1960s, the appreciation of residential land prices beginning in 1973, and the appreciation of land prices in cities, suburban areas and subsequently local regions throughout Japan beginning in 1980 and ending with the bursting of the Japanese real estate bubble in 1990-91. Due to the general uptrend in real estate prices until the early 1990s (as well as other factors such as landlord-tenant relations prior to 1950), current Japanese law provides relatively strong protections for tenants of land and buildings, since the overall trend of rising prices and scarcity of properties was thought to give landlords the opportunity to drive up rents.

However, the balance of power between landlords and tenants started changing in the early 1990s. As a response, parallel legal rules allowing for a new type of lease, a 'fixed-term' lease, were enacted in 2000. These rules assist landlords by giving them an optional set of leasing rules which, if agreed to in lieu of a 'traditional' lease, can allow them to retain a higher degree of control over their leased properties. Nevertheless, Japanese laws with respect to leasing still retain their relative bias for tenants. This is one of the reasons why landlords traditionally have required the payment of 'key money' (*reikin*, a separate, non-refundable payment for the right to lease a property) and relatively high deposit amounts (in the past, up to two years of rent for commercial leases was customary).

The basic philosophy of Japanese law with respect to leasing is that the landlord-tenant relation is one of trust and mutual commitment. Consequently, for a landlord to be allowed to terminate a lease due to breach, typically the tenant's breach must be so egregious that the act itself is considered to rise to the level of a violation of trust under Japanese law (*i.e.*, only a severe breach is generally deemed to suffice). For example, in the event of an unauthorized sublease by a tenant, the general legal rule is that the landlord may not terminate the tenant's lease where there are 'extenuating circumstances' which make such subleasing *not* rise to the level of a 'betrayal of trust' (*haishinteki koui*) in the landlord-tenant relation. Furthermore, landlords are commonly advised to provide multiple notices and wait a reasonable time (at least several months) before taking legal action to try to evict a tenant delinquent in paying rent. Even if a tenant files for bankruptcy, generally the landlord may not terminate, regardless of whether the lease agreement so provides.

Either a **Leasehold Interest** (*chinshakuken*, a type of *saiken* or quasi-in personam right) or a **Superficies** (*chijouken*, a type of *bukken* or *in rem* right) can be used to create a land lease for an owner of a building located on land owned by another party. In Japanese, both of these can be referred to as a right to lease land (*shakuchiken*), although the word '*shakuchiken*' is usually used to refer to the former since leasehold interests are created much more frequently than superficies. Reasons for this include the fact that a superficies can be freely transferred without the landowner's consent, and that the holder of a superficies has a legal right to compel the landowner (or the authorities) to register the superficies on the relevant land register. As a rule, superficies give beneficiaries much more of the bundle of legal rights to property than leasehold interests, so they are disfavored by landowners and rarely used in practice.

There is no Japanese custom of the 'triple net lease' as there is in the United States, although common area maintenance (CAM) fees, insurance fees, and utility fees (for water, electricity, HVAC, etc.) are often borne separately by tenants. In many commercial leases, utility fees are paid directly to the landlord as a fixed amount which may not reflect actual expenses. In addition, lease renewal fees are not uncommon for both residential and commercial properties in major metropolitan areas, although there is a trend for landlords not to require such fees.

II. Rules regarding Application of the Japanese Civil Code and the Law on Leasing Land and Buildings

The **Japanese Civil Code** ("JCC") contains the default rules which apply to all leasing transactions in Japan (both commercial and residential). However, most of the JCC rules have been amended and superseded by the **Law on Leasing Land and Buildings** (*shakuchi shakuyahou*, "Land and Building Law") to protect two types of tenants: (1) tenants of buildings, and (2) tenants of land to construct and own a building situated on the land. Tenants with a land lease to own a building enjoy special protection under Japanese law since constructing and owning a building on leased land is so commonplace. Please note that the ownership of a parcel of land and the ownership of a building are separately registerable legal rights in Japan.

Leases to construct and own a building on someone else's land are relatively common because purchasing land is particularly expensive in Japan, and it is usually much easier and cheaper to find suitable land to rent and build on. Further, there is a considerable amount of desirable land (and buildings) controlled by a relatively small number of companies, which do not always market their holdings for sale (for example, currently four companies own approximately 65% of all 'Grade A' office buildings in Tokyo). The large number of land leases to own a building has spurred a separate market in Japan for land with such leases (*sokochi*), where investors buy encumbered land in order to acquire the stable rental income paid by the building's owner.

Generally with respect to building leases and land leases to own a building (including any subleasing arrangements), the contents of the Land and Building Law prevail over any conflicting rules in the JCC. For example, the maximum contractual term of a lease in accordance with the JCC is 20 years, but the Land and Building Law modifies this rule by mandating the *minimum* legal term for land leases to own a building as 30 years (and no maximum term), and for leases of buildings, no minimum or maximum legal term. The JCC rules are still significant, however, because they regulate basic legal matters such as contract formation, land leases where the Land and Building Law rules do not apply, and matters not specifically covered by the Land and Building Law. For instance, matters regarding the repair of properties (*e.g.*, any make good provisions at the time a tenant vacates a property) are regulated by the JCC since this matter is not expressly covered in the Land and Building Law.

Application of the Land and Building Law to land leases generally depends on whether the main purpose of the lease is to own a building on the land. Accordingly, a land lease in order to operate a parking lot is not subject to the Land and Building Law (*i.e.*, it is only subject to the JCC rules), since the main purpose of the lease is not to own a building. Further, a land lease entered into in order to operate a golf course is also generally not subject to the Land and Building Law, even if buildings are built on the leased land, provided ownership of the buildings is merely tangential to the purpose of the lease agreement.

In addition to applying to land leases without a building, the JCC rules exclusively regulate all leases of land or buildings without any charge of rent (known as *shiyou taishaku* and usually existing between blood relations), and leases of buildings which are temporary in nature (such as the stalls in front of Japanese supermarkets). Please note there is a special type of land or building lease as well, a **Lease for Provisional Use** (*ichiji shiyou mokuteki no shakuchiken* or a *ichiji shiyou mokuteki no shakuyaken*), which is not automatically subject to most of either the JCC rules or the Land and Building Law rules. This type of lease is meant for the construction and use of provisional facilities which the parties intend to exist for a short time only. There are also leases that were entered into prior to August 1st, 1992 (the date the Land and Building Law came into effect) which continue to be governed by the legal rules existing prior to August 1st, 1992.

When the Land and Building Law applies to a lease, as a general rule any legal issues which are specifically covered by the law are mandatory and may not be amended by special agreement between the parties, unless the change is more favorable to the tenant than the minimum rules in the Land and Building Law. Consequently, any changes to the detriment of the landlord are in principle valid and enforceable. In the event a lease agreement contains a provision not as favorable to the tenant as the mandatory rules, the agreement is still enforceable, but generally the offending provision is automatically replaced by the Land and Building Law rule. This is in contrast to the JCC rules, which normally may be changed by special agreement between the parties when they apply.

III. Traditional Building Leases

Traditional Building Leases (*futsuu chintaishaku keiyakusho*) contain many favorable rights for tenants due to the Land and Building Law protections. For example, at the time of expiration of a traditional lease agreement, the landlord must have a **Justifiable Reason** to refuse to renew the lease if the tenant would like to renew. There is a very high threshold for what constitutes a landlord's justifiable reason not to renew, and consequently as a practical matter, traditional leases only expire if the tenant consents to vacate. In addition, after a traditional lease is renewed, it automatically becomes a lease with an indefinite term under the Land and Building Law. Further, traditional leases with a term of less than one year are also considered legally to be leases with an indefinite term.

At a minimum, the following four factors are weighed to determine whether a justifiable reason exists for a landlord to refuse to renew a traditional lease: (1) the landlord's need and the tenant's need to use the building, (2) the prior history of leasing of the building (whether key money or any renewal fees were paid, etc.), (3) the current use and condition of the building, and (4) whether the landlord has offered any financial assistance or compensation to the tenant (*e.g.*, moving expenses) in consideration for the tenant to move out (Art. 28, Land and Building Law). (Traditionally there has been a custom of landlords paying a large lump sum called 'eviction money' (*tachinokikin*) to compensate the tenant for the inconvenience of having to vacate.) In practice, other factors are considered as well such as in the case of residential buildings, the number of family members, their ages, the tenant's profession, and the financial situation of the tenant. In the event of dispute, the courts are usually very tenant friendly, and in fact, a finding of a justifiable reason for a landlord is rare.

Even if a landlord has a justifiable reason not to renew a traditional lease, the landlord must still notify the tenant of the landlord's intention not to renew within six months to one year prior to expiration. The notice must also indicate the landlord's justifiable reason. In the event of a lease with indefinite term, a landlord may terminate any time during the lease by giving notice six months in advance and indicating a justifiable reason.

If the landlord fails to deliver the required notice within the prescribed time, the lease agreement will be renewed under the same conditions as the previous lease. A general exception here, however, is when the landlord notifies the tenant in the prescribed time that the lease will not be renewed unless the terms are amended (along with the landlord's justifiable reason). Further, even if the landlord provides advance notice in the above time frame, indicating the justifiable reason and the landlord's intention not to renew, a traditional lease may still be renewed in certain circumstances. That is, if the tenant continues to use the property after the lease expires, and the landlord fails to object 'without delay,' the lease may be deemed to have been renewed under the same conditions as the previous lease.

The legal protections for tenants in a traditional lease make leasing fraught with uncertainty for landlords. As a result, if a landlord wants to lease out a building under a traditional lease for any period of time, basically the landlord has to be prepared to lease out the property *in perpetuity* at the option of the tenant. Even a promise by a tenant to let a traditional lease expire in consideration for receiving a payment in the future would not necessarily bind the tenant, and in general the landlord would only be able to cause the lease not to renew if the landlord also had a justifiable reason and gave the prescribed notice.

IV. Fixed-Term Leases

In 2000, this lopsided situation changed when the Land and Building Law was amended to create the optional rules for a **Fixed-Term Building Lease** (*teiki chintaishaku keiyakusho*). The innovation of the fixed-term lease agreement is that it gives landlords the right to end a tenancy conclusively at the end of the contracted term, provided the minimum legal requirements set forth below are met. The legal requirements are (1) the contract must be written, notarized (*kousei shousho*), and clearly state the lease is for a fixed term and will not be automatically renewed, (2) at the time of contracting, the landlord must provide a separate written notice and explain verbally to the tenant that at the end of the term the lease will not be renewed, and (3) only in the case where the lease term is at least one year, the landlord must provide notice to the tenant no more than one year or less than six months before the end of the term that the lease will end at expiration. Although in principle a fixed-term lease may not be terminated during the term by either party (unless agreed otherwise), please note that the legal purpose of a fixed-term lease is not to lock a tenant in for the entire term, and damages for a claim of lost profits in the event of a tenant's early termination may not result in a judgment covering the entire remaining term of the lease (depending on the circumstances, damages exceeding one year of lost rent may be deemed excessive, and any damages awarded will usually be offset by any rent received during the term from a new tenant for the property).

In the event either condition (1) or (2) above is not fulfilled, then generally the executed agreement will be considered a traditional lease under Japanese law (and a justifiable reason will be needed for the landlord not to renew). If (3) above is not carried out, the fixed-term lease will only expire six months after the written notice is sent to the tenant. Of course, at the end of a fixed-term lease, a landlord and tenant are not prohibited from renewing their lease agreement. However, without the fixed-term lease option, in practice some landlords may not want to lease out a property at all (since generally the landlord will lose the right to use the property for any other reason until the tenant agrees to vacate). Moreover, the fixed-term lease rules now make it possible for a landlord to effectively rent out a building for less than one year, provided the tenant agrees to a fixed-term lease.

A majority of new leases are still traditional leases, although fixed-term leases are used commonly in commercial deals and real estate securitizations to enhance stability and predictability. One reason why traditional leases are still so prevalent is because for the most part, rent levels in Japan remained flat or falling during the 2000s, and landlords typically have wanted their buildings leased up and tenants remaining as long as possible. In addition, landlords sometimes give new tenants the option of entering into either a traditional lease or a fixed-term lease along with a variety of other leasing conditions (such as varying deposit amounts). Tenants sometimes benefit from the fixed-term lease option because it can facilitate a landlord charging cheaper rent (since the tenants do not acquire a quasi-perpetual right to renew).

There are also several new types of **Fixed-Term Land Leases** which are similar to the fixed-term building lease in that they create a way for landowners to effectively end a land lease at the end of the term. In a traditional land lease under the Land and Building Law, the agreed term must be at least 30 years (shorter terms are automatically extended), and, as long as the tenant owns a building on the land, the tenant has a legal option to renew the lease at expiration (for an initial 20-year term and then 10-year terms *in perpetuity*), unless the landowner has a 'justifiable reason' not to renew. In the alternative, at expiration the tenant may decide to force the landowner to purchase the building at market price to extinguish the leasehold interest. Prior to the land leases explained below, any changes to the above rules to the detriment of the tenant were generally unenforceable.

Since the early 1990s a **Fixed-Term Land Lease** (*teiki shakuchiken keiyakusho*) has been possible, which must be in writing and can be used to create a land lease of at least 50 years. If explicitly agreed to by the parties, the land tenant has no general right to renew (*i.e.*, the landowner doesn't need a justifiable reason not to renew), and no right to demand the landowner buy any buildings on the land at the end of the term. In addition, there are also **Land Leases with Purchase Commitment** (*tatemono jouto tokuyakutsuki shakuchiken keiyakusho*) which do not need to be written, must last at least 30 years, and at expiration, the landowner agrees to purchase the building to extinguish the building owner's leasehold interest.

Further, since January 1st, 2008, two types of **Fixed-Term Land Leases for Commercial Use** (*jigyouyou teiki shakuchiken*) have been available. In the first type, the lease term must be 30 or more years and less than 50 years, and the parties are allowed to amend any of the tenant's rights under a traditional land lease to own a building (for instance, the perpetual right to renew the lease and the right at expiration to put the building to the landowner at market price). In the second type, the lease term must be ten or more years but less than 30 years, and the tenant's two rights mentioned directly above do not automatically apply, regardless of whether specifically excluded or not. Both of these types of land leases must, however, be for business use only and in the form of an officially notarized document (*kousei shousho*).

V. The Legal Right to Increase or Decrease Rent

Under Art. 32 of the Land and Building Law, both the landlord and the tenant have the right to amend the rent amount during the term of a lease, *irrespective of the terms of their agreement*, provided the amendment is due to (1) a change in taxes or some other costs, or (2) a change in the value of the land and/or building or some other economic circumstances (*e.g.*, a change in the cost of living), or (3) the rent level has become inappropriate when compared to the rent levels of similar land or buildings in the vicinity. In the event of dispute, the issue must first be brought to a panel of third-party real estate arbitrators under the **Civil Conciliation Law** (*chouteihou*), before proceeding to the courts. In general, Art. 32 creates an advantage for landlords in a rising market (and an advantage for tenants in a falling market), since rents may be raised or decreased unilaterally regardless of the parties' agreement, as long as the "amount is reasonable" (*soutou to mitomeru gaku*) (and provided in the event of dispute, the real estate arbitrators agree with the reduction or increase).

Another important difference between traditional building leases and fixed-term building leases is that in a fixed-term building lease, it is possible for the parties to be bound by a written promise that *neither party* will carry out a rent decrease or increase during the lease term under Art. 32 of the Land and Building Law. However, a clause in a traditional lease that there will be no rent *decreases* during the lease term would likely be unenforceable, because this would be an amendment of the tenant's Land and Building Law rights to the detriment of the tenant. As a consequence, the potential right to decrease rent under a traditional lease agreement can generally be regarded as a non-waivable right of tenants. Nevertheless, Art. 32 expressly provides that a clause in a traditional lease agreement where the landlord promises no rent *increases* during the term is valid and enforceable.

VI. Tenant Rights after Foreclosure on a Mortgage

Under the Land and Building Law, as a general rule a tenant who is occupying a space in a building pursuant to a valid lease has the right to assert its contractual rights with respect to any subsequent third-party purchaser, regardless of whether the leasehold interest is actually registered in the building register maintained at the local Legal Affairs Bureau. However, in the event a tenant leases a space in a building that is subject to a *prior* registered mortgage, the tenant may be forced to vacate the building within six months if the mortgage is foreclosed on and a third party takes ownership. Previously in such case, a building tenant had a three-year grace period after sale, and a tenant of land a five-year grace period, but this was changed in 2004 (except for leases which began prior to the change and have been continuously renewed thereafter). It is for this reason that landlords are required to disclose to prospective tenants in the Explanation of Important Matters discussed in Chapter 2 whether there is a prior registered mortgage on the subject building.

There is, however, a way for new tenants of already-mortgaged buildings to be protected (although rarely carried out in practice). If a tenant rents a space in a building which is subject to a previously registered mortgage, and (1) registers the leasehold interest on the building register, (2) obtains a specific agreement from all of the mortgagees of the property, (3) registers this specific agreement on the building register, *and* (4) obtains consent from any other parties which could be negatively affected by such registration, after a sale of the building due to foreclosure and auction (or private sale etc.), the tenant would generally be able to assert its contractual rights over the third-party purchaser. However, this is oftentimes not an issue because the third-party purchaser would like for the tenant to stay and continue paying rent on the property. In addition, please note that an owner of a registered building with a land lease to benefit the building may assert the land leasehold interest over a subsequent purchaser of the land, irrespective of registration, except in the event the land is sold due to execution on a mortgage that was already registered before the building was constructed (as discussed in Chapter 3, Section VI).

12 Latent Defect Liability

Latent Defect Liability (*kashitanposekinin*) refers to an implied warranty under the **Japanese Civil Code** ("JCC") which protects good-faith purchasers of land and buildings. In general, it applies to all real estate transactions and creates seller liability provided the purchaser has no prior notice of the latent defect, and provided that the latent defect is not so obvious that it should be easily discoverable through normal inspection by the purchaser prior to closing. Unlike legal jurisdictions where *caveat emptor* ('let the buyer beware') is the norm, the general rule in Japanese real estate transactions is that a seller should not be able to benefit from the non-disclosure of a material latent defect. Consequently, a disclaimer of latent defect liability is not effective with respect to any undisclosed latent defects known by the seller prior to closing.

Issues concerning latent defect liability arise when real property subject to a contract for sale contains a hidden material defect. Interestingly, the defect does not have to be a physical defect in a building, but may concern a defect in the legal rights concerning land as well. For example, a seller may incur latent defect liability in the event land is sold to construct a building, but the seller fails to disclose the fact that construction on the land is prohibited under city planning regulations.

Upon discovery of a latent defect (such as the existence of termites), a good-faith purchaser may make a claim against the seller for damages (*i.e.*, the cost of repairs, etc.) under the JCC, or may rescind the sales agreement in the event the latent defect is so significant that the purpose of the contract cannot be fulfilled. In general, a purchaser may make a claim against the seller under the JCC anytime after delivery of the building, provided that the claim is brought within ten years, and provided the claim is made within one year of discovery of the defect by the purchaser. A purchaser with prior knowledge of the defect, however, has no recourse under the latent defect rules, regardless of whether the seller notified the purchaser of the defect or the purchaser found out about the defect from another source.

For transactions between merchants (which tend to have heightened legal duties under Japanese law), a seller's duty to compensate a purchaser for latent defects is balanced by an affirmative duty of the purchaser to inspect the property after delivery. Art. 526 of the **Japanese Commercial Code** (not the JCC) provides that in order for a merchant purchaser to make a valid claim against a merchant seller, the purchaser must not only inspect the land and buildings without delay after delivery, but the purchaser should also promptly inform the seller upon discovery of any latent defect. In the event of a latent defect which is not reasonably detectable at delivery, the merchant purchaser has a mere six-month window from the time of delivery to discover and notify the merchant seller of the latent defect claim. Thus generally speaking, latent defect liability only becomes an issue in transactions between merchants when there exists a latent defect in real property, not known or reasonably discoverable by the purchaser at delivery, which only becomes conspicuous within the first six months after transfer of the property.

Both merchant and non-merchant sellers may insert a disclaimer in a property sales agreement to eliminate all latent defect liability. However, the disclaimer is only effective in the event the seller does not have knowledge of any latent defects prior to execution of the agreement. If the purchaser can demonstrate that the seller had knowledge and did not tell the purchaser prior to closing, then generally the ten-year window of potential liability under the JCC will still apply with respect to such known defects, regardless of the disclaimer.

There are special rules regarding disclaimers of latent defect liability in the event a licensed **Real Estate Transactions Law** ("RETL") business operator is 'self-dealing,' that is, selling its own property to a third party other than another licensed RETL business operator. In the case of 'self-dealing,' an RETL business operator may disclaim all latent defect liability only after a two-year period from delivery of the property. Other than this permitted shortening of the period of potential liability from ten years to two years, any other contract provisions which modify the JCC's latent defect rules to the disadvantage of a purchaser in a self-dealing transaction are invalid (for example, a clause limiting a latent defect claim only to within three months of discovery). Accordingly, if the agreement contains a disclaimer of latent defect liability after, for example, one year has passed from delivery, the JCC's ten-year period of potential liability would apply by default. However, please note that a disclaimer of all latent defect liability in a transaction between two RETL business operators is valid and enforceable (Art. 78, Paragraph 2, RETL).

To supplement the JCC rules concerning latent defect liability, purchasers of new residences benefit from enhanced protections pursuant to the **Law regarding the Promotion and Maintenance of Quality Building Materials, etc.**, first promulgated in 1999. This law applies to all latent defects in the materials or parts of new residential buildings which are significant to their structural integrity, and obliges both sellers and contractors to be liable (to the initial purchaser only unless agreed otherwise) for repairs and other potential damages for at least ten years after delivery. This term may be extended per contract up to twenty years, but may not be shortened to less than ten years. However, this law only applies to latent defects in the materials for new residences, and latent defect liability in all other cases is still regulated primarily by the JCC.

13 Selected Real Estate Transactions Law Topics

I. The Role of Deposits in Japanese Real Estate Purchase Transactions

When parties enter into a **Real Estate Purchase and Sale Agreement** ("PSA") in Japan, usually the buyer agrees to pay a deposit (known as 'earnest money' in the United States) to the seller. Payment and receipt of this deposit not only creates evidence of the parties' intent to make a binding legal contract (demonstrating the 'earnest' intention of the parties), it can also serve other purposes depending on the contents of their agreement. For example, the buyer and seller may agree to designate the deposit as a **Liquidated Damages Deposit** (*iyaku tetsukekin*) or a **Cancellation Money Deposit** (*kaiyaku tetsukekin*). Generally what constitutes a suitable amount of deposit depends on various market factors such as desirability of the property, and deposits are usually 10-20% of the total purchase price. Also, it is common for any deposit paid to be used to offset part of the purchase price at closing, and as a general rule parties do not use escrow agents in real estate transactions in Japan.

The purpose of a 'liquidated damages deposit' is to function as an approximation of the damages either party would suffer if a closing were not completed due to a breach of the PSA. Significantly, if a deposit is designated as a liquidated damages deposit, the non-breaching party doesn't have to prove the amount of damages suffered from the other party's breach. Rather, in the event of a material breach, the non-breaching party is entitled to terminate the agreement and receive an amount equal to the liquidated damages deposit from the breaching party, but is generally restricted from claiming any damages above this amount unless specifically agreed otherwise. If the buyer were to terminate, the seller can keep the deposit, and if the seller were to terminate, the buyer is entitled to recover the deposit as well as the same amount again from the seller.

Most deposits in Japanese PSAs are, however, designated to function as a 'cancellation money deposit' (*kaiyaku tetsukekin*) pursuant to Art. 557 of the **Japanese Civil Code** ("JCC"). Use of a cancellation money deposit facilitates the right of either party to terminate a PSA *for any reason* prior to closing by payment of the cancellation money, without any further liability. An important caveat is that a cancellation money right may only be exercised prior to the other party taking a 'significant step' in carrying out its closing obligations. For example, generally a seller may not validly exercise a cancellation money right if the buyer has already completed preparations for full payment of the purchase price. Nevertheless, cancellation money deposits are useful because in the absence of a cancellation money deposit, generally a PSA may not be justifiably terminated (*i.e.*, without liability on the part of the terminating party), unless there is a material breach by the other party. In sum, by validly exercising a cancellation money deposit right, not only can a person terminate a PSA for any reason, the terminating party may also cut off any damage claims in excess of the cancellation money deposit (similar to the effect of a liquidated damages deposit).

Unlike a liquidated damages deposit clause, the mere existence of a cancellation money deposit clause in a PSA does not generally affect the amount of damage claims a non-breaching party may make against a breaching party. If a PSA contains a cancellation money deposit clause, upon a material breach by the other party, the non-breaching party may return the cancellation money deposit to the buyer and sue the breaching party for damages in an amount in excess of the cancellation money deposit. However, if the breaching party were to first terminate by validly exercising its cancellation money deposit right, the non-breaching party would generally only be entitled to receive the cancellation money deposit (either through waiver by the buyer or return of the deposit and an additional payment by the seller). In sum, if a deposit is designated as cancellation money, it may be returned to the buyer and a damages claim initiated against the breaching party, however if it is designated as liquidated damages, only the amount of the deposit may be claimed, and generally neither party may sue for additional damages (unless specifically agreed otherwise). Please note that if the buyer and seller do not clearly specify the nature of a deposit in a PSA, under Japanese law there is a presumption that the parties intend it to function as a cancellation money deposit.

The **Real Estate Transactions Law** ("RETL") modifies these deposit rules when a licensed RETL business operator (*takkengyousha*) is selling a property it owns to any person other than another licensed RETL business operator (known as **Self-Dealing**). In this case, any deposit may not exceed 20% of the total purchase price of the relevant property. (In transactions between non-licensed parties, there is no statutory ceiling.) In addition, in the event a licensed RETL business operator is self-dealing, legally any deposit may only be treated as a cancellation money deposit, regardless of any agreement to the contrary. Further, depending on the total amount of deposit, the licensed RETL business operator is required to: (1) use a holding agent (*i.e.*, an escrow agent), (2) arrange for insurance, or (3) obtain a bank guarantee for the benefit of the non-professional buyer.

II. The Cooling-Off Period

Under Art. 37-2 of the RETL, generally buyers of properties from a licensed RETL business operator (*takkengyousha*) enjoy a statutory **Cooling-Off Period**, provided the operator is self-dealing (selling its own property and not selling to another RETL business operator). The cooling-off period is an automatic eight-day period in which a buyer may terminate a signed agreement or application to purchase without fault or penalty whatsoever (including the right to recover any deposit and the restriction of all damage claims by the seller). The cooling-off period begins when the buyer signs a PSA or an application to purchase and also receives written notice of the cooling-off period rights. In addition to expiration of the time limit, there are other circumstances which may prevent a buyer from being allowed to exercise cooling-off rights.

Termination by a buyer during the cooling-off period must be in writing to be effective, and a buyer may not use cooling-off rights to terminate after the purchase price has been paid in full and delivery of the property to the buyer completed. Also, in principle a buyer only obtains cooling-off rights if the PSA or application to purchase is signed in a place other than a specially set up information office (*annaijo*) or a licensed RETL business operator's office (which are deemed to be places so serious that it is reasonable to assume the buyer used due care in making a financial decision there). Another condition is that the buyer has not requested the seller to visit the buyer's residence or place of business for signing (in which case there will generally be no cooling-off period). There are other situations in which the cooling-off rules may not apply as well, but in general the rules do help protect consumers from unscrupulous self-dealing RETL business operators.

III. Real Estate Broker Agreements

When a person selling a property desires to use a broker to locate a buyer, there are three types of representation the person can choose from: (1) general (*ippan*), (2) exclusive (*sennin*), and (3) restricted exclusive (*senzoku sennin*). **General Representation** denotes a type of representation where the seller is not restricted from engaging multiple brokers simultaneously with respect to the same property, and a general representation agreement may or may not require the seller to inform the broker of the names of any other engaged brokers. An **Exclusive Representation** agreement bars the seller from engaging any other brokers simultaneously with respect to the subject property, either as an agent or an intermediary, and a **Restricted Exclusive Representation** agreement not only bars the seller from engaging any other brokers for the property during the term of the agreement, but also prohibits the seller personally from finding a buyer during the term. In practice, only exclusive representation and restricted exclusive representation are common, since it is very hard to find a broker who will consent to enter into a general representation agreement.

In addition to the above types of broker representation, the scope of representation may vary; a broker may be authorized to act as either an agent (*dairi*) or an intermediary (*baikai*) for a seller. An **Agent** is generally authorized under the JCC to conclude a binding sales agreement directly with a buyer with respect to the seller's property. (Generally if a seller enters into an agency agreement, the seller will indicate a minimum acceptable amount, among other matters, as guidance for the agent.) An **Intermediary** may only introduce the buyer to the seller but has no legal authority to bind the seller. Thus, sellers desiring a broker's services can choose from one of the following forms: (1) a general agency or general intermediary agreement, (2) an exclusive agency or exclusive intermediary agreement, or (3) a restricted exclusive agency or restricted exclusive intermediary agreement.

There are various statutory limits for fees charged by real estate brokers. For example, in a real estate purchase transaction, generally brokers may charge their fee as a percentage of the purchase price of the property as follows (after deducting consumption tax which is levied on buildings only): 5% on properties costing up to JPY two million, 4% + JPY20,000 on properties costing more than JPY two million but not more than JPY four million, and 3% + JPY60,000 on properties costing over JPY four million. Typically brokers charge lower percentages as the property becomes more expensive (*e.g.*, 1% for properties over JPY100 million).

As a maximum, a broker may negotiate to receive up to the statutory limit from each the seller and the buyer (in other words, in total double the statutory limit but only up to the statutory limit from each) in the event of acting as an intermediary. When a broker acts as an agent, the broker may negotiate to receive up to double the statutory amount as well, but the entire amount can be from one client or apportioned as desired between the buyer and the seller. If there are multiple brokers however, in total their fees may not exceed two times the statutory amount. In addition, brokers may charge to their clients the applicable consumption tax they must pay on any fees they receive.

There are special reporting rules under the RETL for brokers when they enter into either an exclusive representation agreement or a restricted exclusive representation agreement with a seller or a person desiring to exchange a property. Please note that these rules are only mandatory with respect to representation agreements with sellers or parties to a potential exchange, *not* with respect to agreements with landlords. Under Art. 34-2 and Art. 34-3 of the RETL, after concluding either an exclusive representation agreement or a restricted exclusive representation agreement, a broker should send a written notice without delay notifying the seller, etc. of details such as the broker's fee, the term of the agreement, the customer's rights concerning termination, and the matters which need to be registered with **REINS**, the Real Estate Information Network System for Eastern, Kinki, Central, or Western Japan. (REINS is the Japan multiple listing service with access restricted to licensed

RETL business operators only.) Matters concerning an exclusive representation agreement need to be registered with REINS within seven days of concluding the agreement. Matters concerning a restricted exclusive representation agreement should be registered within five days.

When a buyer is found and a sales agreement concluded, the broker should update the REINS entry without delay. In addition, brokers have a duty to provide to their customer an update of the status of their search either once every fourteen days or once every seven days, depending on whether the agreement is an exclusive representation agreement or a restricted exclusive representation agreement. Under the RETL, both of these types of agreements can only be effective for a three-month period (longer agreements are automatically shortened to three months), and may not be automatically renewed (although they may be renewed if the parties agree separately).

14 Japanese Common Ownership and the Law on Sectional Ownership

I. Japanese Common Ownership (*kyouyuu*)

The **Japanese Civil Code** ("JCC") sets forth the default legal rules governing the rights and duties of concurrent owners of real property. In Japanese, this legal relation is called **Common Ownership** (*kyouyuu*), and can arise, for example, when a father dies and bequeaths ownership of a building to his two sons. In this case, each of the sons would obtain a 50% ownership interest in the undivided property, and each would have the right to use the *entire* property in accordance with his interest (*e.g.*, generally each son would be entitled to use the entire building for six months out of the year unless agreed otherwise). That is, under Art. 249 of the JCC, each common owner is entitled to use the entire property in proportion to such owner's ownership interest unless agreed otherwise.

Common ownership under the JCC is similar in some respects to the legal relationship called 'tenants in common' found in many common law jurisdictions ('tenant' here means a co-owner of a property). Like tenants in common, common owners in Japan have an undivided, fractional ownership interest but are entitled to occupy and use the entire subject property (in general, no common owner has the legal right to exclusively use any portion of the property). Each common owner may transfer or mortgage an interest in the property without the consent of any of the other common owners, and a common ownership interest may also be devised to one's heirs. There is no right of survivorship among common owners, however in the event a common owner were to die without an heir (or a person deemed under law to have "a special connection to the deceased"), generally the other common owners would receive the deceased's common ownership interest. Common owners hold a percentage of ownership in the subject property (with a pro rata right to receive any income from the property such as rent), and the ownership percentages are presumed to be equal but may be amended by agreement (for instance, three investors may buy a property and agree to a 60/30/10 ownership interest split based on their differing invested amounts).

When a property is subject to common ownership, the multiple common owners will on occasion need to make a decision regarding matters such as repairing a broken window, renovating the property, etc. The JCC divides such property matters into three categories: (1) **Acts of Preservation** (*hozon koui*), (2) **Acts of Management** (*kanri koui*), and (3) **Acts of Transformation** (*henkou koui*). However, please note that these matters, and the ownership percentages needed to approve a decision, may be changed per agreement among the parties.

Under the JCC, an 'act of preservation' would be, for example, a common owner causing the removal of a squatter from any part of the property. Each common owner has the legal right to do this individually without consent from any of the other common owners. An 'act of management' concerns more important matters such as entering into or terminating a lease agreement with a third party, and may only be decided by a person or persons holding a majority of all common ownership interests (a majority owner or group of owners with a majority). Agreements to sell the property or carry out a large-scale renovation are examples of 'acts of transformation,' and may only be decided with the consent of all common owners.

Because acts of management may be carried out by a majority common owner alone, minority interest holders may become dissatisfied with the default common ownership rules. For instance, the decision to execute an improvement to the property is a type of act of management, and all common owners have a legal duty to pay a proportion of the costs of an improvement based on the percentage of their common ownership interest. In the event a common owner doesn't pay within one year (*e.g.*, a minority common owner who doesn't agree with the improvement in the first place), the other common owners may purchase the delinquent common owner's interest at fair market value.

Although the JCC sets forth a legal framework for reaching decisions regarding a property held in common ownership, it is still easy for disputes to arise among common owners. Accordingly, each common owner has the legal right to petition a court to partition the property, unless agreed otherwise by all of the common owners in writing. An agreement not to partition is only valid for a maximum of five years, however the parties may agree to renew the agreement at its expiration. Also, please note that a third-party purchaser of a common ownership interest is only bound by a non-partition agreement if it is noted on the property's legal register prior to the purchase. Even if all of the common owners agree to a partition, it may still be very difficult to physically divide a property, and common owners applying for a partition may find that they have to either sell their interests or buy out all of the other common owners.

As a general rule, disputes regarding common ownership properties tend to occur more frequently than disputes regarding properties owned through **Sectional Ownership** (also known as 'strata title' or 'condominium law rights' in English and explained in the next Section). Nevertheless, investors may be able to enjoy a significant financial advantage from utilizing a common ownership structure. Since a purchaser of a common ownership interest acquires the right to possess and use the *entire* property for a period of time (as agreed with the other common owners), a seller of a common ownership interest may be able to receive compensation that would exceed the percentage of the purchase price the seller would receive in a sale of the entire property to one party. Consequently, investors wishing to purchase a property together should consider whether this potential financial benefit of using a common ownership structure would outweigh the practical difficulties of having to work together in using and owning the property.

II. The Law on Sectional Ownership etc. of Buildings

Due in part to the growth in the number of multi-family residential buildings in the post-war period, in the early 1960s there was a need for new rules for the collective ownership of buildings. As a practical matter, the JCC common ownership rules were not detailed enough to provide a clear answer to every issue which came up among common owners. This was compounded by the oftentimes large number and differing backgrounds of common owners of large-scale buildings. Many lenders also disliked providing loans collateralized by a mortgage on a minority common ownership interest, since in the event of default, the lender's rights to the whole property would be encumbered by the other common owners' interests. As a result, on April 4th, 1962 the **Law on Sectional Ownership etc. of Buildings** (*tatemono no kubun shoyuutou ni kansuru houritsu* or "Sectional Ownership Law") was enacted to create a legal framework for the exclusive ownership of sections of buildings as well as for securing the common ownership of essential common areas. In addition, one innovation of the Sectional Ownership Law is that it enables different sections of the same building to be specified for different uses (*e.g.*, a building may be designated on the property register as part residence, part office, part retail space, etc.).

For individuals desiring to own a portion of a building for use as a primary residence, the Sectional Ownership Law represents a significant improvement over the JCC common ownership rules. One reason for this is that in a building subject to sectional ownership, co-owners with a co-ownership interest of less than 50% are provided significant legal protections when compared to common owners with a minority ownership interest. One of the most important of these protections is also one of the most basic: the legal right to own a partitioned section of the building (called an 'exclusive area') to the exclusion of all third parties (including in most cases the ability to freely transfer, devise and encumber such right).

There are other ways the Sectional Ownership Law provides special protections for minority co-owners. The decision-making body of a building under the law is called the **Homeowners' Association** (*kanri kumiai*), and each co-owner is given the right to vote in the homeowners' association meeting. The homeowners' association is responsible for maintaining common areas and reaching decisions affecting the building as a whole in accordance with its **Bylaws** (*kiyaku*), and as a general rule, the law requires a minimum approval of over 50% of all co-owners *as well as* over 50% of all co-ownership interests in order for the homeowners' association to pass a resolution (such percentages may be reduced by the Bylaws in limited circumstances only, and there are required higher approval thresholds for certain important matters). Consequently, the law generally mandates a system whereby many minority co-owners can vote together to block the actions of one or several co-owners holding over 50% of all co-ownership interests in a property.

The purpose of the Bylaws is to create rules for resolving conflicts of interest among the co-owners of a building, and as such, the Bylaws operate as a constitutional document indicating the rights and duties of all co-owners. Although some of the rules of the Sectional Ownership Law may be modified by the Bylaws, there are many important rules to which the Bylaws must conform. Further, after the Bylaws of a building are established by the homeowners' association, in practice it is generally very difficult to amend the contents (as a matter of law, no less than a 75% approval of both all co-owners and all co-ownership interests in the building are necessary).

For buildings owned under the Sectional Ownership Law, there are two types of designated areas: (1) **Exclusive Areas** (*sen'yuu bubun*), which legally must be separate or separable in a structural sense and have functional independence from other parts of the building and (2) **Common Areas** (*kyouyuu bubun*), which are typically sections of the building that should be designated for common use due to their collective purpose or function (such as hallways and elevators). Certain areas are deemed common areas as a matter of law, while some areas have functional independence from other parts of the building but may be designated as common areas through agreement among the co-owners (for example, a separate conference room to be used to hold homeowners' association meetings). In addition to exclusive areas and common areas, co-owners also have a co-ownership right to any land appurtenant to the building (called a **Site Right** or *shikichi riyouken*). This right is based on the percentage of all exclusive areas in the building owned by such co-owner, and site rights may not be transferred or encumbered separately from the co-owner's exclusive area(s) unless so provided in the Bylaws. This is in contrast to common area rights, which may not be separately transferred or encumbered regardless of the contents of the Bylaws.

Ownership of exclusive areas is separately registered on the building register at the local Legal Affairs Bureau, and these interests may be transferred and encumbered without the consent of any third parties unless the Bylaws provide otherwise. The Bylaws may also provide for a right of first refusal for existing co-owners in the event a co-owner wants to sell an exclusive area right. Each co-owner has an indivisible ownership interest in all common areas based on his or her ownership of an exclusive area. Generally the use right for common areas for each co-owner is based on the total floor area of all exclusive areas owned by such co-owner divided by the total floor area of all exclusive areas in the building, although this may be modified in the Bylaws as well.

Both site rights and the ownership of exclusive areas are governed by the Sectional Ownership Law. However, the rights to common areas are governed by the JCC common ownership (*kyouyuu*) rules. Nevertheless, if the homeowners' association resolves any significant act of management concerning the building's common areas, all co-owners who would be particularly affected by such act have a special veto right to protect their interests under Art. 17, Paragraph 2 of the Sectional Ownership Law.

Among the most important mandatory rules for the Bylaws are (1) the requirement that incorporation of the homeowners' association necessitates no less than a 75% approval of both all co-owners and all co-ownership interests in the building, (2) the requirement that no less than a 75% approval of both all co-owners and all co-ownership interests in the building are necessary to establish, amend or abolish any parts of the Bylaws, with a veto right for all co-owners who would be specially affected, (3) the requirement that for the approval of any 'major' act of transformation of the common areas (defined as any act of transformation which constitutes a conspicuous change in form or function of the building), no less than a 75% approval of both all co-owners and all co-ownership interests in the building are necessary (in this case however, the Bylaws may reduce the approval percentage of all co-owners to more than 50%), with a veto right for all co-owners who would be specially affected, and (4) in the event the homeowners' association were to resolve to demolish the building in order to reconstruct a new building on the site, no less than an 80% approval of both all co-owners and all co-ownership interests in the building would be necessary. Please note that a resolution to demolish a building (without the intent to rebuild) requires the unanimous consent of all co-owners (since this is not specifically addressed in the Sectional Ownership Law, it is considered to be an act of transformation under the common ownership rules of the JCC).

In the event any co-owner were to not want to participate in the demolition and reconstruction of a new building, within two months after such resolution, the other co-owners would have a call option to buy the non-participating co-owner's interest at the prevailing market price, but the non-participating co-owner would have no put option to sell his or her individual interest. In case of a resolution to restore the common areas of a property that has suffered over a 50% diminution in value due to 'large-scale' damages (which requires at the minimum a 75% approval of all co-owners and all co-ownership rights), an objecting co-owner has a put option to sell his or her co-ownership interest in the building to the other approving co-owners at the prevailing market price. However, if the other co-owners appoint a certain co-owner or co-owners to buy such co-ownership interest, the objecting co-owner may only exercise the put option with respect to such co-owner or co-owners.

A homeowners' association meeting must be held at least one time per year, and unless provided otherwise in the Bylaws, is typically responsible for appointing a building manager to oversee maintenance of the common areas, take care of administrative work for the homeowners' association, and carry out any other rights and duties set forth in the Bylaws. Any co-owner holding at least 20% of the co-ownership interests, or any group of co-owners which make up at least 20% of all co-owners, may call a meeting of the homeowners' association (although these percentages may be reduced in the Bylaws). The Bylaws and all resolutions of the homeowners' association bind all current co-owners of the building, including all future heirs and transferees of co-ownership interests.

Please note that currently the Japanese government is considering amending the Sectional Ownership Law. One reason amendments are being contemplated is that under the current rules, it is very difficult for homeowners' associations to obtain enough votes to remodel or rebuild older buildings to enhance earthquake resistance. For example, there is discussion of reducing the 80% threshold for demolishing and reconstructing buildings which are especially susceptible to earthquake damage to no less than a 66.6% approval, and reducing the requirement for a major act of transformation where the purpose is to increase earthquake resistance from 'at least 75%' to a 'more than 50%' approval. The unanimous approval requirement for demolishing a heavily-damaged building (without the intent to rebuild) may also be changed to an 80% approval requirement. The government is also considering revising the current rules so that an executive officer of the homeowners' association would be authorized to decide on repairs to the building in the event of disaster (rather than the homeowners' association), in order to speed up the repair process.

15 Real Estate as Collateral

I. Introduction

Owners use land and buildings in Japan to secure obligations to creditors in a variety of ways. Although placing a **Mortgage** (*teitouken*) or a **Revolving Credit Mortgage** (*neteitouken*) on a property to secure a loan is the most common way of using real estate as collateral, there are alternative methods such as using a **Provisional Registration** (*kari touki*), a **Real Estate Pledge** (*fudousanshichiken*), a **Sale and Right to Repurchase** (*kaimodoshiken*), or a **Collateral Assignment** (*jouto tanpo*, which refers to a non-statutory security interest arising through contract between the parties). Despite the fact that real estate pledges (*fudousanshichiken*) are only rarely used in practice, pledges (*shichiken*) are the primary security interests employed with respect to **Trust Beneficiary Interests** ("TBIs"), and accordingly they frequently play an important role in commercial real estate transactions. In addition, since land and buildings are considered separate property, with separate land and building registers maintained at the local Legal Affairs Bureau, it is possible for a building to be used to secure one debt while the land under the building is used to secure a debt to a different creditor.

II. Mortgages (*teitouken*)

A **Mortgage** (*teitouken*) is a property right (*bukken*) created by contract between a real estate owner (the 'mortgagor') and a creditor or lender (the 'mortgagee') with respect to specific real estate. It is used to secure an obligation to the mortgagee such as to repay a loan or satisfy a legal judgment, and generally the mortgagee's power to exercise rights over the collateral asset(s) is contingent upon the mortgagor's default on the secured obligation. Oral mortgage agreements are valid, but they need to be written and registered in order to be effective against subsequent purchasers and maintain priority with respect to subsequent mortgagees.

A mortgage agreement may be executed to secure an obligation of the mortgagor or a third party, and a basic characteristic of mortgages is that mortgagors may continue to use the collateral asset(s) during the term of the mortgage agreement. In the event of a default on the secured obligation, the agreement typically gives the mortgagee the right to cause a court to sell the collateral, with the mortgagee receiving a priority right to the sale's proceeds to satisfy the secured obligation. For example, commercial loan agreements contain a section defining certain events of default which, if triggered, give the lender (the mortgagee) the right to make the entire loan amount immediately due and payable (called 'accelerating the loan'). If the borrower cannot repay the loan after acceleration, the borrower is said to be 'in default' on the loan. In this case, depending on the contents of the mortgage agreement, the mortgagee will usually have the right to cause a **Private Sale** (*nin'i baikyaku*) or institute a legal proceeding (sometimes called a foreclosure proceeding in English) under the **Civil Execution Law** (*minji shikkouhou*) in order to sell the mortgaged property.

In the legal proceeding under the Civil Execution Law, the local municipal court verifies the mortgage claim and, after the property's value is appraised by a third-party appraiser, manages a public auction of the property, with the mortgagee receiving satisfaction from the auction proceeds. The entire foreclosure process and auction can take anywhere from three months to over a year depending on factors such as the ease of valuation of the asset, desirability of the asset, speed of the courts, etc. Please note that under Japanese law, the collateral asset must be sold through the court-led process (as opposed to a private sale), unless stipulated otherwise in the mortgage agreement.

As a general rule, the mortgagee bringing the action is paid off in full before any other creditors are paid (except, for example, where there are unpaid fixed asset taxes arising prior to registration of the mortgage). It is possible for several mortgagees to hold a mortgage with respect to the same asset, and upon completion of the auction in this case, the priority of payments would follow a first in time rule: the mortgagee bringing the action would be paid in full before any junior registered mortgagees, with any unregistered mortgagees having the lowest priority. (It is, however, possible for mortgagees to agree among themselves to change the order of priority.) If there is any remaining amount after all mortgagees are paid off, the mortgagor (*i.e.*, the prior owner) receives such remainder. Further, if some junior mortgagees are not paid off in full, they become general, unsecured creditors of the mortgagor for the remaining balance of their claims. Thus, properties sold through the legal foreclosure process are transferred free and clear of all junior mortgages.

In the legal proceeding, the mortgagee bringing the action may claim all loan amounts specified and registered in the land or building register (principal, interest, delinquency penalties, etc.) which are due and payable as a result of the mortgagor's default, provided, however, that generally claims for interest and penalties for delinquent payments are limited to a two-year period from the acceleration date, unless there are no other mortgagees and certain other conditions are satisfied. Also, in the event a mortgage on a building is foreclosed on, tenants with valid leasehold interests (*chinshakuken*) prior to the mortgage being registered, and any tenants recorded in the building register with leasehold interests, may continue their lease under the same leasing conditions. However, tenants with leases beginning after the mortgage was first registered may be forced to vacate the building within six months after sale. In addition, if a parcel of land is mortgaged and subsequently a building is constructed on the land without consent of the mortgagee, upon an event of default, generally the mortgagee may initiate the legal foreclosure process with respect to both the land and building. However, in this case the mortgagee will only have a priority right to the sale proceeds derived from the land (Art. 389 of the **Japanese Civil Code**, "JCC").

The bidding process in the public auction is not openly competitive and bids are only disclosed to the court, which initially indicates a minimum bidding amount based on a third-party appraisal. Prior to the auction, the court prepares and makes public an information circular (*bukkenmeisaisho*) specifying details of the subject real estate. Please note that any parties wishing to bid must pay a deposit (usually 10-20% of the desired purchase price) along with the submission of their bid in writing.

It is legally permissible for a mortgagor to agree in a mortgage or side agreement that, in the event of default, the mortgagee may obtain **Direct Ownership** of the mortgaged asset (*teitou jikinagare*) (with a legal duty to compensate the mortgagor if the value of the asset is more than the secured debt), or cause a sale of the asset directly to a third party in a private sale (*nin'i baikyaku*), without any legal proceeding. Although the direct ownership method may seem preferable to a private sale, after a default has occurred, as a practical matter it can be very difficult to obtain a valuation of the asset to which both parties agree. Also, one advantage to using a private sale is that usually the mortgaged asset is sold at a relatively higher price than assets sold through the court-led public auction. The private sale process may also, depending on the circumstances, be cheaper and less time-consuming than instituting a legal proceeding to foreclose on a mortgage. Accordingly, many creditors prefer using this option.

The main drawback to using a private sale, however, arises in cases where there are multiple registered mortgagees. In this event, the asset will be sold still encumbered by all junior mortgage interests, unless the junior mortgagees agree to release their mortgages. This is in contrast to the court-led execution process, where junior mortgagees who are not paid off become general creditors of the mortgagor, but the asset is sold free of any such encumbrances. Accordingly, senior mortgagees arranging a private sale may find the negotiation process impractical where there are multiple registered junior mortgagees demanding to be paid off in full at the time of sale, and where the prospective buyer only wants to buy the asset unencumbered with such interests and naturally for as low a price as possible. As a result, oftentimes lenders include a boilerplate clause in their mortgage agreements restricting all subsequent mortgages without the lender's prior consent, and then elect the private sale process upon loan default.

A mortgage may be created under Japanese law not only with respect to ownership of land or buildings, but a **Superficies** (*chijouken*, a right to own something on another's land) and **Farming Rights** (*eikosakuken*, the right to use another's land for farming or grazing) may also be subject to a mortgage. In addition, a mortgage may also be placed on mining rights, fishing rights, factories, and timber under specific laws. A leasehold interest (*chinshakuken*) on land or buildings however, whether registered or not, may not be mortgaged.

A **Joint Mortgage** (*kyoudou teitouken*), where many different assets are used as collateral to secure a single obligation, is also available and quite common (although all assets subject to a mortgage must be specified for registration purposes, and a comprehensive mortgage covering all of an obligor's current and undetermined future assets is not legally effective). Generally, a mortgagee has no right to occupy or use a mortgaged property, and the mortgagor has a duty to avoid physical **Waste** (unusual actions which could cause a diminution of value in the encumbered asset). Further, a mortgagee has the right to bring a legal action to stop a mortgagor from causing waste (called a *bougai haijo seikyuuken*).

Since a mortgage is used to secure an obligation, as a rule its efficacy is tied to such obligation. Consequently, if the obligation is transferred, the benefit of the mortgage follows the obligation to the new creditor by operation of Japanese law (this is called **Adhesion**, *zuihansei*). If the obligation is extinguished through repayment, etc., the mortgage right is also deemed to have been automatically extinguished (*fujuusei*). Unless agreed otherwise, a mortgagee may transfer its mortgage right, and a mortgagor may transfer an encumbered property, freely and without the consent of any other parties (including other mortgagees). Generally a new owner of the property would take the property subject to all registered mortgages, and any unregistered mortgages would not be effective after transfer.

A registration tax (*touroku menkyozei*) is levied at the time a mortgage is initially registered (generally 0.4% of the secured amount) and at the time a transfer to a new mortgagee is registered (generally 0.2% of the secured amount). The registration tax for recording a mortgage is much lower than the registration tax for registering a change of ownership (*shoyuuken iten touki*) (generally 1-2% of the purchase price of the property). The mortgagor customarily pays the registration tax for recording a new mortgage.

In the event a mortgaged property is destroyed, under Art. 304 and 372 of the JCC, a mortgagee may use the Japanese legal concept of **Material Subrogation** (*butsujou dai'i*) and attach (*sashiosae*) the mortgagor's right to receive any proceeds from related insurance policies. However, as a general rule, to be effective the mortgagee must attach the mortgagor's right to receive such proceeds prior to the mortgagor actually receiving any payments. Similarly, in the event a mortgaged property is sold or leased, a mortgagee may compel satisfaction of the mortgagor's obligations (provided the mortgagor has already defaulted) by attaching the right to receive the proceeds prior to payment by using the material subrogation concept.

III. Revolving Credit Mortgages (*neteitouken*)

A **Revolving Credit Mortgage** (*neteitouken*) is a special type of mortgage used by lenders to secure a fluctuating loan amount, for instance as occurring with a line of credit. Unlike a floating lien (which is frequently used in common law jurisdictions), rather than the collateral for the security interest changing over time (like assets in a warehouse subject to a floating lien), in a revolving credit mortgage, the collateral is constant but the secured amount varies under a certain maximum amount until it becomes fixed. Revolving credit mortgages are useful in that they save the time and expense of registering and re-registering a regular mortgage in the event a loan is made, repaid, and then borrowed again. (In contrast to regular mortgages, a revolving credit mortgage is not automatically extinguished upon repayment in full.)

In a revolving credit mortgage agreement, the mortgagor and mortgagee agree to a **Maximum Credit Amount** to be secured (*kyokudogaku*), which is then recorded in the land or building register for the relevant asset. This results in the creation of a security interest which covers not only the current draw-down amount, but also can cover future potential drawdown amounts up to the maximum credit amount. Legally, a revolving credit mortgage may be used only where there are potential future obligations arising (1) from a specific agreement regarding continuous transactions between the mortgagor and the mortgagee, (2) from a certain type of transaction between the mortgagor and the mortgagee, (3) continuously between the mortgagor and the mortgagee due to a specific reason, or (4) from transactions in commercial paper or notes (Art. 398-2, JCC). It is also possible for a mortgagee and a mortgagor to enter into a **Joint Revolving Credit Mortgage** agreement (*kyoudou neteitouken keiyaku*) using several different real estate assets as collateral.

The date in which the secured amount (known as the **Principal** or *ganpon*) becomes fixed is significant because from this point forward, the revolving credit mortgage is generally treated as a regular mortgage for most intents and purposes. The date for **Fixing the Principal** (*ganpon no kakutei*) can be agreed in the revolving credit mortgage agreement, although in this case the date must be within five years of execution of the agreement under the JCC. If the date is left unspecified, the mortgagor may make a written request to fix the principal any time after three years from execution, and the principal will be fixed with effect two weeks after the mortgagee receives the request. However, the mortgagee may request to fix the principal at any time with immediate effect if the date is left unspecified (for example, if the mortgagee wants to end all future drawdowns, or in the event the mortgagee wants to foreclose on the mortgage due to the mortgagor's breach of loan covenants). Until the principal is fixed, the parties are allowed to amend the scope of obligations which are secured by their agreement (Art. 398-4, JCC), but an increase in the registered maximum credit amount requires the consent of all parties who could be affected by such change (such as subsequent secured creditors) (Art. 398-5, JCC).

Revolving credit mortgages differ from regular mortgages in that if the secured loan is transferred, a revolving credit mortgage does not follow by operation of Japanese law (there is no adhesion), unless the principal is already fixed. Also in contrast to a regular mortgage, as a matter of law a revolving credit mortgage may not be assigned by the mortgagee without the prior consent of the mortgagor. However, once the principal is fixed, the mortgagee may transfer the mortgage right without the mortgagor's prior consent (like a regular mortgage), unless the parties agree otherwise. To foreclose on a revolving credit mortgage, the principal must already be fixed, and the mortgagee may include in the related legal claim any interest, late fees, etc. up to the maximum credit amount. That is, in principle there is no two-year rule for limiting claims for interest, penalties for delinquent payments, etc., as generally applicable to regular mortgages.

IV. Pledges (*shichiken*)

A **Pledge** (*shichiken*) is another type of property right (*bukken*) created by contract and used to secure an obligation to a creditor (the 'pledgee'). There are different types of pledges under the JCC such as real estate pledges, pledges on movable assets (*dousan*), and pledges on intangible assets such as receivables and intellectual property rights. Depending on the contents of the pledge agreement, in the event of a breach of the pledgor's (or a third party's) secured obligation, the pledgee may carry out a private sale or cause a sale of the pledged asset under the Civil Execution Law (*minji shikkouhou*), with a priority right to repayment from the proceeds. Please note that in addition to regular pledges, there are also **Revolving Credit Pledges** (*neshichiken*) similar in function to revolving credit mortgages.

One of the main legal differences between a real estate pledge (*fudousan shichiken*) and a mortgage (*teitouken*) is that in order to create a valid real estate pledge, not only do the pledgee and the pledgor need to agree, but the pledgee must also take delivery (*i.e.*, custody) of the collateral (Art. 344, JCC). Further, it is expressly prohibited for a pledgee to appoint the pledgor to occupy the pledged real estate on behalf of the pledgee (Art. 345, JCC), and it is not possible to create a real estate pledge for longer than ten years (Art. 360, JCC), although the term may be renewed at expiration. Consequently, since lenders and debtors almost always want a long-term security agreement where the debtor retains the right to occupy and use the collateral (typically to earn income to pay off the secured loan), and the lender doesn't want to incur the extra costs associated with taking delivery and maintaining a pledged property, real estate pledges are rarely used in Japan.

Nevertheless as mentioned above, TBIs are frequently used as collateral in real estate financing transactions, and in this case a pledge is normally used to secure the lender's right to repayment. A TBI pledge is a pledge of a type of personal right (*saiken*) where the beneficiary is specified (*shimei saiken*), and in this case, pursuant to amendments to the JCC in 2004, there is no requirement that custody be transferred to create an enforceable pledge (unlike a real estate pledge). A TBI pledge is perfected with respect to the pledgor by agreement between the TBI beneficiary (*i.e.*, the pledgor) and the pledgee, and obtaining the trust bank's consent to the pledge. With respect to third parties, a TBI pledge is normally perfected by getting the trust bank's written consent to the pledge notarized with a *kakutei hizuke* (certified date) stamp affixed by a notary public (*koushou yakuba*) in accordance with Art. 364 and Art. 467 of the JCC.

One advantage of using a TBI pledge scheme is that it is much cheaper (the cost of the *kakutei hizuke* stamp is JPY200) than registering a mortgage on a property register (which is generally 0.4% of the secured amount). However, please note that usually in the event of default and execution on the TBI pledge, the pledgee (the lender) will still need to get the trust bank's separate consent to sell and transfer the TBI to a third party (in accordance with the contents of the trust register (*shintaku mokuroku*)). In addition, if the trust register restricts the creation of a TBI pledge, a pledge may not be created.

Typically a pledge on a TBI is not used in isolation, since for a variety of reasons a trust can be dissolved and the trust principal (*i.e.*, the entrusted real estate) returned to the beneficiary (the pledgor or borrower). Accordingly, usually a lender will receive benefit of (1) a pledge over the TBI, (2) a separate conditional mortgage (*teishijoukentsuki teitouken*) agreement (with the borrower agreeing to record the lender's mortgage on the property register in the event the trust is dissolved), and (3) a pledge agreement covering any insurance proceeds the borrower may receive in the event the collateral real estate is destroyed by fire, etc. In most cases, in the event of default on the secured obligation, the pledgee is authorized to carry out a private sale of the TBI to receive repayment.

V. Collateral Assignment (*jouto tanpo*) Transactions

A **Collateral Assignment** (*jouto tanpo*) is a security transaction recognized under Japanese case law in which a borrower and a lender agree to use a transfer of ownership in certain collateral to secure a debt to the lender. In the collateral assignment agreement, the borrower is usually required to register a transfer of ownership (*shoyuuken iten*) to the lender in the collateral's land or building register. Nevertheless, in their agreement the parties clearly indicate that the intention of the transfer is only to serve as part of a financing transaction, and in the event the lender is repaid under the relevant loan agreement, the lender promises to release its claim to title in the collateral (and register ownership of the collateral back in the borrower's name). The parties also typically agree that, upon default on the loan, either the lender may sell the asset to a third party (and return any amounts over the secured amount to the borrower), or the lender may receive full ownership of the property (with any difference between the fair market value of the collateral and the secured amount returned to the borrower).

A collateral assignment is similar to a mortgage in that generally the collateral remains in the hands of the borrower. However like a regular sale, in the usual case a transfer of ownership is recorded in the relevant land or building register. Nevertheless, according to much of the case law on collateral assignments, the assignment is considered only to be a superficial transfer of ownership, and in principle the lender has no legal right to use, encumber or transfer ownership of the collateral (*i.e.*, to change the contents of the land or building register) prior to the borrower's default. In essence, recording a collateral assignment acts as a marker on the property register, giving notice that ownership of the collateral may change in the future if certain conditions are fulfilled (in the recording of the transfer of ownership to the lender, the reason for the transfer can be recorded as "collateral assignment"). As a result, any potential third-party purchaser of the collateral reviewing the register would not know whether clear title has passed to the lender, or still rightfully remains in the borrower.

Not only does a lender not have clear title to collateral subject to a collateral assignment until the borrower's default, but the borrower would also generally not be able to sell the subject collateral or use it for any other financing during the term of the collateral assignment agreement. The reason is that ownership of the property would no longer be registered in the borrower's name, and any subsequent buyer, mortgagee, or other secured party would normally not be able to have its interest recorded in the land or building register. (In general, the borrower would not be able to authorize any new recordings on the register since the recorded owner (the lender) would be a different person or entity.)

Using a collateral assignment transaction can save a lender significant time and expense since there is no need to initiate a legal proceeding to foreclose on a mortgage, etc. in the event of the borrower's default. In addition, the value of the collateral can be determined by the parties in advance, rather than depending on what a third party would pay. A collateral assignment may also be used like a floating lien with respect to movable assets in a warehouse, etc., provided, among others, that the warehouse, collateral, etc. are sufficiently specified in the collateral assignment agreement (this is called a **Collective Movables Collateral Assignment** or *shuugou dousan jouto tanpo*).

Nevertheless, there can be significant registration tax expenses in a collateral assignment deal, and there are also unsettled legal issues which can pose a potential risk to lenders in the event of dispute. This is due to the fact that a collateral assignment is not a legally defined property right (*bukken*) under the JCC like a mortgage or a pledge (the exact scope and extent of a collateral assignment is more uncertain and open to debate than the security interests set forth in the JCC). For example, in the event the borrower files for bankruptcy during the collateral assignment, depending on the circumstances the lender may not be treated as a secured creditor in the bankruptcy proceeding. Also, borrowers generally prefer a mortgage or other security interest because it is very difficult to further encumber or transfer ownership of collateral after a collateral assignment is recorded, and over time there can be excess value in the collateral that is not used efficiently. On the other hand, from a lender's perspective, use of a collateral assignment can put economic pressure on the borrower to pay off the secured loan as soon as possible. The fact that in practice, assets subject to a collateral assignment are very hard to transfer or further encumber is a distinctive factor of a collateral assignment transaction.

VI. Sale and Right to Repurchase (*kaimodoshiken*) Transactions

A **Sale and Right to Repurchase** (*kaimodoshiken*) transaction is another way a borrower can provide security to a lender. In a sale and right to repurchase transaction, the borrower receives the full purchase price (as a loan) for the property, and the period for the right to repurchase is similar to the term for repayment of a loan. In the event the purchase price (the loan) is not repaid by the end of the term, the parties agree that the right to repurchase will lapse and ownership of the collateral will be free and clear from this encumbrance.

In a sale and right to repurchase transaction, a transfer of ownership (*shoyuuken iten*) in the collateral land or building is registered in the name of the lender. However, the borrower's right to repurchase is recorded at the same time as a note registration (*fuki touki*) to the transfer of ownership registration. A right to repurchase is a recognized property interest under Art. 579 of the JCC, and as a general rule, a party with a right to repurchase can assert the right against the lender or any subsequent third-party purchaser. (In the event a right to repurchase is exercised, in effect the prior transfer to the lender is rescinded.) Thus, using a sale and a right to repurchase can provide a high degree of security for a lender while also giving the borrower the ability to fully benefit from the value of the collateral (since generally the borrower can receive full market value for the collateral).

Because a right to repurchase can be asserted against a third-party purchaser, the JCC sets forth relatively strict rules for registering this right. For example, the right to repurchase must be recorded in the collateral property's register at the same time the transfer of ownership to the lender is recorded. It may not be longer than ten years, and any agreement to repurchase longer than that is automatically shortened to ten years. The term of a right to repurchase may not be extended or renewed, and if no term is agreed between the parties, the term for repurchase shall be five years. Also, the purchase price for the right to repurchase is to be agreed at the time of the initial transfer, and may only be comprised of the original purchase price and any contract costs (as a rule, no extra fees or interest from the related loan agreement are allowed).

VII. Provisional Registration (*kari touki*) and a Sale and Commitment to Sell Back (*saibaibai no yoyaku*)

In addition to the more conventional security interests such as a mortgage or a revolving credit mortgage, there are other non-statutory or provisional methods which can be used to secure an obligation. One of the most frequent of these is the use of a **Provisional Registration** (*kari touki*). A provisional registration is recorded in the property register of an asset and provides a conditional right of priority to the person benefiting from the registration. For instance, a provisional registration of a transfer of ownership can be entered into a land or building register, and the provisional registration can be changed to a full (*hontouki*) transfer of ownership (generally creating clear title) if certain future conditions are met. In this case, full transfer of ownership would take effect as of the time of the provisional registration on the property register, and thus would be perfected over any subsequently recorded transfers. A provisional registration of a mortgage can also be used to save the cost of registering a full mortgage at the time of a loan transaction (with the lender receiving in advance all documents necessary to unilaterally turn the provisional registration mortgage into a regular mortgage in the event of default, etc.).

Although the registration tax for a provisional registration is less than the tax for a full registration of a transfer of ownership, there are potential risks for lenders. For example, in the event the collateral is attached in a legal proceeding by a third-party creditor of the borrower, as a general legal rule the provisional registration may not be changed into a full registration. Further, if the borrower files for bankruptcy, a holder of a provisional registration is generally only left with a claim for monetary damages (and loses the chance to turn the provisional registration into a full registration). It is also important to note that a sale of land or buildings in a legal foreclosure proceeding will automatically extinguish all provisional registrations on the relevant property register.

The **Law regarding Contracts for Collateral subject to Provisional Registrations** (*kari touki tanpo keiyaku ni kansuru houritsu*) additionally regulates some of the rights and duties of creditors and obligors in provisional registration agreements. Pursuant to this law, upon default the beneficiary of a provisional registration must wait at least two months after notice has been provided to the borrower, before being allowed to turn a provisional registration of transfer of ownership into a full registration. Still, compared to a sale and right to repurchase, there is no statutory ten-year time limit, and the registration tax for a provisional registration is significantly lower.

Another option that can be used by creditors is to carry out a financing transaction with a contractual **Sale and Commitment to Sell Back** (*saibaibai no yoyaku*). This method involves an outright sale and a promise to sell back like a sale and right to repurchase, however the resale price, term, etc. are not set in advance. There is also no statutory ten-year limit as with a sale and right to repurchase.

Nevertheless, a commitment to sell back is created by contract (*i.e.*, it is not registered), and an unscrupulous lender could transfer the collateral to a third party before the commitment to sell back has lapsed. This would result in the borrower only having a legal claim for monetary damages against the lender for breach of contract, but no legal claim to repurchase the property from the third party. For additional security, a sale and commitment to sell back can be combined with a provisional registration. Another option is for the lender to receive in advance all of the documents necessary for recording a transfer of ownership in the legal register (*i.e.*, the title deed or confidential identification number card, a signed power of attorney, etc.), to be held in trust until the borrower repays the loan in full, but this arrangement involves a certain amount of risk as well.

16 The FIEL and its Impact on the Japanese Real Estate Industry

I. Introduction

On September 30th, 2007, the **Financial Instruments and Exchange Law** (*kin'yuu shouhin torihikihou*, "FIEL") came into effect to amend and replace the prior **Securities and Exchange Law** ("SEL"). Introduction of the FIEL had a significant effect on the real estate business in Japan, and to allow for a transition there were grace periods for companies to comply with the new legal and licensing regulations. Along with implementation of the FIEL, four prior laws were abolished and eighty-nine laws were amended. Some were incorporated into the FIEL; for example, the SEL was completely amended and renamed the FIEL. Others were either partially amended or abolished because they were superseded by the contents of the FIEL.

The impetus for the new law was to increase investor protections by broadening the regulation of investment services and modernizing the former patchwork of financial laws. The FIEL was enacted with four main goals in mind: (1) to create one comprehensive legal framework for financial transactions by expanding coverage of *the types of financial instruments* (such as trust beneficiary interests for real estate, "TBIs") and *the types of business activities* (such as the offering of quasi-limited partnership (*tokumei kumiai*) interests for collective investment schemes in TBIs) subject to regulation under Japanese law, (2) to strengthen internal compliance and disclosure requirements for listed companies by mandating quarterly financial disclosures, amending the prior tender offer bid regulations, changing the rules for the

Report on Substantial Shareholding (*tairyou hoyuu houkokusho*), and requiring regular internal control reports through introduction of a Japanese version of the United States's Sarbanes-Oxley legislation (dubbed 'J-SOX'), (3) to improve the self-regulation of financial instrument exchanges such as the **Tokyo Stock Exchange** ("TSE"), and (4) to increase penalties for fraudulent transactions, etc.

The Japanese real estate industry was most directly affected by (1) above, since through implementation of the FIEL, certain previously unregulated real estate investment products and business activities became subject to regulation and supervision by the **Financial Services Agency** ("FSA"). (As a general rule, the FSA has jurisdiction over financial laws which affect entities such as banks, securities firms, and insurance companies whereas the Ministry of Land, Infrastructure, Transport, and Tourism ("MLIT") enforces laws concerning real estate.) It should be noted that foreign funds with Japanese investors, or foreign funds that solicit investment from Japanese investors, are also in principle subject to the regulations of the FIEL. In addition, there is some flexibility in application of the FIEL regulations with respect to certain professional investors (known as "qualified institutional investors" under the FIEL) as opposed to retail investors (who need pre-contract written explanations and receive a post-contract 'cooling-off' period, among other protections).

The FIEL sets forth new broadly applicable legal definitions for **Financial Instrument** and **Financial Instrument Activities** to extend jurisdiction over generally all prior regulated and unregulated securities firms, financial advisory businesses, asset managers, special purpose companies ("SPCs"), investment funds, etc., and subsequently designates four categories of **Financial Instrument Businesses** depending on the type of financial instrument they deal in and the scope of their financial instrument activities. Previously there were many laws which could be relevant to such businesses: the SEL, the Securities Investment Advisory Law, the Financial Futures Trading Law, the Mortgage Business Law etc., but the FIEL does away with this segmentation by instituting a new, comprehensive regulatory framework. In this way, the FIEL consolidates prior rules while significantly increasing the breadth of real estate investment products and services regulated under Japanese law.

The four categories of financial instrument businesses under the FIEL are: (1) **1st Tier Financial Instrument Businesses**, (2) **2nd Tier Financial Instru-**

ment Businesses, (3) **Investment Advisory and Agency Businesses** (*toushi jogen dairi gyousha*), and (4) **Investment Management Businesses** (*toushi un'yougyousha*). The definition of **1st Tier Financial Instrument** includes shares in listed companies and derivatives such as interest rate swaps, whereas **2nd Tier Financial Instrument** refers to generally less liquid instruments such as TBIs and interests in quasi-limited partnerships (*tokumei kumiai*). As a general rule, each of the four types of financial instrument businesses is required to register with the Office of the Prime Minister and satisfy registration criteria which vary depending on the category of FIEL registration. Typically there are minimum capital requirements, personnel requirements, etc. Pursuant to amendments to the FIEL in 2011, there is also a new type of investment management business for qualified investors. For these businesses, the registration requirements are less strict than for regular investment management businesses (*e.g.*, there are reduced personnel and capital requirements (from JPY50 million to JPY10 million)), provided the company applying to register only deals with certain qualified investors, and the total amount of assets under management does not exceed a certain maximum amount.

1st tier financial instrument businesses are authorized to engage in largely all traditional securities business activities such as the underwriting and offering of listed securities for sale. As such, they are the most strictly regulated of the new financial instrument businesses. To register as a 1st tier financial instrument business, an entity must be organized as a joint stock company (*kabushiki kaisha*) and have at least JPY50 million in both capital and net assets, among other conditions. In addition to the registration requirements, 1st tier financial instrument businesses are also required to obtain a special FIEL permit (*ninka*) to engage in certain business activities. As a result of their enhanced regulation, 1st tier financial instrument businesses are the only type of FIEL business permitted to use the Japanese words 'securities firm' (*shouken kaisha*) in their corporate names.

The other three categories of financial instrument businesses, namely 2nd tier financial instrument businesses, investment advisory and agency businesses, and investment management businesses, are generally the most relevant for the Japanese real estate investment industry. The reason the 2nd tier financial instrument business category is so important is that the FIEL designated certain financial interests commonly used in the real estate business (such as TBIs and interests in 'collective investment schemes') as 2nd tier financial instruments. (A **Collective Investment Scheme** under the FIEL is generally any legal structure where capital or assets are contributed by two or more passive investors, and such capital or assets are used in a business or invested with the aim of distributing profits to such investors.) The FIEL rules concerning the two remaining FIEL business categories (investment advisory and agency businesses and investment management businesses) generally affected services provided by the traditional real estate advisory and fund management industry.

II. Effects on the Japanese Real Estate Business

Most pre-existing real estate investment structures were significantly affected by implementation of the FIEL. Perhaps the greatest impact came from the new 2nd tier financial instrument business regulations over TBIs and investments in collective investment schemes through quasi-limited partnership interests (*tokumei kumiai mochibun*), quasi-general partnership interests (*nin'i kumiai mochibun*), and other types of quasi-partnership interests such as interests in limited partnerships for investment(*toushi jigyou yuugen sekinin kumiai mochibun*). (Please note, however, that businesses acting as an agent or intermediary in third-party TBI transactions were previously subject to regulation primarily under the Trust Business Law.)

In addition to the new definition of 2nd tier financial instrument, the FIEL expanded the scope of regulations concerning real estate business activities. For example, it did this by *newly* covering (1) the offering (*i.e.*, the marketing and solicitation) of investment opportunities in 2nd tier financial instruments, either for third parties or on one's own behalf, (2) the buying and selling as a business of 2nd tier financial instruments on one's own behalf, (3) the acting as an agent or intermediary for third parties in transactions in certain 2nd tier financial instruments that were not previously regulated, and (4) the management of third-party investments in 2nd tier financial instruments. Consequently, entities registered as a 2nd tier financial instrument business may engage in the business of buying and selling 2nd tier financial instruments on their own account, act as an agent or intermediary for such buying and selling, and offer and market investments in 2nd tier financial instruments on their own behalf or for third parties. (To manage third-party investments in 2nd tier financial instruments, generally a company must register as an investment management business or an investment advisory and agency business depending on the level of discretion exercised over the investment assets.)

The new definition of 1st tier financial instrument was also significant in that Japanese law now directly regulates transactions in interest rate swaps, interest rate caps, and credit derivatives. As a general rule, in the past only financial futures transactions and securities derivatives were regulated. However, because acting as an intermediary for a derivative transaction is now an activity for registered 1st tier financial instrument businesses, companies wishing to arrange an interest rate swap or interest rate cap agreement for an SPC (*e.g.*, to hedge a non-recourse loan) may need to register as a 1st tier financial instrument business in advance, depending on the company's level of involvement in negotiations, etc.

Enactment of the FIEL also had far-reaching effects on many prior laws by establishing new industry-wide standards of conduct. For example, Art. 21-2 of the **Real Estate Syndication Law** ("RESL") incorporates many of the minimum FIEL conduct rules such as the rule prohibiting the solicitation of investments in products which are reasonably considered 'inappropriate' in view of the purpose of the contract and the target investor's level of experience, wealth and sophistication (known as the "principle of compatibility" or *tekiaisei no gensoku*). Additionally, introduction of the FIEL caused the modification of much of the Japanese terminology used in the real estate industry, for example, trust beneficiary interest dealers (*shintaku juekiken hanbai gyousha*) are now called financial instrument business operators (*kin'yuu shouhin torihiki gyousha*).

III. Impact of the FIEL on Asset Managers

Asset Managers ("AMs") are practically ubiquitous in the real estate investment industry in Japan, since using an SPC to own an asset with operations delegated to a separate AM company is such a common investment structure. An important reason for this is that generally lenders require real estate investment schemes utilize a bankruptcy-remote SPC structure for non-recourse financing. This is so that in the event of default, the lender can more quickly and easily obtain all rights to the underlying real estate.

GK-TK structures almost always utilize an outside AM to provide investment and valuation advice, and additionally often delegate significant authority over their portfolio to be able to benefit from the AM's network and real estate management expertise. (A "GK-TK" (*goudou kaisha-tokumei kumiai*) is a type of investment scheme where the GK (*goudou kaisha*) acts as a corporate vehicle for quasi-limited partnership (*tokumei kumiai*) investors benefiting from pass-through taxation and limited recourse.) **TMK** schemes (a "TMK" or *tokutei mokuteki kaisha* is a type of statutory SPC) own asset portfolios managed in accordance with a written asset liquidation plan registered with the Ministry of Finance, and operation of their portfolios must be delegated to a third-party AM in accordance with the TMK Law. **J-REITs**, another type of SPC, are also legally required to delegate the management of their portfolios to specially-licensed AMs.

After implementation of the FIEL, AMs typically need to be registered as either (1) an investment management business or (2) an investment advisory and agency business *and* a 2nd tier financial instrument business (to solicit investments and act as an agent in TBI deals). This can be an important distinction because entities registering as an investment management business must satisfy registration criteria which are almost as strict as those for 1st tier financial instrument businesses. (If an AM is registered as an investment management business, a 2nd tier financial instrument business registration may not be necessary (unless, for instance, the AM wants to solicit third-party investments), since acting as an agent or intermediary in 2nd tier financial instrument transactions for client portfolios is considered to be part of the AM's investment management business.) Companies registered as investment advisory and agency businesses are allowed to give general valuation and investment advice to their clients, and to act as an agent in entering into discretionary investment contracts (*toushi ichinin keiyaku*) with investment management businesses and investment advisory agreements (*toushi komon keiyaku*) with other investment advisory and agency businesses, but may not act with full discretion over the operation and management of their clients' assets like investment management businesses. In addition, companies which are registered as an investment management business must register with the MLIT as a **Comprehensive Real Estate Investment Advisor** (*sougou fudousan toushi komon gyousha*).

Whether an investment advisory and agency business registration or the more comprehensive investment management business registration is required depends on the level of authority the AM exercises over the financial instrument portfolio. Specifically, in a legal sense the difference is whether in substance both 'the decision to invest' and 'the authority to invest' have been delegated by the SPC to the AM, or whether the AM merely provides the SPC with analysis and/or investment and valuation advice. This distinction generally depends on the individual circumstances and the contents of the relevant asset management agreement.

A regular difficulty for GK-TKs here, however, is the degree to which *tokumei kumiai* (TK) investors may be involved in the *tokumei kumiai* operator's business (*i.e.*, the GK) and still retain the *tokumei kumiai* legal relationship. Depending on the situation, a GK set up as an SPC may not have sufficient capacity on its own to make the decision to invest *and* exercise the authority to invest. However, if the TK investor were to be actively involved in either, there is a risk that the *tokumei kumiai* legal relationship may be re-characterized as a quasi-general partnership (*nin'i kumiai*). In this case, the investor could incur unlimited liability for the TK operator's activities in carrying out the TK business.

Only joint stock companies (*kabushiki kaisha*) may register as an investment management business (although under Japanese law, it is possible to transform an existing GK into a *kabushiki kaisha*). Even if a GK-TK delegates management of all assets to a third-party investment management business, in principle the GK would still need to be registered as a 2nd tier financial instruments business to buy and sell TBIs as a business or to offer TK interests to potential investors. To overcome this, there are various exceptions to the FIEL registration requirements which are explained in Section V below. Also, please note that in the event an SPC completes the procedures for the 'QII Business Notification' exception explained below, any AM acting for the SPC is only obliged to register as an investment advisory and agency business.

IV. Impact on Existing Investment Schemes

The FIEL's impact on investment schemes such as J-REITs, TMKs, GK-TKs and RESL structures very much depended on the specific scheme. Investment schemes licensed under the RESL were perhaps the least affected. One reason for this is that RESL structures may not use an outside AM to manage their real estate portfolio. Another reason is that RESL structures involve real estate held directly in fee simple, meaning the underlying assets are not in the form of financial instruments in any event. Although typically quasi-limited partnership interests (*tokumei kumiai mochibun*) and quasi-general partnership interests (*nin'i kumiai mochibun*) for collective investment schemes fall under the regulations of the FIEL, the rules of the RESL have priority with respect to such financial interests (now considered 2nd tier financial instruments), provided they arise in a RESL-licensed investment structure. This is due to the fact that prior to the FIEL, the RESL already had licensing requirements and other legal rules which were considered sufficient to protect retail investors in RESL schemes. Consequently, business operators licensed under the RESL do not need a separate FIEL registration to carry out their business (although as explained previously, certain FIEL standards of conduct do apply to such schemes).

Similar to RESL structures, J-REITs are collective investment schemes mainly regulated by a law other than the FIEL. Prior to enactment of the FIEL, J-REITs were considered to be already well regulated under the J-REIT Law and the TSE rules, among others. Also, since J-REITs are legally required to delegate all operations to third parties, including the entire asset management function to their AM company, when the FIEL was being drafted it was concluded that the J-REIT vehicle did not generally need further regulation.

The AM company of a J-REIT must, on the other hand, register as an investment management business under the FIEL, and may need to register as a 2nd tier financial instrument business if, among others, it intends to market and solicit investments in J-REIT investment units or J-REIT bonds for the J-REIT. (J-REIT investment units and J-REIT bonds are 1st tier financial instruments under the FIEL, and for this reason a J-REIT would normally need to appoint a 1st tier financial instrument business to solicit third-party investments in such instruments, but there is an exception for AM companies of J-REITs, so they only need to be registered as 2nd tier financial instrument businesses to perform such activities for their J-REITs.) In addition, please note that the FIEL was amended in 2011 to allow a 2nd tier financial instrument business registration to suffice in circumstances where a registered investment management business intends to solicit investments in certain 1st tier financial instruments from qualified investors only.

The collective investment scheme that was most affected by introduction of the FIEL was the GK-TK structure. In general, GKs acting as a *tokumei kumiai* operator and *directly soliciting capital* from investors in quasi-limited partnerships (*tokumei kumiai*) became subject to regulation as a 2nd tier financial instrument business, since *tokumei kumiai* interests for collective investment schemes are considered 2nd tier financial instruments. (Such solicitations are usually done as a private placement, *i.e.*, offered to be sold to a limited number of persons, etc., otherwise a prospectus, securities notice, etc. may be required under the FIEL.) In addition, since GKs *buy and sell TBIs in real estate* on their own account, rather than transacting in direct legal title in real estate (otherwise they would have to acquire an RESL license), from this perspective as well GKs generally need to be registered as a 2nd tier financial instrument business. Further, since GK-TKs *manage TBI portfolios* for third-party investors, as a general rule they must also be registered under the FIEL as either an investment advisory and agency business or an investment management business. However, investment structures using a GK can oftentimes satisfy the requirements for one of the exceptions to FIEL registration explained in the next Section.

For TMKs, the situation is very different from GK-TKs. Under the FIEL, the offering by a TMK of preferred equity or TMK bonds does not fit the definition of 'an offering of an interest in a collective investment scheme,' regardless of whether the TMK invests in TBIs or direct real property. As a result, TMKs do not have to be registered under the FIEL. However, since TMK preferred equity shares (and TMK bonds) are considered 1st tier financial instruments, if a TMK were to employ a third party to market or solicit investments in such instruments, the third party would need to be registered as a 1st tier financial instrument business.

In addition, since TMKs must delegate the management of their assets to a third party under the TMK Law, generally such third party must be registered as an investment management business (or an investment advisory and agency business) if the TMK holds TBI assets. An AM company acting for a TMK may also need to register as a 2nd tier financial instrument business if it solicits buyers for TBIs held by the TMK or acts as an agent or intermediary in TBI transactions for the TMK. However, if a TMK holds all of its real estate assets in direct fee simple ownership and not as TBIs, the AM for such TMK would not need to be registered under the FIEL (since the TMK would not be investing in financial instruments). In sum, by utilizing a TMK holding real estate assets in direct fee simple only, the entire real estate investment scheme (AM and TMK) may be structured to avoid registration under the FIEL. (Nevertheless, the AM would need to be registered as a 1st tier financial instrument business if it were to arrange derivative transactions for the TMK, or market or solicit investments in TMK bonds or preferred equity.)

V. Exceptions to the FIEL Requirements

SPCs are generally set up to provide a bankruptcy-remote vehicle in real estate securitization schemes, and as such they are usually thinly capitalized. Upon implementation of the FIEL, it was thus not practical for pre-existing SPCs to try to restructure to meet the various personnel and minimum capital requirements to qualify for FIEL registration (let alone the internal control and compliance requirements, or in the case of registration as an investment management business, the joint stock company (*kabushiki kaisha*) requirement). In a real estate investment scheme in the form of a GK-TK holding TBIs, under the FIEL the SPC (the GK) generally would need to register as a 2nd tier financial instrument business to solicit investment capital (and buy and sell TBIs in its portfolio). In addition, typically the GK would need an investment management business registration to manage the TBI portfolio. To assist such GK-TKs, there are several exceptions to the 2nd tier financial instrument business and investment management business registration requirements.

In many ways, the simplest exception to FIEL registration is for a company to delegate the relevant FIEL activities to a third-party service provider already registered under the FIEL. In this case, the SPC could delegate both the marketing and solicitation of investment capital and the management of the investment scheme holding TBIs. However, there may be situations where a company does not want to completely delegate all of these activities, especially given the extra costs involved in engaging a third-party service provider.

The second exception, submitting a *tekikaku kikan toushikatou tokureigyoumu todokede* (a qualified institutional investor special ordinance business notification or "**QII Business Notification**"), can be used by a GK in a GK-TK scheme to be excepted from *both* the 2nd tier financial instrument business registration and the investment management business registration. In general, to qualify under the QII Business Notification exception, a GK must (1) have at least one investor considered to be a **Qualified Institutional Investor** ("QII") under the FIEL, (2) have forty nine or fewer *other* investors, (3) have no disqualifying investors, such as a TK operator with any non-QII TK investors or a TMK with any securities issued to non-QII investors, etc., and (4) submit the requisite notification to the finance bureau commissioner (*zaimukyoku-chou*). For the purposes of this exception, a QII is an entity which is considered to have specialized knowledge and experience in investing in negotiable securities under Art. 2, Paragraph 3, Item 1 of the FIEL and as designated by cabinet ordinance. Generally insurance companies, financial institutions, trust banks, foreign insurance companies, and corporate pension funds may qualify. Importantly, this means that practically anyone who can find one investor that qualifies as a QII under the FIEL can set up an asset management company (relatively cheaply as a GK), and solicit and manage capital from up to forty-nine retail (*i.e.*, non-sophisticated) investors.

The third FIEL registration exception only applies to companies seeking exemption from an investment management business registration. This exception is designed for application to the lower GK-TK in a double GK-TK structure (where the lower GK holds TBI assets and receives TK investment capital from the upper GK, and the upper GK acts as a TK investor in the lower GK and obtains investment capital from third-party TK investors). This type of scheme is relatively common because it allows the upper GK to act as a fund manager, and the lower GK to function as a specialized asset vehicle, enabling the lower GK to receive non-recourse loans with covenants tailored to its individual TBI assets. This structure also protects the upper fund manager GK from any issues arising from a single asset affecting the entire investment structure. For the lower GK to apply to receive this exception, (1) it must only hold TBIs, (2) the upper GK must submit the QII Business Notification for an FIEL exception as described above, and (3) the lower GK may only have one parent fund investor (the upper GK).

In addition to the three options above, there are other exceptions to the FIEL registration requirements. The FIEL definition of collective investment scheme generally covers structures where there is capital collected from two or more people to carry out an investment scheme or conduct a business, with the aim of distributing profits to its passive investors. The law expressly excludes interests where (1) all investors directly participate in operating the investment scheme, (2) any distributions, redemptions, etc. to each investor will in no case exceed the capital invested by such investor, (3) the capital invested is for insurance or a mutual aid program, or (4) the capital investment is for an employee shareholder association, trade group, etc., where legally no significant investor protection issues are considered to exist.

Based on the exclusion in (2) above, *ippan shadan houjin* (the bankruptcy-remote vehicle explained in Chapter 19 on TMKs, which on their face may be a type of collective investment scheme under the FIEL) can avoid application of the FIEL rules, provided their articles of association are drafted (or amended) so that the *ippan shadan houjin* may not return any distributions to contributors in excess of the amount contributed by such contributor. Also, the FIEL generally only regulates companies that are engaged in financial instrument activities 'as a business' (that is, where there are repeated and continuous actions towards the general public). Accordingly, there may be special circumstances where a company buying or selling TBIs merely 'to improve its own portfolio' (not 'as a business') is able to avoid registration under the FIEL.

The main impact from the introduction of the FIEL was that it increased the scope of regulated business activities and the types of regulated real estate investment products. It does this by generally regulating transactions in financial interests described or enumerated in the law, but does not generally affect business activities which concern the management of real estate owned directly in fee simple. For this reason, the activities of property managers that take care of the maintenance and upkeep of real property only were largely unaffected by implementation of the FIEL. In addition, asset managers which merely analyze or give advice regarding the value, etc. of *real estate* only, not TBIs or other financial instruments, generally do not need to be registered under the FIEL. For instance, an asset manager only giving valuation advice to a licensed RESL operator would not need an FIEL registration.

17 The Real Estate Syndication Law

I. Introduction

The **Real Estate Syndication Law** (*fudousan tokutei kyoudou jigyouhou*, "RESL") came into effect on April 1st, 1995 in order to create new legal protections for Japanese investors in real estate syndications. The impetus for the law was to implement new regulations for such investment schemes after the Japanese real estate bubble burst in the early 1990s. As a consequence, all companies wishing to organize or operate a real estate syndication in Japan are obliged to obtain a license under the RESL prior to commencing their syndication business.

II. What is a Real Estate Syndication?

Broadly speaking, a **Real Estate Syndication** is a type of collective investment scheme where multiple investors provide capital to a **Syndication Operator** ("Operator") to buy, sell, and/or lease certain properties on the investors' behalf, with the aim of distributing revenue or profit from such transactions to all members of the syndication. Syndication may therefore be considered a means for a group of investors to secure and exercise mutual ownership of an asset, and as such, a real estate syndication may be operated under a variety of contractual and legal forms. The rights and duties of the Operator and the individual investors vary depending on the legal structure chosen to carry out the syndication.

In practice, syndication can be used as a type of financing since it enables Operators to develop a business project or execute a transaction using investment capital from third-party investors. Syndications may be structured so that the investors extend nearly all of the investment capital, although in other cases Operators make a substantial investment as well. Typically, Operators earn significant professional fees from acting as an agent to the syndication in the buying, selling, and management of the syndication's assets. However, this can lead to conflicts of interest between the Operator and the investors, which is one reason for the enactment of the RESL. The types of assets which may be financed through syndication are not limited to real estate, and the concept of syndication can be used in almost any situation where investors desire to pool their money for developing, purchasing, managing, and/or operating an asset.

Real estate syndication offers Operators an alternative to debt for leveraging their own equity to increase profits and obtain control of large-scale real estate assets. In addition, syndications can be beneficial to Operators in that they can be used to lessen the impact of depreciation expenses on an Operator's balance sheet or to extract equity from existing real estate projects. Retail investors benefit from participation by obtaining the chance to invest in business opportunities which, on the whole, would exceed their own individual investment resources. Real estate syndication also provides retail investors with the opportunity to earn profits directly from the skill and know-how of real estate professionals.

III. What existed prior to the RESL?

Prior to the RESL coming into effect, it was common for collective real estate investment schemes in Japan to be carried out with **Small-Lot Real Estate Products** (*fudousan koguchika shouhin*). In these schemes, generally the arranger sold all or a substantial part of the common ownership interests (*kyouyuu mochibun*) in a property to investors, and then either leased the property back to sublease it to third parties, or used a quasi-general partnership (*nin'i kumiai*) arrangement among the investors to operate the investment asset(s) as the agent/quasi-general partner (*gyoumu shikou kumiaiin*). When the real estate bubble burst in the early 1990s, a large number of Operators went bankrupt and many retail investors suffered heavy losses. Some of these losses were due to the investors not being able to recover their capital because it had been diverted by the Operator to other uses. In other cases, the investment scheme or Operator had been undercapitalized from the outset. In addition, many of the investors who suffered losses complained of a lack of accurate information regarding the scheme at the time of contracting. Against this backdrop, the RESL was enacted in 1995 with the objective of "safeguarding the financial interests of investors and contributing to the sound development of real estate syndication enterprises."

IV. When does the RESL apply?

The RESL was enacted in order to regulate investment schemes where cash and/or assets from a large number of passive investors are combined for executing real estate transactions. Since real estate syndications can take many different contractual and organizational forms, the RESL has been drafted to cover a variety of syndication structures, and in general, application of the RESL is triggered by the contractual relationships indicated in Art. 2.3 of the law. Nevertheless, application is not triggered by merely using a certain form of contract, and there are many exceptions designated in the RESL Enforcement Ordinance. Further, Art. 2.3(5) contains a catch-all enabling application of the RESL to any new, similar contractual relationships designated by cabinet ordinance in the future. (To date however, no new contractual relationships have been so designated.)

The RESL applies when an investment structure in real estate is operated 'as a business' and uses one of the types of investment contracts defined in Art. 2.3 ("**RESL Contract**"). Similar to the **Real Estate Transactions Law** ("RETL"), there is no express requirement that a business be intended 'for profit' to be subject to the RESL. However, unlike an RETL license, there is no need to renew an RESL license (since an unintended expiration of an RESL license could harm investors). It is also important to note that the RESL applies not only to companies directly concluding RESL Contracts, but also any company acting as an agent or intermediary in the execution of RESL Contracts under Art. 2.4, Paragraph 2 of the law.

The three main types of RESL Contracts can be thought of in English as a **Quasi-General Partnership Structure** (*nin'i kumiai*), a **Quasi-Limited Partnership Structure** (*tokumei kumiai*, which is further described in Chapter 18 covering GK-TKs) and **Two Permutations of a Leasing Structure** using real estate held in common ownership (*kyouyuu*). In addition, pursuant to Article 2.3, Paragraph 4, the RESL may apply to contracts based on the laws and ordinances of foreign countries which are deemed to correspond to the three contractual types above. For example, the RESL generally applies to limited partnership agreements under US state law entered into in Japan with the aim of investing in real estate in the US or Japan.

In practice, the quasi-limited partnership structure (*tokumei kumiai*) is by far the most popular syndication form due to its relative tax merits and the high degree of freedom it affords Operators. This investment structure also offers limited liability to each of the individual investors. (In principle, all investors in a quasi-general partnership structure (*nin'i kumiai*) have unlimited liability, although this can be changed by agreement.)

An important caveat to application of the RESL is that it does not apply to investment structures where the intention is for investors to only receive revenue or profits arising from transactions other than 'real estate transactions' (**Real Estate Transactions** are defined in Art. 2.2 of the RESL to mean the buying, selling, exchanging and/or leasing of real estate). For example, a collective investment scheme involving a hotel or golf course (such as individuals conveying parcels of land for a golf course operator to operate a golf course) would not generally be subject to the RESL, provided the goal of such scheme is to make a return to investors from the proceeds of *operating* the hotel or golf course, as opposed to making a return from engaging in real estate transactions. Similarly, the RESL is generally not applicable to double special purpose company ("SPC") investment structures, where one SPC collects funds from investors in a quasi-limited partnership structure (*tokumei kumiai*), and then *loans* the proceeds to a second SPC to carry out real estate transactions (since any profits paid to the investors would arise from lending activities).

Furthermore, the RESL does not apply to investment schemes where investors are already considered to be sufficiently protected under other laws. Contracts for Japanese real estate investments concluded abroad, for instance, are not generally subject to the RESL, provided the laws of such foreign jurisdiction are deemed to be sufficient to protect those receiving distributions of revenue or profit, and provided the parties were not solicited in Japan and the contracts executed on a brief trip abroad. In the converse however, the

RESL does generally apply to structures which solely use foreign real estate, provided the RESL Contracts are physically signed in Japan, regardless of the governing law of the documents.

Collective investment schemes in **Trust Beneficiary Interest Certificates** ("TBIs") are excepted from application of the RESL, since these structures are already effectively regulated by the various Japanese laws regulating trusts. Moreover, transactions in TBIs are not transactions in real estate as defined under the RESL, but transactions in 2nd tier financial instruments under the **Financial Instruments and Exchange Law** ("FIEL"). Accordingly, not only are investment schemes dealing exclusively in TBIs not subject to the RESL, but RESL investment schemes may also not invest in or hold TBIs. Collective investment schemes based on the leasing of sections of buildings held under the Law on Sectional Ownership etc. of Buildings (*tatemono no kubun shoyuutou ni kansuru houritsu,* "Sectional Ownership Law") are also not subject to the RESL, since the rights of investors in such schemes are already sufficiently protected under the Sectional Ownership Law.

Art. 1 of the RESL Enforcement Ordinance specifies five investment structures not subject to regulation under the RESL. Generally these are schemes where: (1) a quasi-general partnership structure (*nin'i kumiai*) is used, and the investors are shareholders in the Operator and the Operator is organized as a joint stock company (*kabushiki kaisha*) (since presumably the investors are sufficiently protected under Japanese company law), (2) a quasi-limited partnership structure (*tokumei kumiai*) is used, and the Operator is a 100% subsidiary of the investor parent company, (3)a leasing investment scheme under common ownership (*kyouyuu*) comes about for some reason other than a prior sales scheme (*e.g.*, if it comes about due to inheritance of a property), (4) the structure is already sufficiently regulated by the (former) Japanese Securities and Exchange Law, a similar Japanese law (*i.e.*, the FIEL) or a similar foreign law, or (5) the RESL Contracts are concluded abroad, and it is deemed that the laws of such foreign jurisdiction sufficiently protect the syndication investors. In addition, Art. 3 of the RESL Enforcement Regulations indicates a further condition to (5) above that the only RESL Contracts which qualify for this exception are contracts other than contracts where the solicitation for investment occurs in Japan, but the contracts are executed outside of Japan as part of a "temporary" (*ichijiteki*) trip abroad.

In September 1999, there was an important revision to the RESL allowing for a change in the assets subject to an existing RESL Contract, provided the relevant licensing authority (either the **Ministry of Land, Infrastructure, Transport, and Tourism** ("MLIT") or the prefectural governor) approves the change. Pursuant to this legal revision, it became possible to sell and replace a syndication's assets (generally syndication assets are fixed at the time of applying for an RESL license), or acquire new, additional assets through soliciting additional investment capital. Please note however, that in the event of a replacement of assets, the new assets must be purchased within one year of sale of the prior assets. Nevertheless, thanks to this legal revision it is now possible to set up and operate a type of private real estate fund under the RESL.

V. Why are other investment schemes used more often than RESL structures?

There are many reasons why investment schemes such as *goudou kaisha-tokumei kumiai* ("GK-TKs") and *tokutei mokuteki kaisha* ("TMKs") outnumber real estate syndications in Japan. Probably the first and foremost is that currently it is not possible to create a non-recourse (bankruptcy-remote) investment structure in a real estate syndication. In practice, Operators usually both own and manage all of a syndication's assets (except where a quasi-general partnership (*nin-i kumiai*) is used, in which case all investors are common owners), since any SPC employed in a syndication must be a 100% subsidiary of the Operator, and the Operator must be joint and severally liable for all acts of the SPC, under Art. 7 of the RESL Enforcement Regulations. Typically, syndication investors must therefore depend not only on the investment judgment and real estate acumen of the Operator, but also the Operator's creditworthiness. Accordingly, there is a legal rule that Operators may not comingle syndication assets with their own assets or the assets of any other syndication under Art. 27 of the RESL.

To counter this non-recourse limitation, the MLIT has announced plans for far-reaching amendments to the RESL which, if passed by the Japanese Diet, could become effective sometime in 2013. Under these plans, a *goudou kaisha* ("GK"), which is often used in Japan as an SPC vehicle, would be allowed to acquire real estate assets directly in fee simple without a prior RESL license, provided the GK were to delegate certain services to an RESL-licensed entity, and other special conditions were met (such as filing a notification to the MLIT and limiting participation in the investment scheme to 'sophisticated investors' only). This means that, if passed, the amendments will create the possibility for a new non-recourse RESL investment scheme.

The MLIT has explained that it is proposing the RESL amendments to facilitate real estate companies working with private capital providers in "renewing the functionality of metropolitan areas." Specifically, the intent is for such SPC investment structures to be used for the renovation and/or remodeling of existing properties, including the implementation of measures for enhanced earthquake resistance. Many of these properties are currently not acceptable for entrustment by Japanese trust banks, and the related investment risk, etc. makes them challenging to target in other possible collective investment schemes.

Another drawback of RESL investment structures is their relative lack of liquidity, since syndication interests are generally not as easy to transfer as preferred equity in TMKs or listed J-REIT investment units (although sometimes Operators give investors a put option to provide a degree of liquidity). For example, in order to transfer a quasi-general partnership interest (*nin'i kumiai mochibun*), consent of all other syndication investors is necessary, although to transfer a quasi-limited partnership interest (*tokumei kumiai mochibun*), only the Operator's consent is required. An additional disadvantage of RESL investment schemes is that there are no reduced real estate acquisition taxes or reduced registration taxes, unlike for TMKs, J-REITs, or GK-TKs dealing in TBIs. Also, for quasi-general partnership (*nin'i kumiai*) syndications, the basic legal rule that all investors have unlimited liability can pose an obstacle, although this can be mitigated by contract.

VI. RESL Licensing and Operational Requirements

Because the RESL was enacted with the aim of protecting Japanese retail investors, entities wishing to receive an RESL license must satisfy many prerequisites such as first acquiring an RETL license, being organized as a juridical person (unlike under the RETL, individuals may not be licensed), and employing personnel with the requisite experience and qualifications (an RESL

Operation Manager or *gyoumu kanrisha*) at each office to be used for RESL business activities. Moreover, the entity applying for the license must have at least JPY100 million in paid-in capital, and continue to meet a minimum solvency test during the term of operation of the syndication. The minimum solvency test is calculated by subtracting total liabilities from total assets of the licensed entity and then subtracting 90% of total paid-in equity. The remainder must remain equal to or more than zero during the entire term of the syndication.

All RESL Contracts must incorporate the **Real Estate Syndication Contract Standard Terms and Conditions** (*fudousan tokutei kyoudoujigyou keiyaku yakkan*) approved by the MLIT, and Operators generally must provide investors with pre-contract and post-contract written disclosure materials in accordance with the RESL Ministerial Ordinance. There is also an eight-day 'cooling-off' period for most investors under Art. 26 of the RESL. Additionally, Operators must provide explanations to investors upon request regarding the status of the syndication assets, and send out regular written asset management reports, among other requirements.

For more information about the RESL, please refer to the English translation found at the back of this book. Although there are current plans to amend the law, the RESL resembles other real estate laws such as the Real Estate Transactions Law, and the translation is a good example of a Japanese real estate law in English.

18 An Overview of Real Estate Collective Investment Schemes and a discussion of GK-TKs

I. A Short Overview of Collective Investment Schemes in Real Estate

In Japan, collective investment schemes in real estate are generally organized based on (1) special statute, (2) use of a trust structure, or (3) use of a combination of corporate and commercial law. Schemes structured based on special statute include real estate syndications under the **Real Estate Syndication Law** ("RESL") and securitization structures such as **J-REITs** and **TMKs** (*tokutei mokuteki kaisha*, a type of special purpose company which is generally bound by the contents of its registered asset liquidation plan). Use of a trust structure involves the transfer of title in real estate to a licensed trust bank (or trust company) in exchange for a **Trust Beneficiary Interest Certificate** ("TBI"), and a majority of the real estate investment schemes using corporate and commercial law use the GK-TK (*goudou kaisha-tokumei kumiai*) structure described in the following Sections. Please note that sometimes several of the above five structures are present in one scheme (such as a J-REIT holding a TBI), and there are other structures less common (such as a limited partnership for investment or *toushi jigyou yuugen sekinin kumiai*), which are not discussed here. All of these structures can provide tax advantages for investors over a collective investment scheme utilizing a simple joint stock company (*kabushiki kaisha*).

There are many factors which should be considered in order to determine which investment structure is most appropriate for a specific transaction. For instance, a GK-TK is not a statutory scheme like a TMK or a J-REIT, but is created pursuant to corporate and commercial law. It may therefore be affected in an unforeseen manner by changes to the Commercial Code, the Company Law, or the Trust Business Law (since GK-TKs are generally used to hold TBIs only). Nevertheless, there are many J-REIT Law and TMK Law rules which make J-REITs and TMKs not as flexible or simple to operate as GK-TKs. This is one reason that GK-TKs are often used to acquire an asset temporarily before transferring the asset to a J-REIT or TMK, thereby assisting the J-REIT or TMK time its acquisition appropriately in view of its balance sheet and cash flow strategy. An umbrella GK-TK scheme can also be set up so that a 'mother' GK focuses on raising funds and making TK investments into 'children' GKs, which hold certain properties and obtain non-recourse loans with covenants tailored to such properties.

There is a notable distinction under Japanese law between **Asset Liquidation** (*shisan ryuudoukagata)* **Collective Investment Schemes** and **Asset Operation** (*shisan un'yougata*) **Collective Investment Schemes**. If the main impetus for a transaction is to move a real estate asset off the original owner's balance sheet in a one-time exchange for cash (an asset liquidation scheme), traditionally a TMK scheme has been used since the TMK Law was drafted with such transactions in mind. However, if the goal is to set up a vehicle for the continual acquisition, operation and disposition of real estate assets (an asset operation scheme), with projected frequent additional capital raising and profit distributions, then a J-REIT scheme or a GK-TK scheme has been the preferred structure. This is changing somewhat due to recent amendments to the TMK Law, but this distinction between asset liquidation schemes and asset operation schemes can still be meaningful in many situations.

Depending on the investment project and issues such as the planned number of investors and their level of sophistication, the desired degree of involvement of investors in management of the vehicle, the costs of set up and operation, tax and compliance issues, the likelihood of soliciting future investment capital, the desired allocation of profits and losses, and the projected frequency of buying and selling investment properties, certain structures may be more cost-effective and suitable than others. Still, as a general rule a

GK-TK structure can be a reasonable choice for almost any type of real estate investment scheme. As a consequence, the GK-TK structure (including its predecessor, the YK-TK scheme) has been the most commonly used structure for real estate investments since real estate securitizations started in Japan in the late 1990s.

According to the Ministry of Land, Infrastructure, Transport, and Tourism's "Survey on the Status of Real Estate Securitization Schemes" (*fudousan shoukenka no jittai chousa*), for the fiscal year ending March 31st, 2011, GK-TKs were used to acquire roughly 43.8% of the total asset value of all real estate acquired (direct acquisitions and/or TBIs) during the term, followed by J-REITs next at approximately 27.5%, TMKs at approximately 21.7%, and RESL syndications at approximately 7%. In the fiscal year ending March 31st, 2012, J-REITs acquired approximately 33.8%, GK-TKs 31.7%, TMKs 26.7%, and RESL schemes 7.8%. (The 2012 survey was the first one in which the amount from J-REIT acquisitions exceeded the other schemes since the survey was started in 2003.) It should be noted that since introduction of the **Financial Instruments and Exchange Law** ("FIEL") in late 2007, GK-TKs have become subject to new legal regulations, which may at least partially account for the drop in their popularity.

TMKs are basically most suitable for securitizations of developmental assets or assets specified at the outset of an investment (although as explained in Chapter 19 on TMKs, the situation is changing). This is because there are restrictions against TMKs receiving unspecified tranches of capital as well as making certain types of additional acquisitions. J-REITs can be used as a vehicle for carrying out largely unlimited real estate transactions, but in general they are designed to be listed on the Tokyo Stock Exchange. The disclosure requirements and practical considerations (*e.g.*, maintenance of liquidity for investors) of operating an open-ended (*i.e.*, non-listed) J-REIT have led to a large majority of all J-REITs being listed. (In fact, as of June 2012 there were only three non-listed J-REITs in operation.) It can also be difficult to operate a J-REIT or a TMK as a fund for future acquisitions, since to receive special tax treatment they may not hold significant retained earnings from year to year.

These obstacles to using either a TMK or a J-REIT as a private vehicle for unlimited and unspecified future real estate acquisitions are important reasons why the GK-TK structure (coupled with the acquisition of TBIs to avoid application of the RESL) is so commonly used for private investment schemes in Japanese real estate. In short, in a GK-TK it is possible to structure cash flows so there is little taxation at the GK level (the operator of the real estate investment business), while ensuring that the TK Investors have limited liability. Also, since GK-TKs generally transact their business in TBIs, lenders may monitor and control rent receivables and reserves paid or held in the trust account at the trust bank. However, such GK-TK investment structures must take into consideration the payment of trust bank fees in the investment scheme waterfall. (Please refer to the end of this Chapter for a simple example of a TBI waterfall.)

Using a trust bank (or trust company) for a real estate investment scheme should be considered a special category because an entrustment can be used as a stand-alone investment scheme (for securitization of a real estate asset and sale of the resultant TBI(s) to an investor or investors), or in combination with almost all of the above structures. A TMK, J-REIT, GK-TK, and a stand-alone entrustment scheme itself can all be a beneficiary of a TBI. However, a licensed real estate syndication under the RESL may only invest directly in real estate (not TBIs). In addition, please note that both TMKs and J-REITs may hold direct real estate interests without being subject to the RESL.

One reason the GK-TK structure has generally been regarded in the past as the most flexible of any of the above structures is that it is not explicitly regulated by a specific statute like J-REITs or TMKs. However, in September 2007, the new FIEL came into effect to regulate the offering of TK interests in collective investment schemes as well as transactions in TBIs and other financial instruments. Consequently, GK-TKs investing in real estate are now generally subject to the FIEL regulations, and therefore supervision of the Japanese Financial Services Agency.

II. What is a *goudou kaisha* ("GK")?

The **Company Law** (*kaishahou*, "Company Law") was amended on May 1st, 2006 in order to create a new, flexible form of limited liability company called a *Goudou Kaisha* ("GK"). Subsequently, GKs have become a preferred corporate vehicle for private real estate investments in Japan. In a GK, all investors (called "members") have limited liability as well as the right to participate in management and represent the GK in outside dealings (although these rights can be limited to certain members in the GK's articles of incorporation). Because there is no basic separation of ownership from management in a GK, there is no legal obligation to appoint any directors or auditors, and no requirement for regular corporate resolutions or any member (shareholder) meetings. As a general rule, all matters of a GK are left to its members' discretion as agreed in the GK's articles of incorporation.

A major reason why GK real estate investment schemes are so popular is the flexibility they offer. Unlike the other main Japanese corporate form, the joint stock company or ***Kabushiki Kaisha*** ("KK"), GK profits may be allocated freely in the percentages agreed by its members, regardless of each member's financial contribution. In addition, setting up a GK is usually much simpler (only one member is required) and a little less expensive than setting up a KK. Although a GK cannot be listed on the Tokyo Stock Exchange like a KK, GKs do not have to disclose their balance sheets (and sometimes income statements) to the public as KKs must pursuant to Art. 440 of the Company Law. It is also possible to change the company form of an existing GK to a KK.

In contrast to J-REITs and TMKs, there is no explicit limitation on the types of assets a GK may acquire. A key limitation, however, is that in a real estate investment scheme using a GK (or a KK) as a vehicle for investors in a quasi-limited partnership (*tokumei kumiai*), generally the investment properties must already be entrusted to a Japanese trust bank. This is because such schemes can only deal in TBIs, unless the GK (or KK) is licensed under the RESL. Also, in principle entities soliciting or managing third-party investments in collective investment schemes, or directly engaging in the business of transacting TBIs, must first be licensed under the FIEL. Moreover, any entity engaging in the business of real estate transactions must first obtain a **Real Estate Transactions Law** ("RETL") license, unless certain exceptions apply.

Concurrently with the legal change to create the GK company form, the prior law governing ***Yuugen Kaisha*** ("YK," a type of limited liability company) was abolished. YKs established prior to abolishment of the law still continue to exist as a special corporate form called a *tokurei yuugen kaisha*, but for most intents and purposes they are now legally considered KKs. Please note that in the past, YKs generally performed the function in real estate investment schemes that GKs currently do.

There are several important differences between GKs and the former YKs. For example, the allocation of profits may be freely determined in a GK's articles of incorporation, but for YKs, the distribution of profit to each equity holder had to be in proportion to the amount of capital contributed by such equity holder. Moreover, YKs were not authorized to issue corporate bonds, but GKs are. (Nevertheless, GK schemes are usually funded on the debt side through non-recourse loans, and on the equity side through quasi-limited partnership or *tokumei kumiai* ("TK") contributions.) Another important difference between YKs and GKs is that YKs were managed by a board of directors, and YK equity holders were not provided the legal right to directly manage the company.

The new GK corporate form was loosely modeled on the limited liability company ("LLC") form popular in the United States. However, a significant difference between LLCs and GKs is that a GK is a regular taxable entity in Japan (just like a KK), and there is no 'pass-through' to GK members as there is in an American LLC. Nonetheless, by utilizing a GK-TK (*goudou kaisha-tokumei kumiai*) structure instead of a stand-alone joint stock company (*kabushiki kaisha*), investors can enjoy limited liability while significantly reducing the amount of distributable profit subject to double taxation (at the vehicle level and the investor level) as explained below in Section IV on *tokumei kumiai*. Further, since GKs have an inherently flexible governance structure, they can be set up so that certain matters are decided by certain groups of investors, depending on criteria such as the amount of their investment. It should also be noted that in the event a GK is set up for investing capital received from TK investors into TBIs for real estate, as a general rule it must either delegate asset management services to a third-party investment manager licensed under the FIEL, or carry out procedures to comply with one of the exceptions to the FIEL licensing requirements, as explained in detail in Chapter 16 on the FIEL.

III. Why not use a *kabushiki kaisha-tokumei kumiai* ("KK-TK")?

The main reason GKs are usually used in real estate investment schemes instead of KKs is that in the event of financial difficulty, KKs may file for court protection under the **Corporate Reorganization Law** (*kaisha kouseihou*), whereas GKs may not. In a legal proceeding under the Corporate Reorganization Law, existing security interests in a debtor's property may be voided or have their scope reduced. In addition, if a debtor files under this law, generally any secured creditors are prohibited from executing on their security interests outside of the legal proceeding (for instance, they may not foreclose on a mortgage irrespective of the occurrence of an event of default), although depending on the circumstances this may be possible during legal proceedings under similar laws such as the **Civil Rehabilitation Law** (*minji saiseihou*).

Accordingly, using a KK instead of a GK in a real estate investment scheme can create an unnecessary risk for lenders and secured creditors. Indeed, the usual reason for using a GK in a real estate investment scheme is to set up a bankruptcy-remote vehicle (with an *ippan shadan houjin* as explained in Chapter 19 on TMKs) to function as a **Special Purpose Company** ("SPC") for TK investors and lenders. (It should also be noted that the former YKs, now *tokurei yuugen kaisha*, are generally subject to the Corporate Reorganization Law by virtue of their presently being considered quasi-KKs, although previously YKs were not subject to the law.)

There are other reasons to avoid using a KK in a collective investment scheme as well, for example, the requirement that KKs must make their balance sheets public. However, the other main reason KKs are typically not used is that they are subject to certain legal rules which apply when a company has at least JPY500 million in paid-in capital or at least JPY20 billion in total liabilities (the "**Large Corporation Rules**"). The Large Corporation Rules regulate such companies by requiring them to have at least three directors on their board of directors, financial records audited by an outside audit firm, and an internal control framework which greatly increases administrative costs. Consequently, the KK form is oftentimes inappropriate for a company being used as an SPC. If a KK is nevertheless used, the total amount of liabilities and paid-in capital should be strictly controlled to avoid triggering the Large Corporation Rules.

IV. What is a *tokumei kumiai* ("TK") and why use one with a *goudou kaisha*?

A *Tokumei Kumiai* or "TK" (sometimes translated as a 'quasi-limited partnership' or 'silent investor arrangement') is a type of two-party agreement under the **Japanese Commercial Code** ("JCC") entered into by a passive investor ("**TK Investor**") and a business entity or operator ("**TK Operator**"). Pursuant to the TK agreement, the TK Operator uses investment capital (or property) contributed by the TK Investor to carry out a certain business activity ("**TK Business**"), either as part of or separately from the TK Operator's main business, and distributes profits derived from the TK Business. Please note that a TK is merely a contractual arrangement, not a legal organization or entity, and the TK Investor is liable for debts of the TK Business only up to the contributed amount, unless agreed otherwise.

There are always only two parties to a TK, although TK Operators may enter into TK agreements with multiple investors. The various passive TK Investors, however, have no legal relationship to each other, and their identities usually remain undisclosed. There is no requirement that a TK Operator be engaged only in the TK Business, and a TK Operator may carry out the TK Business as a side business to its main business as long as certain minimum fiduciary duties to the TK Investor(s) are met. Also, a TK Operator may generally only use TK investment capital in furtherance of the TK Business, although in all other respects TK Operators enjoy a high degree of freedom in implementing the TK agreement.

There is an important tax benefit to using a TK investment scheme. Distributions to a TK Investor are deducted and paid from the total profits generated from the TK Business (typically TK Operators use an accounting ledger separate from their own businesses to calculate profit and loss for the TK Business), and the remaining profits are included in the TK Operator's income, prior to being subject to Japanese corporate tax. In this way, using a TK arrangement enables the parties to avoid double taxation on profits, since all profits generated by the TK Business are only taxed after distribution to the TK Investor and the TK Operator. TK agreements thus serve as a **Pass-Through** arrangement for corporate tax purposes. Combining a TK with a GK is a popular real estate investment structure since a GK-TK is comprised of a very flexible corporate vehicle that can be structured as a bankruptcy-remote SPC, and any profit generated by the GK (from investing in real estate as a TK Operator) can be distributed to the TK Investors prior to being taxed at the GK level. In addition, properly structured TK investments generally do not create 'permanent establishment' issues for foreign investors under Japanese tax law.

Since profits from a TK Business are distributed after expenses are deducted from revenue, it is possible for TK Investors to benefit from the depreciation of buildings and other depreciable assets owned by the TK Business. TK losses may also be passed through to the TK Investor if so agreed in the TK agreement. However, please note that TK distributions may be treated differently for foreign, non-resident investors than TMK dividends or J-REIT dividends, depending on the applicable cross-border tax treaty.

For TK Operators, entering into a TK agreement can create a source of funds between debt and equity. Generally, TK Investors take the risk of loss up to their invested capital (as agreed in the TK agreement), but have no legal right to an allocation of TK profits other than the agreed profit percentage. Further, since a TK agreement is not an actual loan agreement, the profit percentage agreed between the parties can be considerably higher than the interest percentages paid under regular commercial loans subject to Japanese usury laws. The TK Investor can also be obligated in a TK agreement to provide additional investment capital to the TK Business based on the occurrence of certain future events. A TK Investor's interest in a TK Business may be encumbered by a pledge to benefit a third-party lender, and sometimes lenders require the full repayment of the non-recourse loan, including all interest, as a condition precedent to any distributions being made to TK Investors.

Because TK interests are legally considered to be 2nd tier financial instruments under the FIEL, companies making an offering of TK investments to the general public may be subject to certain public disclosure requirements. In addition, as a general rule companies must obtain a special FIEL license (a 2nd tier financial instruments business license) to carry out an offering of TK investments (*i.e.*, to solicit TK Investors) for a collective investment scheme, and there is a separate FIEL license in the event the TK Operator intends to manage and operate a collective investment scheme (*e.g.*, to buy and sell TBIs) with the investment capital raised from the TK investment offering. However, please note that there are several exceptions to these FIEL requirements (for example, a TK Operator can delegate the offering of TK investments, and operation of the collective investment scheme, to licensed third parties to comply with the FIEL licensing rules).

V. The Extent of TK Investor Rights

It is important to note that a TK Investor has no ownership rights in a TK Business, and all assets of a TK Business are registered in the name of the TK Operator. In addition, a TK Investor generally may not participate in any of the business activities of the TK Business, although TK Investors do have certain supervisory rights under the JCC. TK Investors also have certain quasi-creditor rights such as the right to demand payment of TK profits in accordance with the TK agreement, and the right to demand the return of invested capital at the end of the TK agreement (provided the capital hasn't been lost in the TK Business). Please note that an investment pursuant to a TK agreement must be either in cash or property, and no contribution of services is allowed.

One issue that often comes up in TK arrangements is the extent a TK Investor may be involved in managing the TK Business or controlling TK invested funds. Art. 536, Paragraph 3 of the JCC sets forth the basic principle that a TK Investor may not represent a TK Business in outside dealings nor engage in the TK Business. The risk here is that the Japanese tax authorities will recharacterize the relevant TK agreement as a quasi-general partnership (*nin'i kumiai*) agreement, if the supposedly passive investor is considered to be actively engaged in the TK Business. In this event, the TK Investor could lose the benefit of limited liability for the TK Business, and in the case of a foreign TK Investor, may incur significant tax liabilities due to being deemed to have a permanent establishment in Japan under Japanese tax law.

Art. 539 of the JCC gives TK Investors the right to inspect the TK Operator's balance sheet, and if there is sufficient reason and permission from a competent court, the condition of the TK Business and its assets. This right is important since in the event of bankruptcy of the TK Operator, TK Investors are considered general, unsecured creditors under Japanese law. In addition, depending on the circumstances it may be legally acceptable for TK Investors to be provided with a veto right with respect to a very limited number of important TK Business matters as specified in the TK agreement. Although these rights cannot be compared to the scope of rights enjoyed by J-REIT unitholders or TMK preferred equity holders, the above supervisory rights can still help TK Investors have some limited understanding of how their investment capital is being used in a TK Business. Nevertheless, oftentimes there is a significant issue with management of GK-TKs since the TK investor cannot be directly involved in the TK Business, and the GK is usually set up to function as an SPC with operations delegated to a third-party AM (which in practice may not want to commit to certain actions without instructions from the main investors). As is evident from the above discussion, receiving professional legal and tax advice is an important part of any GK-TK investment scheme.

Example Chart of Waterfall for TBI Investment by a GK-TK

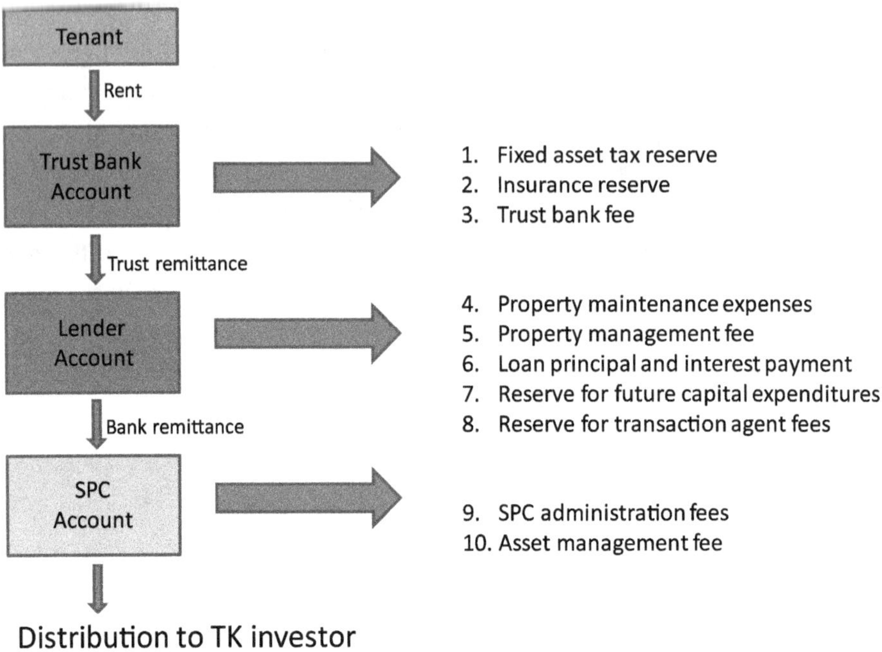

19 Tokutei Mokuteki Kaisha

I. Introduction

A *Tokutei Mokuteki Kaisha* ("TMK," literally a "specified purpose company") is a type of securitization vehicle which was originally designed to assist owners wishing to remove assets from their balance sheet and replenish cash reserves (the prototypical asset liquidation or *shisan ryuudouka-gata* scheme). In Japanese, the law establishing TMKs ("TMK Law") is called the **Law concerning the Liquidation of Assets** (*shisan no ryuudouka ni kansuru houritsu*). 'Liquidation' in this sense means making ownership of an asset more liquid by converting the ownership rights into negotiable securities, *i.e.*, securitization. The TMK Law was established in 1998 primarily to facilitate the disposal of non-performing loans and other illiquid assets by providing a private vehicle for investors wishing to acquire such assets.

Today TMKs are commonly used for securitizing loan obligations as well as commercial real estate assets. They are also frequently used in real estate development projects by developers wishing to set up a bankruptcy-remote entity to receive third-party funding. Please note that in addition to TMKs, the TMK Law created another securitization option called a specified purpose trust (*tokutei mokuteki shintaku* or "TMS"), although TMS schemes are not commonplace in practice.

For investors, a TMK is a type of **Special Purpose Company** ("SPC") which issues securities and employs investment capital to carry out specific projects or purchase certain assets. Investors participate by purchasing TMK preferred equity or TMK bonds (although loans are also possible) with the aim of receiving periodic dividends or interest payments from operation of the TMK's acquired asset(s). Usually they receive the bulk of their invested capital back at the time of final disposition of the TMK asset(s), with the TMK's preferred equity holders receiving any capital gain upon such disposition. Each investor's potential loss is limited to the amount they invest, and investors can benefit from significant tax advantages by utilizing a TMK structure, provided the requisite legal and tax criteria are satisfied.

The TMK Law was drafted to limit the types of risks which can affect TMK investment schemes. TMKs are restricted under the law from engaging in any business activities other than securitization (in general, 'securitization' means issuing securities, acquiring and leasing properties, and paying out interest and dividends), and activities ancillary to such securitization. Further, all business activities must strictly follow the contents of a detailed **Asset Liquidation Plan** ("ALP") adopted by the TMK's specified equity holders and accepted by the Prime Minister's Office prior to the TMK commencing business. (In practice, the ALP is registered at a local finance bureau of the **Ministry of Finance** with jurisdiction over the TMK, and then forwarded to the **Financial Services Agency** ("FSA") in trust for the Prime Minister's Office.) The types of TMK assets and the range of acceptable funding methods are also restricted in the law and must be set forth in the registered ALP (although certain amendments to the ALP after registration are acceptable, and over time the types of assets have been broadened from specified monetary claims and real estate to practically any type of securitizable asset).

TMKs are legally required to outsource the management, custody and disposition of all securitized assets to authorized third parties such as trust banks or qualified asset managers. They are only required to have one director and one auditor (who may not be the same person), and there is no requirement for TMKs to have any employees or even a physical office (most only have a mailing address). In fact, all TMK administrative matters (providing notices to equity holders, calculating and remitting dividends, etc.) are normally outsourced in order for the company to be operated without any regular employees (thereby minimizing expenses and any legal risks which could affect cash flow to the TMK's investors). Thus, the typical TMK is operated as a 'paper' company by third-party service providers delegated with the authority to carry out the TMK's day-to-day business. Because operation of a TMK's business is bound by the contents of the ALP, and all TMK business activities are outsourced to service providers, in a very real sense TMKs are pure asset-holding special purpose entities.

The role of TMK directors is generally supervisory in nature. In almost all cases they have little to no independent authority over a TMK's operations, and the extent of their rights and duties is limited by the ALP and other registered documents such as the TMK's articles of incorporation ("AOI"). Further, they usually waive their right to petition a court to cause the TMK go into bankruptcy. Directors must also be independent and legally may not serve concurrently as a director or officer of the TMK's asset manager or the original owner of any TMK assets.

In contrast to the *goudou kaisha-tokumei kumiai* ("GK-TK") structure, TMKs may own the rights to real estate either directly or by **Trust Beneficiary Interest Certificate** ("TBI"), without triggering the requirements of the **Real Estate Syndication Law** ("RESL"). In the event all TMK assets are held as TBIs, generally the issuing trust bank may manage the assets on behalf of the TMK, otherwise the TMK must appoint a separate third-party asset manager. Since a TMK is intended to be set up as a paper company, it cannot be used as an RESL operator, although a TMK may invest in RESL schemes, and pursuant to recent legal amendments, it may acquire quasi-limited partnership (*tokumei kumiai*, "TK") interests and quasi-general partnership (*nin'i kumiai*) interests in schemes solely involving investments in real estate or TBIs for real estate. Also, it should be noted that registered TMKs are exempted from the legal requirements of the **Real Estate Transactions Law** ("RETL") under Art. 204 of the TMK Law.

II. Structure of a TMK: Equity

TMKs may issue two types of equity, **Specified Equity** (*tokutei shussi*, which loosely corresponds to common shares in the main Japanese corporate form, the joint stock company or *kabushiki kaisha*) and **Preferred Equity** (*yuusen shussi*). Some TMKs only issue specified equity (no preferred) and are primarily funded by TMK bondholders and lenders, however most issue preferred equity as well as specified equity. When preferred equity is issued, practically all equity funding comes from the preferred equity holders. TMKs may issue several classes of preferred equity with differing levels of risk and return, and an in-kind contribution in exchange for the issuance of preferred equity is not allowed (Art. 40, Paragraph 10, TMK Law). Like the other main private securitization vehicle in Japan, the *goudou kaisha*, TMKs may be set up with as little as one Japanese yen in paid-in capital.

Typically in the ALP, preferred equity holders are granted preferential rights to receive dividends and any capital gains on their invested capital. In contrast, specified equity holders generally have the lowest subordinate right to receiving a return on equity, and the subscription amount for specified equity is usually nominal. Further, specified equity holders may freely transfer equity among themselves, but legally they are required to receive consent from a general meeting of all equity holders to transfer their equity to third parties. Preferred equity holders, on the other hand, may freely transfer or pledge their equity to any third party, and under the TMK Law, the right to freely transfer preferred equity may not be restricted (Art. 44, Paragraph 2, TMK Law).

The basic shareholding structure set forth in the TMK Law creates a clear division between ownership and the right to control. Legally, specified equity holders have the right to vote on all equity holder matters in the general meeting of equity holders (such as the election of TMK director(s)), whereas preferred equity holders have only a very limited scope of statutory rights. Still, preferred equity holders may be given the right to vote on almost all TMK corporate matters, if so indicated in the ALP or other registered documents. For example, preferred equity holders do not have a right to vote on the appointment or dismissal of TMK directors, unless provided such right in the AOI. In this way, TMKs have been designed to be a flexible corporate entity where control can be structured more or less as desired by the TMK investors. However, please note that TMKs are often structured so that the preferred equity holders have no voting rights other than their statutory rights to maintain bankruptcy remoteness for non-recourse financing purposes.

Because preferred equity holders put in most of the equity funding when preferred equity is issued, they generally have the power to pass or block all resolutions they are authorized to vote on in a TMK's general meeting. In addition, there is no limit to the percentage of equity that can be issued by a TMK as preferred, unlike Japanese joint stock corporations (*kabushiki kaisha*). Nevertheless, preferred equity holders usually leave management of the TMK to the specified equity holders and TMK directors, since this is a regular condition to the TMK receiving non-recourse debt financing. In addition, preferred equity holders have a variety of automatic rights to protect their interests (as explained below), and specified equity holders and TMK directors are generally limited in their powers by the contents of the registered AOI and ALP in any event. Please note that under Art. 62 of the TMK Law, a TMK may include a provision in the AOI that if a preferred equity holder does not attend or exercise its vote (by proxy) at a general meeting of equity holders, then such equity holder will be deemed to have approved all matters passed at the meeting, except for resolutions with conflicting contents (similar to the **Deemed Approval** (*minashi sansei*) provision for J-REITs).

There are several rights preferred equity holders have to protect their financial interests in a TMK, irrespective of the scope of voting rights given to them in the AOI or ALP. Under the TMK Law, preferred equity holders have the right to vote in a TMK's general meeting on matters such as (1) the preferential issuance of additional preferred equity (Art. 39, Paragraph 3, TMK Law) or convertible bonds (Art. 131, Paragraph 4, TMK Law), (2) any change to the contents of the AOI which "may harm" the interests of the preferred equity holders (Art. 66, Paragraph 1, TMK Law), and (3) any change to the contents of the ALP pursuant to a resolution of the general meeting (Art. 152, Paragraph 3, TMK Law). In addition, they have the legal right to petition a court to overturn any TMK resolution contravening the ALP as well as the right to initiate an equity holder's derivative suit against the TMK's directors. They also have the right to demand the redemption of their equity from the TMK in the event they do not consent to an amendment to the ALP at a general meeting (Art. 153, Paragraph 1, TMK Law).

III. Structure of a TMK: Debt

The most common types of TMK debt are TMK bonds and loans, although specified promissory notes, and other types of TMK bonds such as specified short-term bonds, specified convertible bonds, and specified bonds with equity subscription rights are also possible. There are two types of loans possible under the law: loans for acquiring TMK assets, and loans for certain business purposes (specified in the law) other than acquiring TMK assets (Art. 210, Art. 211,

TMK Law). There used to be a requirement that *all* loans to TMKs had to be issued only by **Qualified Institutional Investors** as defined under the **Financial Instruments and Exchange Law** ("FIEL QIIs"), but now loans for purposes other than acquiring TMK assets may be issued by any institution authorized to engage in such money lending. However, loans for acquiring TMK assets must still be issued only by banks or other FIEL QIIs (Art. 210, TMK Law and the relevant cabinet ordinance). In addition, formerly for a TMK to receive special tax treatment, more than 50% of the TMK bonds and more than 50% of the preferred equity had to be subscribed to by Japanese residents, but this has been changed recently to apply only to "more than 50% of the preferred equity and/or more than 50% of all dividend-receiving or capital gains-receiving specified equity" ('TMK bonds' have been deleted).

TMK bonds play an important role in most TMK schemes. This is because issuing at least JPY100 million in TMK bonds in a **Private Placement** (to avoid application of the public offering requirements under the Financial Instruments and Exchange Law, "FIEL"), to a qualified institutional investor as defined in the relevant Japanese tax laws ("**Tax QII**"), is usually the most convenient way to satisfy one of the requirements for receiving pay-through tax treatment for TMK dividends as explained in Section VII below. However, the FIEL private placement exception that is most frequently used (*tekikaku kikan toushika shibo*) requires that the TMK bonds be placed only with FIEL QIIs. Because the legal definitions of Tax QII and FIEL QII do not exactly coincide, in most cases it is necessary to find a TMK bondholder which will qualify as both a Tax QII and an FIEL QII when setting up a TMK. (Although the legal definitions of Tax QII and FIEL QII differ somewhat, it is possible for most financial institutions to qualify as both.)

Accordingly, in practice TMKs are normally funded on the debt side by either TMK bonds and loans or TMK bonds only. TMK bonds may be issued with different classes and are useful in leveraging equity of the preferred equity holders. However, if a TMK does not issue preferred equity, and issues at least JPY twenty billion in TMK bonds and/or loans, the TMK is required to appoint an external auditor (Art. 67, TMK Law). Most TMKs enter into a contract with an accountant or audit firm to prepare financial statements, etc. for each fiscal year, regardless of whether this requirement is triggered. In addition, TMKs almost always appoint a TMK bond administrator (there are legal conditions which necessitate a TMK bond administrator, but most schemes employ one in any event).

Usually TMK bonds are issued with a **General Lien** (*ippan tanpo*) over all TMK assets, and such general liens have legal priority over all other claims under Art. 128 of the TMK Law, except for certain statutory security interests under the Japanese Civil Code or specified otherwise in the ALP. Typically, TMK bondholders do not receive any security interest over the TMK's assets other than the general lien. One reason for this is that to create a secured bond, the relatively onerous procedures of the **Secured Bonds Trust Law** (*tanpotsuki shasai shintakuhou*) must be followed. (In practice, secured bonds are rarely used in real estate securitizations in Japan.) Loans to TMKs are, however, exempt from the Secured Bonds Trust Law, and thus may be secured with a specific security interest over the TMK's assets.

In any event, most TMK bondholders purchase TMK bonds without setting an additional security interest over the TMK's assets since (1) a TMK may not engage in any business other than the securitization activities notified in the ALP, (2) the bankruptcy risk of TMKs is consequently considered very low, (3) bondholders have a statutory right to consider any amendment to the ALP by the TMK's equity holders, and may demand repayment on the bonds if they do not approve the change, and (4) in the event a TMK issues both TMK bonds and receives loans, the bondholder will have priority over the lenders under Art. 128 of the TMK Law unless provided otherwise in the ALP. Further, a TMK bondholder may receive additional security by using a third party to provide a guarantee on the TMK bonds. In this three-party scheme, the guarantor would receive a guarantee (not directly connected to the TMK bonds) from the TMK, which can then be encumbered for the benefit of the TMK bondholder to be enforceable over any other interests in the TMK assets, without generally triggering the Secured Bonds Trust Law.

From a lender's perspective, investment structures using an SPC such as a TMK or a GK-TK enable the use of **Non-Recourse Loans** (and relatively higher interest rates when compared to regular corporate loans). In a non-recourse loan, the lender's recourse is linked directly to the asset itself (*i.e.*, there is full recourse with respect to the TMK and the TMK assets) rather than the owner of the asset (in an economic sense, the investors in the TMK). This allows the lending decision to be based primarily on the value of the underlying assets rather than the credit risk of any sponsor company, in principle thereby limiting the lender's overall risk. Also, lenders of funds to acquire TMK assets have a statutory right to demand repayment (Art. 157, TMK Law) in the event they do not approve of a change to the ALP by the TMK's general meeting of equity holders (similar to preferred equity holders (Art. 153, Paragraph 1, TMK Law) and TMK bondholders (Art. 154, 155, TMK Law)). In addition, please note that TMKs, like *goudou kaisha*, are not subject to the **Corporate Reorganization Law** (*kaisha kouseihou*). The Corporate Reorganization Law is generally disfavored by lenders since if certain conditions are met, security interests on assets of a company filing for bankruptcy under this law may be voided, and in general they may not be executed on outside of the bankruptcy proceeding.

The use of a non-recourse loan or bond structure has implications for how TMK deals are structured and documented. For example, to complement their general lien, TMK bondholders usually require **Negative Pledge Clauses** (*i.e.*, a promise not to create any security interests with priority with respect to the TMK's assets) in agreements with all equity holders, asset managers, TMK contract parties, etc., so they can swiftly acquire priority rights to the TMK assets if there is a default on the TMK bonds. Although their recourse is usually limited to the TMK's assets in the event of default, in most securitization deals lenders and/or bondholders also receive a **Sponsor Letter** that provides additional recourse to the deal sponsor in the event of certain 'bad boy' acts such as fraud, willful misconduct, intentional waste or damage of assets, intentional breach of the ALP or applicable law, misappropriation of loan proceeds, etc. Furthermore, depending on the scheme it may be possible to structure the relevant documents so that if there is a default on the TMK bonds, the TMK bondholders are given the right to exercise all of the equity holders' rights in the TMK in lieu of such equity holders.

IV. The ALP and Activities Ancillary to the TMK Securitization

Arrangers of TMKs must file a **Notification of Commencement of Business** (including attachments such as the TMK's ALP and AOI), and have such notification accepted and the TMK registered by the local finance bureau, before acquiring any assets, issuing securities, or even generally receiving funding for asset purchases. Please note that registration is only required prior to commencing business, not prior to setting up a TMK. In addition, the types, uses, and maximum amounts of all TMK financing, both debt and equity, must be specified in detail in the ALP. TMKs must carry out their business in strict compliance with the ALP, and any business activities not registered in the ALP are prohibited. TMKs are also obliged to provide a report on operations and a statement of cash flow within three months of each fiscal year to the local finance bureau.

The ALP is a rather long and comprehensive legal document containing basically all relevant details about the prospective securitization. The contents include details concerning: (1) the planned term of securitization, (2) the securities to be issued (specified equity, preferred equity, TMK bonds, convertible bonds, etc., with details such as maximum authorized numbers, maximum amounts, etc.) and any loans for acquiring TMK assets, (3) the TMK assets (to be securitized) and any planned transactions, (4) the planned management and future disposition of the TMK assets, including asset management matters, (5) any loans other than loans for acquiring TMK assets, and (6) any other relevant matters as set forth by cabinet ordinance. Nevertheless, the specific details of each ALP depend to a certain extent on the preparer and the discretion of the officer of the local finance bureau reviewing the ALP. The maximum term for a TMK for real estate is fifty years, although a TMK scheme may be wound up sooner if agreed by the parties.

Documents attached to the notification of commencement of business include the ALP, the AOI, a copy of the executed conditional (*yoyaku*) purchase agreement for the TMK asset(s), a copy of the (conditional) trust agreement or asset management agreement regarding the delegation of management and future disposition of the TMK asset(s), a document evidencing approval of the ALP by the TMK's specified equity holders, various identification documents for the TMK director(s), and other documents designated by cabinet ordinance. The Ministry of Finance publishes a checklist of items necessary for the notification on its website, which in practice can be very useful. Please note that upon acceptance of the notification, and entry of the TMK in the TMK register at the local finance bureau, certain details of the documents are made public.

Because the ALP must contain a detailed outline of all material matters concerning the securitization, and the ALP has to be notified to the local finance bureau prior to the TMK beginning business, all interested parties (including generally all preferred equity holders, TMK bondholders and lenders) need to agree to the important parts of the ALP prior to the ALP being registered. For example, unless provided for in the ALP, a TMK may not loan, transfer, exchange or encumber a TMK asset in any way. In addition, it may not invest any surplus from the TMK business other than in bank deposits, government debt, or other instrument or method designated by cabinet ordinance (Art. 214, TMK Law), and the upper amount a TMK may borrow is set forth in the ALP as well. Given the fact that it is very hard to anticipate every future issue that can arise, successfully completing the pre-transaction discussions for a TMK can be a time-consuming process. It can also be difficult to carry out a material amendment to an ALP after it has been registered, especially since the prior consent of all interested parties is required in the usual case.

The statutory purpose of a TMK is to carry out an asset securitization by acquiring assets with funds obtained by issuing securities or receiving loans, and to engage in 'ancillary activities' for such securitization. One of the important issues under the TMK Law is what constitutes such **Ancillary Activities** (*futai gyoumu*), because these are the only business activities allowed prior to acceptance of the notification of commencement of business by the local finance bureau. In the event TMK securitization activities are begun prior to acceptance of the notification, the responsible party can be subject to a fine of not more than JPY three million and/or incarceration not longer than three years.

In general, ancillary activities are those activities necessary for the securitization process other than specific securitization activities, such as issuing securities or closing on the purchase of TMK assets. For example, incorporating a TMK, requesting appraisal services, and receiving loans to pay a deposit at the time of execution of the (conditional) TMK asset purchase agreement are generally considered ancillary activities. Further, since they are required attachments to the ALP notification, execution of (conditional) purchase agreements and (conditional) asset management agreements should also generally be considered activities ancillary to a TMK securitization.

V. Recent Amendments to the TMK Law

One notable issue concerning the legal and tax rules affecting TMKs is the frequency at which they have been amended in the past. For example, initially after the TMK Law became effective in 1998, it was not permissible to change the contents of the ALP after registration at the local finance bureau. The problem was, however, that such a rigid system was not practical for asset securitizations, and consequently the TMK Law was revised in April 2000 to allow for an amendment process. Nevertheless, there are certain matters which may not be amended, and in general it is important to discuss any material amendment with the local finance bureau in advance. Also, please note that in the event of a change in the ALP or any other matters in the documents accepted by the local finance bureau, the basic rule is that a **Notification of Amendment** (with reasons for such amendment) must be sent to the local finance bureau within two weeks of such change.

There are many significant revisions to the TMK Law which became effective on November 24th, 2011. Although an exhaustive discussion of all of the amendments is outside of the scope of this Chapter, there are five amendments which are perhaps the most important for TMK investors. These legal changes affected the rules regarding (1) director-only amendments to the ALP, (2) loans for purposes other than for acquiring TMK assets, (3) the use of proceeds from TMK asset sales for additional acquisitions during the term, (4) the acquisition of additional TMK assets during the term, and (5) the scope of permissible TMK assets.

With respect to the first amendment, prior to November 2011 it was possible for the ALP to be amended by resolution of the TMK director(s) only (without a TMK general meeting resolution). However, this was only permissible provided such amendments were (1) 'minor' in accordance with the relevant cabinet ordinance ("minor" meaning either (i) formalistic and due to the occurrence of some event outside of the control of the TMK, (ii) formalistic and due to another approved amendment to the ALP, or (iii) a reduction in the term of the TMK due to the full repayment of a loan or bond, redemption of preferred equity, etc.), (2) matters that had the prior consent of all **Interested Parties** (all equity holders, TMK bondholders, specified promissory note holders, and lenders of loans for acquiring TMK assets), or (3) other amendments which did not negatively affect any interested parties in the TMK (and met certain other conditions as designated by cabinet ordinance) (Art. 151, Paragraph 3, TMK Law and Art. 79, TMK Law Enforcement Regulations). Under the new TMK Law, the types of amendments which may be carried out by a director-only resolution have been expanded to include certain additional matters designated under the TMK Law Enforcement Regulations such as the timing of issuance of preferred equity or TMK bonds, and the timing of acquisition of TMK assets, provided the TMK director(s) have been given this right already in the registered ALP.

This new exception increases the types of changes to the ALP which may be carried out through an abbreviated process (reducing the circumstances which require either a resolution of the TMK's general meeting or the unanimous consent of all interested parties), and is intended to apply to TMK business matters which in many cases require frequent amendment. The impetus for this change was to make the TMK system more user-friendly and to overcome one of the traditional difficulties of using a TMK, the cumbersome yet frequently required ALP amendment process. In addition, the ALP itself must still be amended and notified to the local finance bureau for such director-only amendments, but the separate notification of amendment to the local finance bureau has been exempted in this case.

The second important 2011 revision involves loans provided to TMKs for purposes other than acquiring TMK assets as defined under the law. Previously, such loans could only be provided by FIEL QIIs. However, as explained above in Section III, now TMKs may receive such loans from any company, not just FIEL QIIs, provided the company complies with the various Japanese legal requirements.

Notwithstanding the two amendments above, perhaps the most significant effects on TMKs have come about from the changed rules on TMKs acquiring additional assets, and the relaxation of the restriction on using cash from the sale of TMK assets for buying additional assets. Regarding this latter amendment, although previously there was no explicit legal prohibition on the use of sale proceeds for acquiring additional TMK assets during the term, the majority legal interpretation was that TMKs could not sell TMK assets and then use the sale proceeds to purchase new assets. The legal reasoning for this interpretation was that the method for raising capital to acquire a TMK asset should be a method specified in the TMK Law, notified in the ALP, and accepted by the local finance bureau prior to execution.

This is a crucial change for TMKs, since TMKs were not originally designed to be used as a transactional vehicle for the multiple buying and selling of real estate assets over the term of the TMK. Now due to this amendment, in principle TMKs may buy and sell assets on an ongoing basis without always requiring additional capital from investors. Please note, however, that the acquisition of any new additional assets is a matter which requires an amendment to the ALP.

In addition to the categories of ALP matters which may be amended pursuant to a director-only resolution referred to above, most material matters in an ALP may be amended through an equity holder process in the TMK's general meeting (Art. 151, TMK Law). Importantly, any preferred equity holders who do not agree in the equity holder process, and any TMK bondholders, specified promissory note holders or lenders for the acquisition of TMK assets who do not consent to the ALP change in the equity holder process, have the right to demand the TMK buy their preferred equity at fair market value, pay off their loan, or redeem their TMK bonds (Art. 153, 154, 155, and 157, TMK Law). Because of the risk this entails, as a general rule the unanimous prior consent method set forth in Art. 151, Paragraph 3(2) of the TMK Law is the main way that TMKs have their ALPs amended (unless the matter to be amended falls under the director-only category).

Prior to the 2011 legal amendments, there were also significant restrictions regarding the types of additional assets which could be acquired by a TMK. Although not explicit in the TMK Law, the FSA used to enforce a restriction that any assets additionally acquired by a TMK had to have a 'close connection' with respect to the existing TMK assets. This was due to the fact that the original legal intent of creating the TMK vehicle was for it to function as part of an asset liquidation *(shisan ryuudoukagata)* scheme, not a transactional vehicle in an asset operation (*shisan un'yougata*) scheme. A 'close connection' was generally interpreted by the FSA to mean in a geographic sense and/or with respect to the function or use of the additional assets, and such assessment was only made after reviewing each case individually and the background circumstances in their totality.

However, pursuant to the 2011 amendments, the FSA has indicated that TMKs may now make an additional acquisition of any TBIs for real estate assets, regardless of the lack of a close connection with existing TMK assets. Nevertheless, the FSA has announced in its public comments that with respect to non-TBI real estate assets (*i.e.,* assets held directly in fee simple), it will still apply the close connection test in determining whether an ALP amendment for acquisition of such assets will be accepted. In any event, it is recommended to discuss the specific facts in advance with legal counsel and government regulators if investors desire to acquire additional assets through an existing TMK.

The last 2011 amendment to the TMK Law concerns the scope of assets TMKs may acquire. Formerly, TMKs were explicitly restricted from acquiring TK interests or quasi-general partnership (*nin'i kumiai* or "NK") interests, unless the investment was part of an RESL-licensed investment scheme. However, pursuant to the new amendments, TMKs may now acquire any such TK or NK interests, provided the interests are in schemes involving investments solely in real estate assets. Accordingly, it may now be possible to set up a TMK-GK-TK double fund, where the TMK serves as a 'mother SPC' and makes TK investments in a GK holding investments in TBIs for real estate.

VI. Bankruptcy Remoteness and a Description of *ippan shadan houjin*

Bankruptcy Remoteness issues can generally involve at least three risks to an SPC investment scheme such as a TMK: (1) bankruptcy of the cash flow vehicle (the TMK), (2) bankruptcy of the original seller of the securitized asset (the TMK asset) or (3) bankruptcy of the arranger, deal sponsor, or other related third party. The point here is that by one of the above parties filing for bankruptcy, the timing or amount of cash flow from the asset to the SPC investors may be adversely affected. For this reason, TMK securitization structures contain certain preventive measures to lessen the risk that any party will cause the TMK to be declared bankrupt, or any party will file for bankruptcy and thereby negatively affect the TMK cash flow.

In order to lessen the risk that a TMK will become subject to bankruptcy procedures, after notification of the ALP to the local finance bureau, it is common for arrangers to transfer the specified equity of a TMK to a Japanese non-profit legal entity called an ***Ippan Shadan Houjin***. The reason this type of Japanese entity is used is because legally it is obliged to act for the benefit of all of its members, while not being intended to issue any distributions or return any contributions to such members (generally the vehicle is meant to be used by non-profit entities such as charitable organizations which receive contributions but desire to be free from interference or influence from any contributors). Accordingly, an *ippan shadan houjin* is used to separate the act of contributing property or capital from any rights associated with the contribution of such assets, and thus a contributor of TMK specified equity cannot cause the voting member of the *ippan shadan houjin* to use its equity rights in the TMK to petition a court to declare the TMK bankrupt. Use of an *ippan shadan houjin* can also serve as a method for blocking the deal sponsor of a securitization from exerting any potential influence over the TMK. The arranger usually sets up the *ippan shadan houjin* with a neutral person such as an independent attorney or public accountant as the only voting member, with a personal agreement from the person not to apply for bankruptcy of the TMK.

Other measures which are used to prevent a TMK bankruptcy include the fact that the TMK's business is limited to only acting as a cash flow conduit (no other businesses which could create additional liabilities are allowed), appointing a TMK director and TMK auditor who are independent from the arranger and any TMK investors (commonly accountants from a professional accounting firm), and arranging for **Non-Petition Letters** to be signed by such independent director and auditor. (A non-petition letter contains a promise not to petition a court to cause the TMK go into bankruptcy, although the enforceability of non-petition letters has never been adjudicated in Japanese court.) The general division of authority between preferred and specified equity holders and the requirement that limited recourse clauses be included in all contracts with the TMK are additional preventive measures. Further, it is common for TMK bondholders and lenders to require that all sellers of assets to the TMK promise in the relevant asset purchase agreement that under no circumstances will they file for bankruptcy against the TMK.

One of the key bankruptcy remoteness issues is a concept called the **True Sale** issue, which concerns potential effects from the bankruptcy of the original seller of the securitized asset. The 'true sale' issue involves whether the sale to the cash flow vehicle (the TMK) is an actual sale or a disguised financing arrangement (the provision of collateral to secure a loan), whereby the asset should remain in the bankruptcy estate of the seller. This is important because TMK investors would like to avoid the possibility that the sale of an asset to the TMK is reversed in the future by creditors of the original owner.

The decision of whether a transaction constitutes a true sale may be different for legal and accounting purposes, and there are a number of potential issues to consider here (for example, in the event the transaction is a sale and leaseback). In addition to a claim of 'lack of true sale,' there are other potential legal claims in a bankruptcy proceeding under Japanese law which can be used to unwind TMK ownership for the benefit of the seller's creditors (such as a fraudulent conveyance-like action called a *sagai koui*). Therefore, it is important for the purchase of a TMK asset to be properly documented and carried out with professional legal and tax advice. Nevertheless, it should be noted that it is not possible to eliminate every bankruptcy risk to the TMK's cash flow with 100% certainty.

VII. Tax Merits of the TMK Scheme

TMKs (and J-REITs) are considered to be **Pay-Through Vehicles** for tax purposes. This is because dividends may be deducted as an expense on a TMK's income statement prior to profits being subject to Japanese corporate tax, provided the entity and fiscal year tax requirements explained below are satisfied (please note that there are different rules for the deduction of distributions). From the perspective of a TMK's preferred equity holders, this means that it may be possible to avoid double taxation (both at the entity level and in the hands of the investors) on TMK profits. However, please note that TMKs must pay corporate tax on any profits that are not distributed to investors. (In comparison, GK-TKs are considered a 'pass-through' arrangement because in no case can a TK arrangement be subject to corporate tax. Thus, TK investors avoid double taxation on profits in a way substantially similar to J-REIT or TMK investors.) In addition to pay-through taxation, if certain separate tax law conditions are met, TMKs (like J-REITs) may benefit from a reduced basis for the **Real Estate Acquisition Tax** (*fudousan shutokuzei*, until March 2013, two-fifths of the regular tax basis) at the time of acquisition of real estate assets, and a reduced **Registration and License Tax** (*touroku menkyozei*) at the time of registering ownership of real estate assets as well.

There are two separate sets of tax law rules which must be satisfied for a TMK to receive pay-through tax treatment for a certain fiscal year. The first set of conditions concerns the TMK itself, and the second set of conditions applies to the specific fiscal year. Significantly, because the second set of conditions must be satisfied for a specific fiscal year, in the event a TMK's tax returns are revised for prior years, there is a risk that a TMK could lose its special tax status for such prior years (basically no longer satisfy the **90% Rule** explained below), and have to pay corporate taxes on already distributed TMK profits. Also, please note that the rules below only apply to TMKs set up in 2012. As a general rule, TMKs already in operation are subject to the rules effective in the year they were established.

The requirements for a TMK to be allowed to pay-through dividends are the satisfaction of (A) and (B) below.

(A) TMK Entity Requirements

(1) The TMK is listed in the local finance bureau's publicly-available register of notified TMKs; and

(2) Any one of the four conditions (a)-(d) below is met:

- (a) The TMK has offered TMK bonds in a public offering and for a total amount of at least JPY100 million; or
- (b) The TMK bonds are intended only to be held by qualified institutional investors ("Tax QIIs" as defined in the Special Tax Measures Law) or TMKs for the Liquidation of Specified Receivables; or
- (c) The preferred equity has been subscribed to by at least 50 entities; or
- (d) The preferred equity has been subscribed to only by Tax QIIs, and

(3) The Asset Liquidation Plan stipulates that more than 50% of the preferred equity and more than 50% of dividend receiving and/or capital gains-receiving specified equity are to be offered and subscribed to in Japan; and

(4) The accounting year of the TMK is not more than one calendar year.

(B) Requirements Applicable per each Fiscal Year

(1) The TMK's business activities have been carried out in accordance with the notified Asset Liquidation Plan; and

(2) The TMK has not engaged in any business activities other than as notified in the Asset Liquidation Plan; and

(3) All of the TMK assets are held in trust or the management and disposition of all TMK assets has been delegated to a third party; and

(4) The TMK is not considered a 'family corporation' as designated under the relevant cabinet ordinance at the end of the fiscal year (except where the TMK has issued TMK bonds in a public offering and for a total amount of at least JPY100 million or the TMK bonds are intended only to be held by Tax QIIs or TMKs for the Liquidation of Specified Receivables); and

(5) The amount of dividends distributed during the subject fiscal year exceeds 90% of all distributable profit of the TMK for such fiscal year (**the so-called 90% rule**); and

(6) The TMK is not an unlimited liability partner in a *goushi kaisha* or a *goumei kaisha* (two types of Japanese entities); and

(7) The TMK does not own any assets which are not held in trust and/or the TMK does not have any assets where the management and disposition of such assets has not been delegated to a third party.

One investment structure frequently used by foreign investors is to combine a TMK in Japan with an entity set up in Singapore to receive preferred equity dividends. In this way, the foreign investor can oftentimes reduce cross-border withholding taxes by benefiting from the various tax treaties between Japan, Singapore, and the foreign investor's home country. This is also an advantage of the TMK structure over the GK-TK structure, since TK distributions are generally not considered 'dividends' under such treaties. Nevertheless, tax issues affecting the TMK structure change rather frequently, so it is highly recommended to consult with a qualified tax advisor prior to beginning any TMK securitization.

VIII. GK-TKs versus TMKs

The main benefit of GK-TKs is that they are a flexible structure generally created by contract between the parties. Unlike a TMK, the parties can easily change the purpose of the investment structure, number and types of assets, etc. during the term of the deal. However, real estate assets owned by GK-TKs need to be in the form of TBIs, otherwise the scheme will be subject to the RESL. Because the scheme must deal in TBIs, a trust bank has to be paid to hold the assets for the benefit of the GK-TK (an expense which can, depending on the circumstances, outweigh the tax advantages of using TBIs). In addition, trust banks can sometimes lack flexibility in dealing with issues such as regulatory violations in entrusted real estate. It may also be difficult to find a trust bank to accept the entrustment of certain problem assets or assets which are located far from major metropolitan centers. Although TMKs are exempt from the requirements of the RETL, GK-TKs are also generally not affected by the RETL since they transact business in TBIs only.

GK-TK schemes dealing in TBIs are subject to the requirements of the FIEL, a law which generally regulates entities engaging in transactions in financial instruments (such as TBIs), and further regulates entities soliciting and/or managing investment capital for collective investment schemes in financial instruments. For this reason, GK-TKs need to satisfy one of the FIEL licensing exceptions or delegate certain matters to FIEL-licensed entities. TMKs are, however, generally exempted as an entity from FIEL registration (though their asset managers are not, unless the TMK only holds real estate assets in fee simple). Another drawback of the GK-TK scheme is that TK investors only have very limited rights to be involved in a TK business (run by the TK operator), whereas legally TMK investors may more directly control a TMK's business. GK-TK schemes may also be more vulnerable to future legal changes since they are not statutory vehicles like TMKs or J-REITs (although in the past, the TMK Law has been subject to relatively frequent amendment).

Like J-REITs, TMKs may hold real estate assets either in the form of TBIs or as direct real estate without being subject to the RESL, although they must delegate the management, custody, and disposition of their assets to qualified third parties such as trust banks or third-party asset managers. Unlike J-REITs, neither a TMK nor a GK may be listed on the Tokyo Stock Exchange. Because TMKs were not originally designed to be used as a transactional vehicle for freely buying and selling real estate assets, and due to the many restrictions and legal and tax rules applicable to TMKs, TMKs are also less appropriate for buying and selling unlimited and unspecified real estate assets on an ongoing basis. It can also be difficult to change an existing ALP during the term (although the legal rules have been significantly relaxed). Nevertheless, from a regulatory perspective, and depending on the details of the deal, some may still consider a TMK the preferred structure. Both GK-TKs (by transacting in TBIs) and TMKs may benefit from reduced real estate acquisition and registration taxes, and dividends from TMKs and distributions from GK-TKs may be treated differently for cross-border withholding tax purposes.

The legal costs of setting up a TMK are typically higher than for setting up a GK-TK, since in general the details of a TMK securitization must be agreed to in advance by all of the TMK investors, and then a rather lengthy ALP drafted and notified to the local finance bureau prior to beginning business. Also, it may be more complicated to manage a TMK from the viewpoint of the average investor, and the tax requirements explained in Section VII above must be satisfied every fiscal year for the TMK to receive special tax treatment for that year. (For example, TMKs may not hold significant cash surpluses from year to year while still qualifying for the 90% tax rule.)

A TK arrangement can pass through profits or even losses to a TK investor based on the contents of the TK agreement, but in general TMKs can only distribute profits. Also, as a practical matter, it is necessary to have short fiscal years (and thus increased administrative costs) for TMKs in the event the TMK investors would like to receive frequent dividend payments. (TMKs are limited under Art. 115 of the TMK Law to only being allowed to issue half-year dividends, and only if their fiscal years are exactly one year, among other restrictions.)

20 J-REITs

I. Introduction

A **Japanese Real Estate Investment Trust** ("J-REIT") is a limited liability entity organized to issue shares for investment capital, acquire real estate assets, and distribute dividends from profits arising from the operation of such real estate assets. Of the three main types of real estate securitization structures in Japan (*tokutei mokuteki kaisha* or "**TMKs**," *goudou kaisha-tokumei kumiai* or "**GK-TKs**," and J-REITs), J-REITs are the only vehicle that may be publicly listed. Accordingly, a large majority of J-REITs are listed on the **Tokyo Stock Exchange** ("TSE"), although over the last several years a few non-listed J-REITs have been set up (as of June 2012, there were three such J-REITs, and there have been announcements of several new private J-REITs to be formed sometime in late 2012).

The legal framework for J-REITs came into force in November 2000 pursuant to a revision of the **Law on Investment Trusts and Investment Companies** ("J-REIT Law"), which was originally based on the 1951 Securities Investment Trust Law. The amended law enables the formation of three types of J-REITs (one corporate-type J-REIT and two trust-type J-REITs). All listed J-REITs to date have adopted the corporate form, presumably due to its superior shareholder protections. Consequently, this Chapter only discusses the corporate form of J-REIT.

Introduction of the J-REIT Law represented a significant step toward promoting the efficient utilization of real estate over merely holding title to real estate assets. Whereas in the past, Japanese companies (and their lenders) prized the simple ownership of large tracts of land, cash flow from real estate is currently of primary importance. J-REITs are emblematic of this transition in their focus on building steady income streams and promptly distributing profits to investors, and in fact the J-REIT market is presently the 4th largest REIT market in the world.

Non-professional investors can benefit from owning equity in J-REITs (called **Investment Units**) in a variety of ways. Although real estate as an asset class is relatively illiquid, investment units of TSE-listed J-REITs can be easily bought and sold. J-REIT investors also have the chance to benefit from real estate investment opportunities they would not be able to locate or afford individually, and they are able to earn profits directly from the skill and experience of real estate professionals. Further, J-REITs usually qualify for special tax treatment (**Pay-Through Taxation**), which allows them to avoid paying corporate taxes on amounts issued as dividends (*i.e.*, J-REIT dividends generally avoid double taxation). As a result, J-REITs are much more tax efficient than the most prevalent Japanese corporate entity, the joint stock company (*kabushiki kaisha* or "KK"). The fact that listed J-REITs (and their asset management companies) must comply with extensive disclosure requirements and many overlapping laws and regulations adds to their appeal to retail investors.

Although the value of listed investment units can be affected by swings of momentum in the broader stock market, non-professional investors can use J-REITs to diversify portfolio risk. Typically, investment units enjoy a risk profile in between debt and common equity, since their dividends are mainly based on stable rental income arising from long-term real estate holdings. Further, because J-REITs are intended to concentrate on generating and maintaining a consistent dividend stream, investment units may be used to balance out portfolio investments aiming primarily for capital returns.

A real estate fund such as a J-REIT may be operated as an **Open-Ended** or **Close-Ended Collective Investment Scheme**, although at present most J-REITs are close-ended (and only close-ended J-REITs are allowed to be listed on the TSE). In an open-ended fund, investors are granted the right to terminate their investment contracts after a period of time in order to redeem their invested capital directly from the fund (usually in accordance with periodic valuations, a pre-agreed price formula, and other conditions). Close-ended funds, however, do not provide for such a right of redemption, but rather use a public exchange to provide liquidity for investors. All Japanese close-ended J-REITs are listed entities, and one of the requirements for a listing on the TSE is that the J-REIT expects at least 1000 independent unitholders.

One complication with operating an open-ended (unlisted) fund is that real estate assets are not readily disposable, and such funds can run into difficulties if too many investors demand the return of their capital at the same time. In this event, any cash reserves of the J-REIT would be quickly exhausted (since to receive special tax treatment, J-REITs are not allowed to have significant retained earnings), and the fund could be forced to dump properties on the market in a short period of time. It can also be difficult for investors to appropriately value investment units in an unlisted J-REIT, and management fees may be higher than in listed J-REITs due to the less stringent disclosure rules (*e.g.*, no applicable TSE rules). In the end, most investors in open-ended funds participate at least partly based on the creditworthiness of the J-REIT's sponsor company.

The investment units of close-ended (listed) J-REITs, on the other hand, can suffer from significant volatility due to the vicissitudes of the public markets, independent of any changes in underlying leasing fundamentals. In comparison, a potential strength of the open-ended fund model is that the value of its investment units is derived primarily from the value of the fund's real estate assets, with no speculative premium or discount automatically included as is the case with listed investment units. Consequently, several open-ended J-REITs have been set up recently to provide a stable, long-term income alternative to the more volatile equity of listed J-REITs.

J-REITs may be classified legally as a type of **Asset Operation** *(shisan un'yougata)* **Collective Investment Scheme**, since their main purpose is to be operated as a real estate fund, and not to serve as a financing vehicle for originators. That is, rather than being intended for the one-time securitization of certain 'specified' assets with investment capital 'specified' in advance (such as an asset liquidation scheme using a TMK), J-REITs are intended to be operated as an ongoing investment fund for issuing shares, accumulating and replacing properties, obtaining financing, and distributing dividends. Nevertheless, J-REITs are statutory special purpose entities under Japanese law (like TMKs), and as such they have a limited business purpose and the assets they may invest in are restricted.

Under the J-REIT Law, J-REITs must delegate all administrative activities as well as the entire operation and custody of their assets to qualified third-party service providers (J-REITs are intended to function as pure investment-holding vehicles similar to TMKs), and legally they are not allowed to have a branch office or even one employee. Further, J-REITs (like TMKs) may hold real estate assets through a trust beneficiary interest certificate ("TBI") or directly in fee simple, without being subject to the requirements of the **Real Estate Syndication Law** ("RESL"). However, unlike TMK directors, the directors of J-REITs are intended to play an active role in governing the J-REIT in partnership with its unitholders.

J-REITs are really in essence two companies (like most Asian REITs and in contrast to US REITs), because although J-REITs issue equity and own properties, legally they must delegate the operation and management of their asset portfolios to a specially-licensed **Asset Management Company** ("AM Company"). As a result, the financial performance of a J-REIT is very dependent upon the skill and experience of its AM Company. Despite being bound to adhere to their J-REIT's general **Operational Guidelines** (*un'you houshin*, which set forth basic investment parameters such as the eligible types of assets, permitted locations, due diligence policy, etc.), AM Companies still enjoy a wide range of discretion in the operation and management of the J-REIT's portfolio. In addition, the **Sponsor Company** of a J-REIT plays a central role in the J-REIT's success, since usually the Sponsor Company sets up both the J-REIT and AM Company, provides a majority of the AM Company's employees, is the largest unitholder in the J-REIT and a majority shareholder in the AM Company, and supplies most of the investment opportunities to the J-REIT's portfolio. (Please note that in many cases, a trust bank is delegated separate custodial rights to the assets owned by a J-REIT.)

A J-REIT's main purpose is thus (1) to function as a **Special Purpose Company** ("SPC") for holding title to real estate assets, (2) to delegate all business matters and broadly supervise their execution by outside service providers, and (3) to provide a vehicle for unitholders to monitor and influence major business and corporate governance matters. In a sense, J-REITs can be considered to be in between TMKs and GK-TKs, since unitholders are able to exert more control over a J-REIT than TK investors in a GK-TK, but legally J-REITs can more freely acquire and dispose of assets than TMKs. Also, it should be noted that J-REITs cannot be structured with specific bankruptcy protections such as using a Cayman SPC/charitable trust structure or an *ippan shadan houjin* (which often hold common shares in TMK and GK-TK schemes). Bankruptcy risks are kept low by J-REITs having no employees, all operations outsourced, permissible investments restricted, and all J-REIT business matters broadly supervised by the J-REIT's directors, its general meeting of unitholders, and the J-REIT's external accounting auditor.

II. Governance of J-REITs

There are five separate offices or supervisory bodies relevant to the internal governance of J-REITs: the **General Meeting of Unitholders** ("General Meeting"), the **Executive Director**(s), the **Supervisory Directors**, the **Meeting of Directors**, and the **External Accounting Auditor**. Although J-REITs are special purpose entities with a limited scope of permissible business activities (basically obtaining funding and buying, selling, and leasing real estate assets through qualified third parties), they are required to hold official meetings of directors and have an external accounting auditor in all cases, unlike TMK or GK-TK schemes. The external accounting auditor is appointed by the General Meeting and is commonly a well-known accounting firm.

Under the J-REIT Law and as determined under the J-REIT's **Bylaws** (*kiyaku*), unitholders are generally provided with many of the same rights and protections enjoyed by shareholders in KKs. For example, unitholders have the statutory right to cause a derivative lawsuit against the J-REIT's directors, to propose an agenda item for the General Meeting, to inspect certain business records, to vote on the appointment or dismissal of the directors and the external accounting auditor (although there are exceptions in the event the auditor breaches its duties), and, if a certain unit ownership threshold is met, to request the convocation of a General Meeting. The Bylaws indicate matters such as the J-REIT's dividend policy, fiscal year, maximum number of authorized investment units, standards for determining the AM Company's fees, and policies regarding the asset portfolio, etc. Unitholders may vote at the General Meeting in direct proportion to the number of units they own, and each investment unit gives rise to an equal right to receive dividends. Also, like shareholders in listed KKs, each unitholder must be given at least two weeks advance notice prior to a General Meeting, and there are detailed rules regulating what must be provided in the convocation notice.

In accordance with Art. 93-2, Paragraph 1 of the J-REIT Law, important resolution matters such as the approval of an investment unit split, amendment of the Bylaws, dissolution of the J-REIT, or a merger of the J-REIT with another J-REIT necessitate a majority of unitholders present at the General Meeting, and at least a two-thirds affirmative vote. An exemption of liability for the J-REIT's directors (provided they commit no grossly negligent acts or intentional misconduct) is a special General Meeting matter and requires the consent of all unitholders (although such a provision in the Bylaws is not uncommon). It should also be noted that the General Meeting is given the right to vote on the execution (except upon establishment of the J-REIT) and termination of the discretionary asset management agreement with the AM Company, provided, however, in the event of a material breach, the meeting of directors may resolve to terminate by itself. The AM Company, however, may not terminate the asset management agreement without the consent of the General Meeting.

There are nonetheless important differences between KKs and J-REITs. For example, a General Meeting is usually not held during each fiscal year since the meeting of directors, not the General Meeting, is given the authority to approve the J-REIT's financial statements under the J-REIT Law. J-REITs are only obliged to hold a General Meeting once every two years (it must be held at least once every two years because executive directors have a maximum two-year term, and under the J-REIT Law, they must be appointed by the General Meeting). However, it is most common for J-REITs to implement a six-month fiscal year and issue dividends twice a year (currently all listed J-REITs have a six-month fiscal period except for one). Also in contrast to the shares of listed KKs, the investment units of J-REITs are presently not subject to the insider trading rules of the **Financial Instruments and Exchange Law** ("FIEL").

With respect to equity, J-REITs may not issue any class of investment units other than common equity, and a J-REIT may not restrict the transfer of its investment units for any reason (Art. 78, Paragraph 2, J-REIT Law). It should be noted, however, that there are plans for allowing J-REITs to carry out investment unit buybacks starting in 2013, and the issuance of subscription rights, preferred investment units and convertible bonds is also being discussed. Currently, J-REITs generally raise capital by receiving loans, issuing bonds, making a public offering of investment units, or making a private placement of investment units through a third-party allotment. Pursuant to 2007 amendments to the J-REIT Law, J-REITs may also issue short-term bonds, but they must have a term of less than one year and may not be used for refinancing. No in-kind contributions are allowed (Art. 71, Paragraph 9, J-REIT Law), and only close-ended J-REITs may issue J-REIT bonds (Art. 139-2, J-REIT Law).

A significant difference between J-REITs and most other Japanese legal entities concerns the so-called **Deemed Approval** (*minashi sansei*) provision. In the

Bylaws, it is possible to insert a provision allowing for the votes of all unitholders not present at a General Meeting (or represented by proxy) to be counted as present for quorum purposes and to be included in the number of affirmative votes for all resolutions (the deemed approval) under Art. 93 of the J-REIT Law. However, in the event there are several different resolutions with conflicting contents, the deemed approval provision may not apply to these resolutions. The deemed approval provision allows investors who so choose to remain passive owners and not affect decisions or quorum requirements at a General Meeting (sometimes the Bylaws include language to reduce quorum requirements as well). Please note that this deemed approval provision is distinctive and while very common for J-REITs, it is not common for most other legal entities in Japan (although a similar provision is available for preferred equity holders in TMKs).

A J-REIT must have at least one executive director and at least two supervisory directors (the number of supervisory directors must always exceed the number of executive directors), and the maximum term for executive director(s) is two years, and for supervisory directors four years (both can be shortened). Executive directors are given the power to represent the company in dealings with third parties and perform other tasks for the J-REIT. However, many important matters (such as the payment of asset management fees) require a prior approval by the meeting of directors under Art. 109, Paragraph 2 of the J-REIT Law (the meeting of directors is comprised of all executive and supervisory directors). In addition, the J-REIT Law mandates that the meeting of directors, not the executive director(s), must approve an amendment to the discretionary asset management agreement with the AM Company. Supervisory directors have no right to represent the J-REIT in dealings with third parties, and they primarily monitor and act as a check on the executive director(s) through their majority at the meeting of directors. They also have the right to dismiss the executive director(s) in certain situations.

As a consequence of the detailed legal framework of J-REITs, J-REIT directors are required to supervise the entity in a more hands-on fashion than the directors of other Japanese special purpose entities. In fact, the function of a J-REIT's supervisory directors can be compared in some respects to the corporate auditors in a well-functioning KK. The executive director must report on the operations of the J-REIT to the meeting of directors at least once every three months, and supervisory directors have the right to demand the executive director(s) and any J-REIT service providers (including the AM Company) to report on their services or the status of the J-REIT's assets at any time. (Please note that the external accounting auditor also has this right, and is obliged to report any violations of law or the Bylaws to the supervisory directors). In sum, the meeting of directors, the external accounting auditor, and (indirectly) the General Meeting are all intended to supervise the management and operation of the J-REIT.

Supervisory directors are usually professional accountants, tax advisors or attorneys, and sometimes the executive director of the J-REIT is also a representative director of the AM Company. Compared to the rules for executive directors, the rules regarding the appointment of supervisory directors more strictly require their independence from the Sponsor Company and the AM Company. For instance, a J-REIT's supervisory directors may not receive any financial benefit from the AM Company or be employees of the Sponsor Company.

III. Regulation and Set Up of J-REITs

There are a variety of overlapping laws and rules which apply to listed J-REITs and/or their companion AM Companies, including the J-REIT Law, the FIEL, the Real Estate Transactions Law ("RETL"), the TSE rules, the Investment Trust Association ("ITA") regulations, the Financial Service Agency's ("FSA") Comprehensive Supervisory Guidelines for Financial Service Companies *et al*, the FSA's Inspection Manual for Financial Companies," and the Securities and Exchange Surveillance Commission's ("SESC") Inspection Manual for Financial Service Companies *et al.* In addition, prior to beginning business, a J-REIT must be registered with the Office of the Prime Minister. Due to the highly regulated nature of the J-REIT business, getting a listed J-REIT and AM Company up and running is a very complicated affair and can easily take well over a year to complete.

Since the AM Company is given wide discretion over the buying, selling, and leasing of the J-REIT's asset portfolio, the licensing process for setting up an AM Company is particularly strict. As a first step, the AM Company must be legally established and organized as a KK (only KK's may receive an FIEL investment management business (*toushi un'yougyou*) license). Then it must apply for an RETL license, although interestingly the J-REIT entity itself does not need an RETL license since the AM Company carries out transactions on the J-REIT's behalf (in accordance with the Bylaws and the Operational Guidelines). The AM Company must also obtain an FIEL investment management business (*toushi un'yougyou*) license from the FSA and a certification to act as a comprehensive deal agent *(torihiki ichinin dairi)* for the J-REIT from the **Ministry of Land, Infrastructure, Transport, and Tourism** ("MLIT"). Accordingly, the AM Company falls under the direct jurisdiction of both the FSA and the MLIT.

Proper scheduling is essential to setting up a J-REIT with its companion AM Company. For example, the AM Company needs an RETL license and an FIEL discretionary manager's license, however it must already have an RETL license in order to apply for the FIEL license. A J-REIT must also comply with the ITA's regulations and become a member of the ITA prior to being listed on the TSE. In addition, since a J-REIT must only have JPY100 million in paid-in capital to be established under the J-REIT Law, but the TSE listing rules require at least JPY five billion in gross assets, JPY one billion in net assets, and net assets per unit of at least JPY50,000, between the time of establishment and listing on the TSE it is essential to adjust the J-REIT's total capital and asset base (for instance, through a combination of public offering, private placement, bridge financing, and acquisition of new portfolio assets).

To illustrate the complexity of the process, the basic tasks for setting up a listed J-REIT and an AM Company include, without limitation, drafting the relevant Bylaws and internal rules, locating and hiring personnel, legally establishing both entities and filing the J-REIT's Bylaws with the Office of the Prime Minister, drafting the discretionary asset management agreement and Operational Guidelines, applying for and receiving the AM Company's RETL license and certification to act as a comprehensive deal agent *(torihiki ichinin dairi)* from the MLIT, acquiring the AM Company's investment management business (*toushi un'yougyou*) license from the FSA, applying to register the J-REIT with the Office of the Prime Minister prior to commencing business, completing the process of joining the ITA, undergoing the underwriting company's inspection and the TSE listing process (talking with potential investors, preparing the securities registration notification and prospectus for the initial public offering, etc.), securing liquidity facilities for the J-REIT as needed, performing a due diligence on target properties and obtaining bridge financing, etc.

It should also be noted that there are various licensing requirements regarding the number and experience level of the AM Company's employees. In addition, J-REITs and AM Companies need to be structured with an internal organization and rule framework compatible with the FSA's Comprehensive Supervisory Guidelines for Financial Service Companies *et al*, the SESC's Inspection Manual for Financial Service Companies *et al*, and other applicable rules and administrative regulations issued by the MLIT, FSA, etc. Consequently, prior to beginning the J-REIT structuring process, the arranger should consult with both the MLIT and the FSA.

IV. Scope of Business

As of August 2012, there are 35 J-REITs listed on the TSE, with six focusing on investments in offices, two focusing on retail assets, seven residential J-REITs, two industrial J-REITs, one hotel J-REIT, and 17 J-REITs with diversified asset portfolios. J-REITs are defined under Art. 2, Paragraph 12 of the J-REIT Law as entities organized primarily for the operation of 'select' assets (*tokutei shisan*, 'primarily' is interpreted to mean more than 50% of the assets should be 'select' assets). Art. 3 of the Enforcement Ordinance of the J-REIT Law defines 'select' assets as (1) negotiable securities (including TBIs), (2) derivative rights, (3) real estate, (4) leasehold interests, (5) superficies, (6) promissory notes, (7) monetary claims, (8) TK investments, (9) futures instruments, and (10) other investment rights.

The TSE listing rules require that at least than 70% of a listed J-REIT's assets be 'real estate assets', defined as real estate (land, buildings and other structures), leasehold interests, superficies, easements, accounts for construction in progress, and TBIs based on such assets. Additionally, the TSE rules require that at least 95% of a listed J-REIT's assets consist of the above assets plus TK interests, preferred equity in TMKs, investment units in other J-REITs, deposits, unrealized business income, and pre-paid expenses. There is also a TSE rule that at least 50% of a J-REIT's assets are expected to create a stable revenue stream and are intended to be held at least one year. The ITA rules and certain tax rules also mandate that J-REITs mainly focus on holding and operating real estate assets.

Foreign real estate was restricted from the above 'real estate assets' definition until the TSE rules and ITA regulations were amended in 2008, although currently no J-REITs hold foreign assets. Nevertheless, there are plans to amend the J-REIT Law in 2013 to allow J-REITs to acquire a majority shareholding in foreign companies which primarily hold real estate (to accommodate the foreign custom of real estate investments being held in special purpose companies to limit liabilities from affecting other investments). One reason J-REITs have not bought foreign real estate to date is the inherent difficulty in holding foreign assets far away from their AM Company. In addition, managing foreign assets can be difficult for Japanese AM Companies since they usually have little familiarity with foreign legal systems and the monitoring of foreign property management companies.

To further limit the scope of permissible activities, in addition to the requirement that J-REITs primarily invest in real estate assets, in most cases J-REITs may not carry out complicated development projects or large-scale renovations of properties, or make major investments in such projects or properties for renovation. Art. 193 of the J-REIT Law defines 'permissible transactions in select assets' as (1) the acquisition and transfer of negotiable securities, (2) the borrowing and lending of negotiable securities, (3) the acquisition and transfer of real estate, (4) the leasing of real estate, (5) the delegation of management of real estate, and (6) any other transactions *in accordance with the relevant cabinet ordinance.* The relevant cabinet ordinance (Art. 116, Enforcement Ordinance of the J-REIT Law and Art. 220-2, Enforcement Regulation of the J-REIT Law) authorizes all transactions concerning 'select assets' *except for* (1) "the construction of buildings and development of land by J-REITs," and (2) "transactions generally concerning the manufacture, production, etc. by J-REITs of commercial goods." Please note that this ordinance is interpreted to mean that J-REITs may enter into contracts for third parties to construct buildings (including the renovation and remodeling of existing properties), or to develop land on behalf of the J-REIT, and in fact, J-REITs sometimes enter into agreements to purchase buildings upon completion of construction, provided the buildings are pre-leased.

The contents of the above cabinet ordinance are additionally restricted by the FSA's Comprehensive Supervisory Guidelines for Financial Services Companies *et al.* These guidelines generally indicate the following transactions as *inappropriate* for J-REITs (and their delegates): (1) "large-scale renovations and remodelings which require tenants to vacate the premises for a period of time, and the resulting fluctuation in cash flow has an excessive effect on the J-REIT's portfolio as a whole," and (2) "the development of land purchased by the J-REIT for constructing a new building, where in consideration of the development risks (development risk, licensing risk, construction risk, tenanting risk, market price fluctuation risk, interest rate risk, major disaster risk, etc.) to be borne by the unitholders, and the lack of immediate cash flow from the development, there is an excessive effect on the J-REIT's portfolio as a whole." Accordingly, there are significant legal obstacles for J-REITs wishing to carry out large development projects or renovations of large assets, or to acquire such projects or older assets for renovation.

In addition to the above legal restrictions on the scope of a J-REIT's business, there are also tax and operational issues to consider. To qualify for pay-through taxation under applicable tax laws, J-REITs must issue over 90% of their qualifying distributable profit as dividends each fiscal year (similar to the 90% rule for TMKs), which means they may not build up significant retained earnings to use as a cushion for riskier business ventures. Further, because they have to distribute over 90% of their qualifying distributable profit every fiscal year, generally they must be very careful with the degree of leverage they use in their business, since they cannot maintain a large cash buffer to limit potential financing risks. (To wit, most listed J-REITs have an internal rule requiring the loan-to-value ratio of their portfolio not exceed 60% at any time.) Consequently, J-REITs tend to acquire properties which generate a stable income stream rather than chasing short-term profits through quick turnover of their asset portfolios.

V. Delegation of J-REIT Business

J-REITs must delegate all matters concerning the operation of their assets to their AM Company (Art. 198, J-REIT Law), all matters concerning the custody (or maintenance) of their assets to a qualified custodian (Art. 208, J-REIT Law), and all other necessary administrative matters concerning their business to qualified administrative service companies (Art. 117, J-REIT Law). In practice, J-REITs typically enter into contracts with parties such as (1) the AM Company, (2) the Sponsor Company, (3) an asset custodian (usually a licensed trust bank), (4) various administrative service companies (for internal accounting and tax preparation, share handling and transfer agent services, solicitation of unitholders and/or bondholders, operation of the General Meeting, maintenance of the register of unitholders, etc.), (5) J-REIT bondholders and a bond trustee (a bond trustee is required only if a J-REIT issues bonds), (6) the external accounting auditor, (7) lenders, (8) property managers, (9) tenants, and (10) property brokers, etc. It is important to note, however, that AM Companies carry out all important decisions regarding the J-REIT's portfolio, including the decision to invest or divest in a certain property, the selection of service providers with respect to leasing, etc. of properties in the portfolio, and compliance with applicable laws and ordinances.

AM Companies provide asset management services to their J-REIT, but in special cases may also provide services such as administrative services for the General Meeting and services ancillary to the leasing of assets. They also supply general market information and advice to the J-REIT regarding investing, disposition activities, etc. AM Companies may legally subdelegate a portion, but not all, of the matters delegated from the J-REIT to a sub-asset management company, depending on the matter and the licensed status of such sub-asset management company (Art. 202, J-REIT Law).

Although J-REITs must delegate the operation of their portfolio to an AM Company, J-REIT directors still have to establish basic parameters for the J-REIT's business. Among the most important matters decided by the meeting of directors at the J-REIT's inception is the Operational Guidelines for the J-REIT, which oftentimes consist of an asset management policy, sales policy, financing policy, valuation policy and separate J-REIT management policy. (A valuation policy is necessary since J-REITs are legally required to obtain a written valuation from a licensed appraiser prior to buying or selling any portfolio asset.)

The Operational Guidelines become an addendum to the Bylaws, and one of their most important functions is to specify criteria for the makeup of the portfolio (such as age, asset type, holding period, location, price range, etc. of eligible assets). Additionally, J-REIT directors typically determine in advance matters such as due diligence guidelines, an acceptable fee schedule for the AM Company's services, and minimum leasing guidelines (indicating acceptable rent levels, etc.) in accordance with the Bylaws. Through creating the above guidelines and policies, J-REIT directors are better able to monitor and evaluate the performance of the AM Company and thereby meet their fiduciary duties to the J-REIT's unitholders.

Interestingly under the J-REIT Law, a single AM Company is not expressly prohibited from operating more than one J-REIT's asset portfolio. However, unless the delegated portfolios differ materially with respect to asset type (*e.g.*, office buildings and logistics facilities), it can be hard for the AM Company to manage both portfolios while avoiding conflict of interest violations. Nevertheless, there are efficiencies and economies of scale in one AM Company administering multiple portfolios. Provided the AM Company satisfies its duty of loyalty and duty to act as a good manager to each J-REIT under the FIEL (*i.e.*, to always act in the best interests of its clients in the pursuit of profits for each J-REIT's unitholders), the unitholders may be able to benefit from this arrangement.

VI. Conflict of Interest Transactions

A 'conflict of interest' transaction can be broadly classified as any transaction between a J-REIT and an **Interested Party**, which generally refers to the AM Company, the Sponsor Company, any affiliate of the AM Company or Sponsor Company, any director of the J-REIT, AM Company or Sponsor Company, or any major unitholder in the J-REIT. These transactions are subject to particular scrutiny because they involve the risk that the interested party will use its special knowledge or influence to cause the J-REIT to enter into a transaction with irregularly adverse terms, *i.e.*, a non-arm's length agreement. However, sometimes entering into a transaction with an interested party can work to the J-REIT's benefit (for example, a J-REIT entering into a property management agreement with a subsidiary of the Sponsor Company, where the property management fee is reasonable and the subsidiary provides superior property management services). Because of this, there is no blanket prohibition on all types of conflict of interest transactions for J-REITs.

Traditionally, corporate legal rules concerning conflicts of interest have centered on directors self-dealing with company assets. However, a conflict of interest transaction does not necessarily involve the transfer of an asset, but may also arise between a J-REIT and an interested party with respect to property management fees, building management fees, repair or renovation fees, transaction agent fees, etc. A conflict of interest issue may even arise if an employee of the AM Company divulges J-REIT tenant or transaction information to the Sponsor Company or its affiliates.

For J-REITs, the most frequent conflicts of interest arise with the AM Company or among the AM Company, J-REIT, and Sponsor Company. One reason for this is that although employees of the Sponsor Company may not be directors of the J-REIT, they may be directors or employees of the AM Company (most executive directors of AM Companies are in fact seconded from the Sponsor Company). Further, sometimes the executive director of the J-REIT is appointed to be the representative director of the AM Company (ostensibly for efficiency reasons). In this situation, the executive director must be careful to not represent the interests of the AM Company shareholders over the interests of the J-REIT unitholders.

Perhaps the most basic conflict of interest exists simply due to the dual structure of J-REITs: management of the AM Company has a duty to pursue profits for its own shareholders (predominantly the listed Sponsor Company), while also being legally and contractually obliged to seek profits for the unitholders of the (usually listed) J-REIT. However, it should be noted that generally the Sponsor Company always has a substantial holding in both the AM Company and the J-REIT, which can mitigate risks from conflicts of interest to a certain extent. Further, some say this dual ownership allows the Sponsor Company to be better able to assist the AM Company in finding acquisition targets, and is a strength of the J-REIT model. However, one of the easiest ways to reduce conflict of interest risks is for the J-REIT to only acquire properties from outside of the Sponsor Company's group. In any event, the reputation and credit standing of the Sponsor Company is a significant point for some investors when deciding to buy a certain J-REIT's investment units.

Since the Sponsor Company typically enters into a sponsor support agreement with the J-REIT to assist in sourcing target properties, and usually the Sponsor Company or its affiliates supply most of the investment opportunities for the J-REIT's portfolio, transactions with interested parties are both unavoidable and critical to the success of J-REITs. Indeed, without the Sponsor Company's network, it would likely be very difficult for the J-REIT or AM Company to locate appropriate investment opportunities. Nevertheless, a J-REIT's unitholders have no direct legal right to sue the directors of the AM Company or Sponsor Company for damages due to negligence, breach of trust, etc., although they may cause a derivative suit against the J-REIT's directors for breach of their fiduciary duties.

There are certain express legal rules which attempt to weed out especially risky conflict of interest transactions. For example under the FIEL, the AM Company may not enter into any contracts involving the J-REIT's portfolio with terms which materially differ from standard transactions (and potentially harm the J-REIT's interests), and more generally, the J-REIT may not enter into any 'unnecessary' contracts with the AM Company, the Sponsor Company, or generally any subsidiary or related company of the AM Company or Sponsor Company for their profit or benefit. Further under the J-REIT Law, transactions (including property management agreements and leases) between the J-REIT and its directors, the AM Company or the AM Company's directors are *per se* prohibited unless certain narrow exceptions found in the relevant cabinet ordinance apply (Art. 195, J-REIT Law). Finally, all transactions between asset portfolios or funds operated by an AM Company are in principle prohibited under the FIEL (Art.42-2, FIEL), unless all concerned investors consent and/or other specific conditions are satisfied under Art. 129 of the FIEL Cabinet Ordinance (*e.g.*, one of the funds is being wound up, the FSA approves the transaction in advance, etc.).

In cases other than the *per se* prohibited transactions outlined above, it is generally permissible for an AM Company to enter into a conflict of interest transaction with respect to the J-REIT's asset portfolio, provided there is no breach of any of the AM Company's legal duties. (Under the FIEL, the directors of the AM Company owe a duty of loyalty and a duty to act as good managers with respect to the J-REIT and its asset portfolio, and any transactions in breach of these duties are prohibited.) Upon execution of a transaction with an interested party concerning a portfolio asset, the AM Company must also promptly provide written notice of details to the J-REIT under Art. 203, Paragraph 2 of the J-REIT Law.

To further protect investors, the J-REIT Law mandates the AM Company submit to the J-REIT a record of all transactions entered into by the AM Company involving any assets similar to the portfolio assets at least once every three months (Art. 203, Paragraph 1, J-REIT Law). Also, prior to the purchase or sale of any asset in the J-REIT's portfolio, the AM Company must obtain at least one written appraisal from an independent and licensed real estate appraiser ('independent' meaning any party other than a party with a potential interest in the transaction), and disclose the appraisal value and transaction price information to the J-REIT (Art. 201, J-REIT Law). In practice however, this protection may not always be effective due to the potential for the independent appraiser to be influenced by third parties.

To complement the above J-REIT Law and FIEL transactional rules, there are also a multitude of operational and organizational rules designed to protect unitholders from improper transactions. For instance, corporate organizational structures and internal compliance rules for J-REITs and AM Companies should reflect the contents of the FSA's Comprehensive Supervisory Guidelines for Financial Service Companies *et al,* the FSA's Inspection Manual for Financial Companies, and the SESC's Inspection Manual for Financial Service Companies *et al.* There are in addition other applicable rules and administrative regulations issued by the MLIT, FSA, ITA, TSE, etc.

The above rules and guidelines contain recommendations regarding acceptable internal risk structures (for example, instituting multiple layers of decision-making or specific unitholder approvals in certain situations) and appropriate valuation and property due diligence procedures (*e.g.*, requiring adequate engineering and environmental reports in advance of a purchase, etc.). AM Companies should also draft in advance internal rules addressing how conflict of interest issues will be handled as a matter of corporate policy. This is so that when conflicts arise (as they frequently do), rules which ensure a fair resolution are already in place, *e.g.*, rules requiring a special committee of outside professionals to approve conflict of interest transactions prior to execution, rules requiring an acquisition (or sale) to be allowed only at a price significantly below (or above) an independent appraiser's valuation, or rules requiring a transparent bidding process for all services to be provided to the J-REIT.

VII. Disclosure of Information

The main disclosure rules applicable to J-REITs and their AM Companies are found in the J-REIT Law and the FIEL, although the TSE's rules and the disclosure guidelines issued by the ITA also apply to TSE-listed J-REITs. Compliance with these disclosure rules is intended to ensure that both individual investors and the general market have sufficient and accurate information to make informed decisions about a J-REIT's (1) financial performance and (2) internal corporate governance structure. Accordingly, the disclosure rules not only require the distribution of information to unitholders and the general public, but also the filing of various government notifications.

At the end of each fiscal period (usually every six months), J-REITs must have their financial statements audited by the J-REIT's external accounting auditor which also prepares a written audit report. Upon approval of the audit report and the J-REIT's financial statements (the balance sheet, income statement, statement of distributions, and supplementary attachments) at a meeting of directors, the documents are sent without delay to each unitholder (along with an updated asset management report), and a 'flash' financial statement (*kessan tanshin*) is issued through the TSE for the general public (as required of every TSE-listed company). The financial statements and audit report must be stored by the J-REIT for at least five years after approval by the meeting of directors. A J-REIT business report must in addition be notified to the office of the Prime Minister (generally an office of the Ministry of Finance) within three months of the end of each fiscal year in a form set forth in the Enforcement Regulations to the J-REIT Law.

As a general rule, the **FIEL Disclosure Obligations** apply to J-REITs (and their delegates) from the time of offering the issuance of investment units with a total value of at least JPY100 million. Prior to soliciting such investment, the J-REIT must prepare and submit to the Ministry of Finance a securities registration notification (which is made public through the TSE and becomes effective for subscription purposes after a period of examination), and a prospectus (which is sent to individual investors and made available at the securities firm underwriting the offering). Once investment units are issued in the public markets, a J-REIT has the continuing obligation under the FIEL to disclose a securities report within three months of the end of each fiscal year. In addition, an extraordinary report must be issued during the fiscal year in the event of a change in major matters such as the J-REIT's Operational Guidelines or policy on the issuance of dividends.

Since January 2007 there has been a requirement for purchasers of investment units to notify the public of a change in major shareholding through the TSE's "Electronic Disclosure for Investors Network" or "**EDINET**." In general, a **Notice of Change in Major Shareholding** must be posted within five days of any new acquisition of investment units where the unitholder thereby acquires more than a 5% total stake in all outstanding investment units. Thereafter, a Notice of Change in Major Shareholding is required on EDINET in the event such unitholder has a change in held units of 1% or more of all outstanding investment units.

The TSE disclosure rules applicable to J-REITs are very important in that they provide a way for investors to gain up-to-date knowledge of matters which may materially affect their investment decisions. The **Timely Disclosure** (***tekiji kaiji***) **Rules** of the TSE require the prompt written notification to the TSE (and release to the public on the TSE's website called **TDnet**) when (1) material business decisions or actions are taken by a J-REIT or AM Company (*e.g.*, a sale of additional units, announcement of financial results, sale or purchase of an asset worth at least JPY50 million, extension of a loan, etc.) or (2) the J-REIT or AM Company becomes aware that certain material occurrences have taken place (*e.g.*, in the event profit and loss will differ from the forecasted figures by at least 30% or dividends will differ from forecast by at least 5%, a loss or damage to the portfolio valued at 3% or more of the J-REIT's total net assets due to disaster, etc.). There is also an English language service called the **J-REIT Flash Report** available on the Bloomberg Professional website and Reuters Real Estate website where significant TSE releases are published in English, usually the same day as the Japanese release.

To supplement the above timely disclosure rules, the TSE rules require a written report on internal operations of the J-REIT and AM Company, which is published within three months of the end of each fiscal year. The main purpose of this report is to indicate transactional, capital and personnel connections among the J-REIT, the AM Company, and the Sponsor Company, including the relevant internal compliance structures and policies regarding conflict of interest transactions and actual transaction details over the period. Also as mentioned in the preceding Section VI, the AM Company must send to the J-REIT a quarterly notice regarding the AM Company's own asset transactions, a notice of any dealings with interested parties involving the portfolio assets at the time of the transaction, and a notice indicating the appraisal price, etc. at the time of any transaction involving the portfolio assets.

VIII. J-REIT Tax Treatment

Similar to TMKs, J-REITs may deduct distributions to their unitholders from operating income (*i.e.*, **Pay-Through Taxation**) prior to being subject to Japanese corporate income tax, provided certain conditions are met by the J-REIT at both the entity level and during the relevant fiscal year. J-REITs may also benefit from reduced **Real Estate Acquisition Taxes** (*fudousan shutokuzei*) and reduced **Registration and License Taxes** (*touroku menkyozei*) if certain conditions are satisfied. Listed J-REITs generally issue close to 100% of their distributable profit every year and thus customarily pay very little corporate income tax.

In order to qualify for pay-through taxation for dividends, a J-REIT must satisfy the following 11 conditions: (1) issue over 90% of its distributable profit for the relevant fiscal year (*restriction on retained earnings*), (2) indicate in its Bylaws that more than 50% of its total investment units are to be offered domestically (*restriction on majority foreign offering*), (3) have a fiscal year not exceeding one calendar year, (4) not have more than 50% of its investment units held by one investor as of the end of the fiscal period (*restriction on being a subsidiary*), (5) not hold 50% or more of the outstanding shares or equity in any other legal entity (*restriction on holding a subsidiary*), (6) receive any loans only from financial institutions designated as qualified institutional investors under the Special Tax Measures Law (*restriction on eligible lenders*), (7) delegate the operation of the J-REIT's assets to a qualified AM Company (*restriction on J-REIT operations*), (8) delegate the custody of the J-REIT's assets to a trust company or other competent licensed entity (*restriction on J-REIT operations*), (9) cause no breach of Art. 63 of the J-REIT Law (*restriction on J-REIT business activities, no branch offices, etc.*), (10) maintain registration at the Office of the Prime Minister and (11) either place investment units worth at least JPY100 million in a public offering at the time of establishment of the J-REIT, <u>or</u> have at least 50 investors or only qualified institutional investors (under the Special Tax Measures Law) owning investment units.

IX. The Balancing Act of New Acquisitions

To qualify for pay-through tax status, J-REITs are restricted from having significant retained earnings, and this restriction constitutes an important operational and business issue for J-REITs. Complicating this issue is the fact that J-REITs need to grow and acquire new properties over time to diversify portfolio, geographic and tenant risks. Since retained earnings are limited and J-REITs cannot store up 'dry powder,' as a general rule they must either dispose of existing assets, issue additional investment units, and/or arrange for more debt to have the wherewithal to carry out new acquisitions for growth.

Obtaining a loan is oftentimes the most expedient alternative for obtaining new investment capital, because an issuance of additional investment units can take over two months to complete (from solicitation to subscription). Nevertheless, J-REITs must adhere to the maximum loan-to-value ratio set forth in their Bylaws, and a high debt-to-equity ratio can hurt their creditworthiness. An increase in debt can also lead to an increase in financing risks for the portfolio as a whole, and the TSE listing rules require J-REITs maintain a net asset value of at least JPY50,000 per unit. Accordingly, in most cases J-REITs need to issue at least some level of additional investment units to complete new major acquisitions.

Since **Dividend Per Unit** ("DPU") is an important criterion for valuing investment units, and existing unitholders dislike an issuance of new equity without a corresponding increase in the J-REIT's income (*i.e.*, the dilution of their investment units), J-REITs usually strive to acquire new properties with a capitalization rate (net operating income over purchase price) that is at least as high, on average, as the other properties in their portfolio. Properties with significant depreciation charges are also not desirable since they can negatively affect DPUs. In addition, J-REITs frequently obtain financing and try to make new acquisitions at the beginning of their fiscal year. This is to enable the investment of capital as early in the fiscal year as possible, and thereby lessen any negative impact on earnings per unit over the term.

Many J-REIT market participants believe it is necessary for individual J-REITs to reach a market capitalization level of more than JPY100 billion to achieve optimal scale. This size is considered desirable in order (1) to facilitate large investments and sufficient liquidity in the J-REIT's investment units for large institutional investors, (2) to achieve economies of scale in the operation of their portfolio, (3) to be able to access debt markets most efficiently, and (4) to mitigate the impact on DPU levels in the event of issuing additional investment units to fund new acquisitions. (Please note that as of the end of July 2012, there were twelve J-REITs with a market capitalization of over JPY100 billion.)

X. The Potential for J-UPREITs

In November 2010, the MLIT proposed at its real estate investment strategy meeting various amendments to the legal and tax rules concerning J-REITs. One of these proposals concerned amending the rules to enable a Japanese UPREIT-like investment structure modeled on the United States' UPREIT rules. An **UPREIT** (which stands for "umbrella partnership real estate investment trust") is a type of partnership which allows taxes to be deferred when transferring an asset to a REIT in consideration for equity in the REIT. In the US, it is believed that introduction of the UPREIT system in the early 1990s led to a breakthrough in REITs' market capitalization levels, and significant growth in the US real estate market as a whole.

Although currently there is no consensus in the Japanese government on introducing a 'J-UPREIT' structure (in part due to the fear that it will lead to a short-term drop in tax revenues), and there are many existing legal and logistical hurdles to creating J-UPREIT rules, there are still some who believe that such a sea change could give a positive jolt to the Japanese real estate market. However, others doubt that a new J-UPREIT system would succeed in spurring growth without special economic incentives for the big Japanese real estate companies, since they hold a disproportionate amount of all valuable real estate assets in Japan. Proponents nonetheless assert that a new J-UPREIT structure could contribute to significant growth in transactions between Japanese private funds and publicly-listed J-REITs, thereby benefitting the entire Japanese real estate market.

XI. A Brief Comparison of J-REITs, TMKs, GK-TKs and RESL Structures

As explained at the outset of this Chapter, J-REITs are the only securitization structure designed for listing on a public exchange, so in many respects they are more regulated and less flexible than TMKs or GK-TKs. Although a TMK or a GK may not be listed on the TSE, it is possible to set up and list a KK to function as an investor in a TMK or GK. However, for shareholders in the KK this structure would not be as tax efficient as simply investing in a J-REIT, since the KK would be subject to Japanese corporate tax prior to issuing dividends. It is possible to set up and operate an unlisted (open-ended) J-REIT, but even as a private vehicle, the administrative costs and compliance requirements are generally more burdensome than for traditional private funds. Another disadvantage of J-REITs and RESL investment schemes (currently) is that they cannot be structured with bankruptcy remoteness like a GK-TK or a TMK.

Open-ended J-REITs must be set up to handle the need to provide direct liquidity to their investors (by, for example, facilitating sales among private J-REIT unitholders), and all J-REIT unitholders must be prepared to accept potential conflicts of interest with the AM Company. Nevertheless, J-REITs and TMKs can invest directly in real estate or TBIs for real estate, which is an advantage over the GK-TK fund model. (Please note however, there are plans for amending the current legal rules to allow certain GK-TKs to invest in and hold real estate directly (in fee simple), provided they delegate certain services to an RESL-licensed operator.)

Although a real estate syndication allows for the collective investment of capital into a real estate asset (but not a TBI), the investor interests in an RESL business are not as liquid as listed J-REIT investment units or preferred equity in a TMK. The TK interests in a GK-TK are also not as liquid as listed J-REIT investment units or TMK preferred equity, since the TK operator (the GK) must approve any transfer of TK interests. It should also be noted that generally TK investors have much less control over their investments than J-REIT unitholders, and J-REIT unitholders in turn have less control than investors in a TMK. However, since GK-TKs are created primarily through contract, in many respects they are the most flexible form, and both J-REITs and GK-TKs are designed to acquire and dispose of assets on an ongoing basis (although TMKs may now generally acquire additional TBI assets as long as all interested parties agree). TMK schemes were originally intended to be used by property holders securitizing assets in a one-time transaction, and for this reason they still require a level of documentation and administrative work that exceeds that of GK-TKs. In addition, all of the above collective investment schemes can benefit from both reduced real estate acquisition taxes and reduced registration taxes, except for RESL investment schemes.

Securitization Scheme Comparison

J-REIT

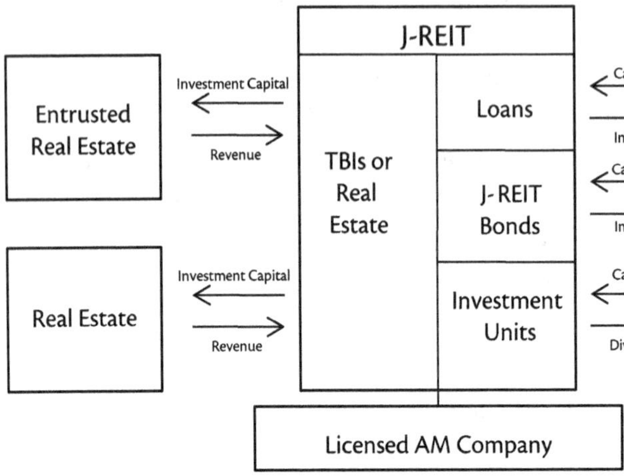

*Large-scale renovations requiring tenants vacate the property, and which create a material disruption of cash flow in the portfolio, are not allowed under the FSA's Comprehensive Supervisory Guidelines for Financial Service Companies *et al*

GK-TK

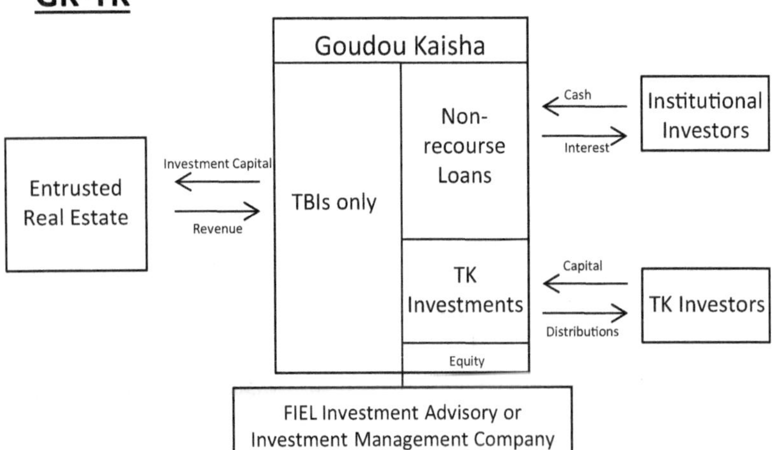

*Properties must pass trust bank inspection (only TBIs may be held), and certain regional assets may not be accepted for entrustment

TMK

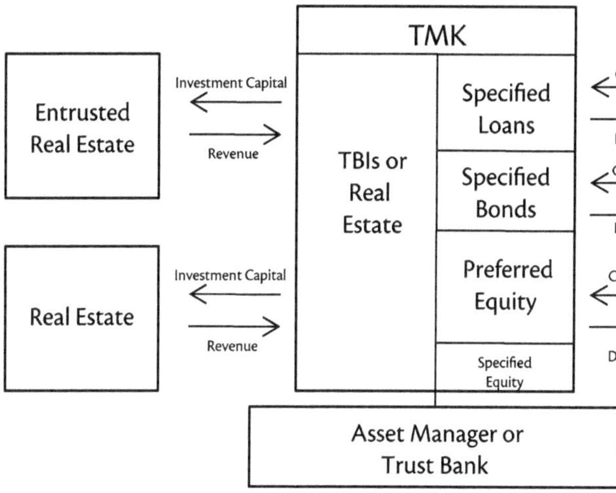

*Changing important matters in the Asset Liquidation Plan requires the unanimous consent of all interested parties in advance

RESL

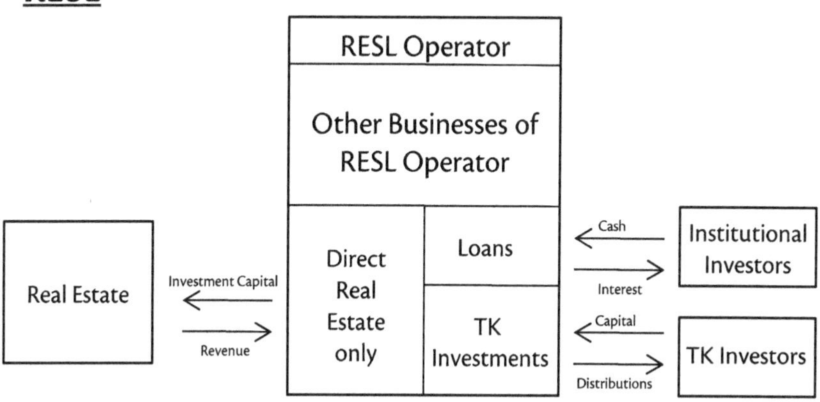

*Need at least JPY100 million paid-in capital and must employ qualified personnel to set up an RESL-licensed entity

Convenience Translation of the Japanese Real Estate Syndication Law

Real Estate Syndication Law
June 29th, 1994
Law No. 77

Final Revisions of Law
June 14th, 2006
Law No. 65

CHAPTER 1 GENERAL PROVISIONS

Article 1 (Purpose)

The purpose of this law is to implement a licensing system for operators of real estate syndication enterprises, to clarify the obligations etc. in the execution of their businesses, and to introduce necessary measures for preventing potential damages to investors, thereby ensuring the proper operation of their businesses, safeguarding the financial interests of investors, and contributing to the sound development of real estate syndication enterprises.

Article 2 (Definitions)

2.1 "Real Estate" means under this law land and/or buildings as defined in Article 2, Item 1 of the Real Estate Transactions Law (1952, Law No. 176).

2.2 "Real Estate Transaction" means under this law the buying, selling, exchanging, and/or leasing of Real Estate.

2.3 "Real Estate Syndication Contract" means under this law any of the contracts below (including promises to agree), excluding any contracts (including promises to agree) designated by cabinet ordinance where, in regard to matters such as the execution process, the parties' relationship, etc., the person(s) receiving revenue and/or profit distributions under the contract (including promises to agree) is deemed to be sufficiently protected.

(1) Contracts containing a promise for each contract party to make an investment for a joint enterprise to be carried out, in which one or more contract parties are to be delegated the authority to conduct business and carry out Real Estate Transaction(s) for the joint enterprise, and revenue from the Real Estate Transaction(s) is to be distributed;

(2) Contracts containing a promise for a contract party to make an investment for the other contract party to conduct Real Estate Transaction(s) with the invested asset(s), and profit from the Real Estate Transaction(s) is to be distributed;

(3) Contracts containing a promise from a contract party or parties with common ownership interest(s) in Real Estate to lease or delegate the right to lease out such Real Estate to another contract party or parties, where the other party or parties conduct Real Estate Transaction(s) based on such Real Estate, and revenue from the Real Estate Transaction(s) is to be distributed;

(4) Contracts based on the laws and ordinances of a foreign country corresponding to any of (1), (2), or (3) above; and

(5) In addition to (1) through (4) above, contracts where there is a promise to distribute revenue or profit from Real Estate Transaction(s) (including contracts based on the laws and ordinances of foreign countries), and such contracts are designated by cabinet ordinance as necessary to secure the impartiality of the

enterprise conducting the Real Estate Transaction(s) and the protection of those to receive revenue or profit from such Real Estate Transaction(s).

2.4 "Real Estate Syndication Enterprise" means under this law any of the following carried out as a business.

(1) The execution of Real Estate Syndication Contracts and distribution of revenue or profit from Real Estate Transactions in accordance with such Real Estate Syndication Contracts (in the case of a Real Estate Syndication Contract under Article 2, Paragraph 3, Item 1, a Real Estate Syndication Contract under Article 2, Paragraph 3, Item 4 which is substantially similar to the contracts indicated in Article 2, Paragraph 3, Item 1, or a contract deemed to be of a similar type pursuant to cabinet ordinance, limited to the juridical person or juridical persons receiving delegation of the right to conduct operations or other similar juridical person); or

(2) The acting as an agent or intermediary in the execution of Real Estate Syndication Contracts.

2.5 "Real Estate Syndication Enterprise Operator" means under this law a juridical person operating a Real Estate Syndication Enterprise after receiving the license indicated in Article 3, Paragraph 1 below.

2.6 "Enterprise Participant" means under this law a party to a Real Estate Syndication Contract not designated thereunder to operate the Real Estate Syndication Enterprise.

CHAPTER 2 LICENSING

Article 3 (License for Real Estate Syndication Enterprises)

3.1 Juridical persons intending to set up and operate an office (main office, branch or other location as designated by cabinet ordinance, hereinafter "Office") for a Real Estate Syndication Enterprise in two or more prefectures are required to receive a license from the competent Cabinet Minister, and juridical persons intending to set up and operate an Office for a Real Estate Syndication Enterprise in one prefecture are required to receive a license from the Governor of the prefecture with jurisdiction over such Office.

3.2 Juridical persons intending to receive a license from the competent Cabinet Minister in accordance with the above Article 3, Paragraph 1 shall pay the registration and license tax at the location indicated in the Registration and License Tax Law (1967, Law No. 35).

Article 4 (Conditions to Licensing)

4.1 The competent Cabinet Minister or Governor may add to or change any conditions to the license in Article 3, Paragraph 1 above.

4.2 Any conditions to licensing instituted under Article 4, Paragraph 1 above shall be limited to the least extent necessary to ensure proper operation of Real Estate Syndication Enterprises, and no unreasonable obligations may be imposed on the juridical person receiving the license.

Article 5 (Application for License)

5.1 Juridical persons applying to receive the license referred to in Article 3, Paragraph 1 hereof shall submit a license application to the competent Cabinet Minister in the event the juridical person intends to set up and operate Offices for a Real Estate Syndication Enterprise in two or more prefectures, and shall submit a license application to the Governor of the prefecture with jurisdiction in the event the juridical person intends to set up and operate an Office for a Real Estate Syndication Enterprise in one prefecture, such license application containing the following matters:

(1) The corporate or business name and address;

(2) The name of directors of the juridical person and any designated employees as indicated by cabinet ordinance;

(3) The name and location of each Office and the name of the employee designated to be engaged in the Office in accordance with Article 17, Paragraph 1 hereof;

(4) The amount of paid-in capital or equity amount;

(5) The matters regarding a Real Estate Transactions Law license indicated in Article 3, Paragraph 1 of such law;

(6) The type of operations (as indicated in Article 2, Paragraph 4 hereof, hereinafter "Type of Operations");

(7) In the event the juridical person engages in other businesses, the types of these businesses; and

(8) Any other matters set forth in an applicable ministerial ordinance.

5.2 The following documents shall be attached to the license application referred to above (in the case of applying to carry out activities only under Article 2, Paragraph 4, Item 2, excluding the document specified in 4 below).

(1) The articles of incorporation or other similar document;

(2) A certificate of registered matters or other similar document;

(3) A document evidencing compliance with the requirements of Article 17, Paragraph 1 regarding each Office;

(4) The Real Estate Syndication Contract Standard Terms and Conditions; and

(5) Other documents containing any matters indicated in an applicable ministerial ordinance.

Article 6 (Reasons for Ineligibility)

Juridical persons which fall under any of the below may not receive a license under Article 3, Paragraph 1 hereof.

(1) Juridical persons which are not juridical persons (including foreign juridical persons without an Office in Japan);

(2) Juridical persons which do not hold the license required under Article 3, Paragraph 1 of the Real Estate Transactions Law;

(3) Juridical persons in which the license referred to in Article 3, Paragraph 1 hereof has been invalidated pursuant to Article 36 hereof, and five years have not elapsed from the relevant invalidation date, or in the event

a juridical has a comparable license (including similar registration and/or administrative dispositions, which also applies to (6) below) based on similar laws of a foreign jurisdiction invalidated, and five years have not elapsed from the relevant invalidation date;

(4) Juridical persons which, with respect to invalidation of the license under Article 3, Paragraph 1 hereof pursuant to a violation of any of the matters in Article 36 hereof, have received a notice pursuant to Article 15 of the Administrative Procedures Law (1993, Law No. 88), and during the period from the date of receipt of such notice until the date a decision whether to penalize has been reached, such juridical person has submitted a notification pursuant to Article 11, Paragraph 1, Item 4 hereof, from which date of submission five years have not elapsed;

(5) Juridical persons subject to a fine pursuant to the Real Estate Transactions Law, the Law concerning Regulation of Receipt of Investment Equity, Deposits and Interest, etc. (1954, Law No. 195), or pursuant to any comparable law of any foreign jurisdiction (including other similar foreign law penalty), and from the time the fine or similar penalty was imposed, or from the time it is possible such fine or similar penalty could be imposed, five years have not elapsed;

(6) Directors (including without limitation employees with executive powers, directors of the board of directors, executive officers and the like, advisors, or other persons regardless of title deemed to have the same or greater corporate authorities than employees with executive powers, directors of the board of directors, executive officers and the like) (such definition of director also applies to Article 7, Item 3 hereof, Article 35, Paragraph 1, Item 6 hereof and (a) through (f) below) or certain employees as designated by cabinet ordinance which fall under any of the following.

   (a) Minors or elderly persons who have legal guardians under law or persons treated similarly under the laws of a foreign jurisdiction;

   (b) Persons who have declared bankruptcy and are still legally subject to bankruptcy or persons of similar situation under the laws of a foreign jurisdiction;

(c) Persons subject to penalty (including comparable penalties under any foreign law) due to a felonious (*kinko*) act where five years have not yet elapsed from the date the penalty was imposed or could be imposed;

(d) Persons violating any of the laws indicated in Item (5) hereof, violating any provisions of the Law concerning the Prevention of Improper Acts, etc. committed by Gang Members (1991, Law No. 77) (except for Article 31, Paragraph 7 thereof), violating a law comparable to the above laws under a foreign jurisdiction, violating the Criminal Law (1965, Law No. 45) Article 204, 206, 208, 208-3, 222 or 247, or violating the Law concerning Penalties for Violent Acts, etc.(1926, Law No. 60), with violation of any of the above laws resulting in the imposition of a fine (or comparable penalty under similar foreign law), and where five years have not yet elapsed from the date the fine was imposed or could be imposed;

(e) Persons who, in the event a Real Estate Syndication Enterprise Operator has the license specified in Article 3, Paragraph 1 hereof invalidated pursuant to the provisions of Article 36 hereof, has served as a director of such Real Estate Syndication Enterprise Operator within the sixty day period preceding such Operator receiving the notice concerning the invalidation process under the provisions of Article 15 of the Administrative Procedures Law, and five years have not yet elapsed from the date of such invalidation;

(f) Persons who have a similar license under a foreign jurisdiction invalidated pursuant to the provisions of comparable foreign laws where five years have not yet elapsed from the date of such invalidation (including persons who served as a director or in a comparable position for a juridical person during the sixty-day period preceding the date of invalidation of such juridical person's license, and five years have not yet elapsed from such date of invalidation).

Article 7 (Minimum Conditions for Licensing)

In the event a juridical person submitting a license application under Article 5 hereof is not deemed to meet all of the following minimum conditions (in the event a juridical engages only in the activities specified in Article 2, Paragraph 4, Item 2, the minimum condition in Item 5 below is excluded), the competent Cabinet Minister or Prefectural Governor may not grant the license specified in Article 3, Paragraph 1 hereof.

(1) The amount of capital and/or contributions for the juridical person is an appropriate and necessary amount to protect the Enterprise Participant for the Type of Operations as designated by cabinet ordinance;

(2) After subtracting the total amount of liabilities from the total amount of assets of the juridical person, the remainder is at least 90% of the total amount of capital or contributions for the juridical person;

(3) The juridical person, its director(s), and/or any employees designated by cabinet ordinance have not committed a fraudulent or conspicuously improper act with respect to a Real Estate Syndication Enterprise within the five years preceding the date of the relevant license application;

(4) Each Office satisfies the requirements indicated in Article 17, Paragraph 1;

(5) The contents of the juridical person's Real Estate Syndication Contract Standard Terms and Conditions are in accordance with the requirements designated by cabinet ordinance;

(6) The juridical person has sufficient financial resources and personnel to carry out the Real Estate Syndication Enterprise in an appropriate fashion.

Article 8 (Change in License)

8.1 In the event a Real Estate Syndication Enterprise Operator receives a license under Article 3, Paragraph 1 hereof and subsequently falls under any one of the following while still engaging in operating a Real Estate Syndication Enterprise, notwithstanding the provisions of Article 5 hereof, such Operator shall send a license application containing the information indicated in Article 5, Paragraph 1, Item 3, in the case of the matters in Item 1 or Item 2 below, to the Prefectural Governor with jurisdiction over the remaining Office or over the Office to be set up, or in the case of Item 3 below, to the competent Cabinet Minister at the location designated by competent ministerial ordinance.

(1) A juridical person with a license from the competent Cabinet Minister has come to have an Office or Offices in only one prefecture;

(2) A juridical person with a license from the competent Prefectural Governor has closed down all of its Office(s) in such prefecture and has set up an Office or Offices in one other prefecture only;

(3) A juridical person with a license from a competent Prefectural Governor has come to have Offices in two or more prefectures.

8.2 Upon submission of a license application in accordance with the preceding Article 8, Paragraph 1, and provided that the juridical person submitting the license application is deemed to satisfy the conditions indicated in Article 7, Item 3 and Article 7, Item 4 herein by the competent Cabinet Minister or Prefectural Governor, notwithstanding the contents of Article 7 hereof, the competent Cabinet Minister or Prefectural Governor shall grant the license indicated in Article 3, Paragraph 1 hereof.

8.3 In the event a Real Estate Syndication Enterprise Operator receives a license under Article 3, Paragraph 1 in accordance with the preceding Article 8, Paragraph 2, the existing license of the Real Estate Syndication Enterprise Operator from the Cabinet Minister or Prefectural Governor with prior competence shall lose its validity.

Article 9 (Authorization of Change)

9.1 A Real Estate Syndication Enterprise Operator shall be required to receive authorization from the Cabinet Minister or Prefectural Governor with competence over the license it received under Article 3, Paragraph 1 hereof in accordance with the competent ministerial ordinance in case such Operator intends to change the Type of Operations or to amend or supplement the Real Estate Syndication Contract Standard Terms and Conditions under Article 5, Paragraph 2, Item 4 hereof (excluding any minor amendments or supplements designated by competent ministerial ordinance, which also applies to Article 46, Paragraph 4 and Article 53, Item 2 hereof).

9.2 A Real Estate Syndication Enterprise Operator shall comply with the preceding Article 9, Paragraph 1 in the event it intends to add or set up a new Office (unless the conditions indicated in Article 8, Paragraph 1, Item 1 through Item 3 apply).

Article 10 (Notification of Change)

In the event there has been a change in any of the matters set forth in Article 5, Paragraph 1 (except Item 5 and Items 6 thereof), the Real Estate Syndication Enterprise Operator shall send a notification of change within 30 days of the change taking place in accordance with the competent ministerial ordinance to the Cabinet Minister or Prefectural Governor with competence over the license it received under Article 3, Paragraph 1 hereof (in the case of a change in the location of an Office set forth in Article 5, Paragraph 1, Item 3, this Article 10 will not apply to situations falling under any of the matters in Article 8, Paragraph 1, Item 1 through Item 3 and Article 9, Paragraph 2).

Article 11 (Notification for Discontinuing Business, etc.)

11.1 Within 30 days of a Real Estate Syndication Enterprise Operator falling under any of the following, the person designated below shall send a notification of such circumstance in accordance with the competent ministerial ordinance to the Cabinet Minister or Prefectural Governor with competence over the license it received under Article 3, Paragraph 1 hereof.

(1) In the event the juridical person ceases to exist pursuant to merger, a director who was a representative of the company which ceased to exist;

(2) In the event the juridical person is dissolved pursuant to the institution of bankruptcy procedures, the trustee of the juridical person during bankruptcy;

(3) In the event the juridical person is dissolved for a reason other than merger or institution of bankruptcy procedures, the liquidator of the juridical person;

(4) In the event the juridical person has ceased its Real Estate Syndication Enterprise (for foreign juridical persons this includes no longer having an Office in Japan), a director representing the juridical person which operated the Real Estate Syndication Enterprise.

11.2 At the time a Real Estate Syndication Enterprise Operator becomes subject to any of the situations specified in Article 11, Paragraph 1 above, the license of such Operator shall lose its validity.

Article 12 (Register of Real Estate Syndication Enterprise Operators)

The competent Cabinet Minister and each Prefectural Governor shall prepare a register of Real Estate Syndication Enterprise Operators (hereinafter "Register of Real Estate Syndication Enterprise Operators"); in the case of the competent Cabinet Minister, such register shall contain all of the matters set forth in Article 5, Paragraph 1, Item 1 through Item 7 and any other matters required under the competent ministerial ordinance regarding each Real Estate Syndication Enterprise Operator to which it grants a license; in the case of the Prefectural Governor, such register shall contain all of the matters set forth in Article 5, Paragraph 1, Item 1 through Item 7 and any other matters required under the competent ministerial ordinance regarding each Real Estate Syndication Enterprise Operator to which it grants a license and any Real Estate Syndication Enterprise Operators with main Office in such prefecture and granted a license by the competent Cabinet Minister.

Article 13 (Inspection of Register of Real Estate Syndication Enterprise Operators etc.)

The competent Cabinet Minister or Prefectural Governor shall offer for inspection by the general public at the location indicated in the competent ministerial ordinance each of the documents indicated in Article 5, Paragraph 2, Item 1 through Item 5 hereof, the Register of Real Estate Syndication

Enterprise Operators, and any other documents set forth in the competent ministerial ordinance.

CHAPTER 3 OPERATIONS

Article 14 (Principles for Execution of Operations)

14.1 Real Estate Syndication Enterprise Operators shall carry out their business with integrity and in good faith.

14.2 Real Estate Syndication Enterprise Operators shall, with respect to their businesses, endeavor to ensure the appropriate and reasonable use of Real Estate as well as make efforts to deter speculative dealings.

Article 15 (Prohibition against Name Lending)

Real Estate Syndication Enterprise Operators shall not permit any other juridical person to carry out a Real Estate Syndication Enterprise under their name.

Article 16 (Display of Placard)

16.1 Real Estate Syndication Enterprise Operators shall place a form of the placard set forth in the competent ministerial ordinance in an easy-to-view location on public display in every Office.

16.2 Persons other than Real Estate Syndication Enterprise Operators shall not place the placard indicated in Article 16, Paragraph 1 above nor any similar placard on public display.

Article 17 (Operation Manager)

17.1 Real Estate Syndication Enterprise Operators shall place in each Office a person registered under Article 18 of the Real Estate Transactions Law and who fulfills all other requirements under applicable ministerial ordinance to carry out the operations specified in Article 24, Paragraph 2, Article 25, Paragraph 2, and Article 28, Paragraph 3 hereof as well as to provide advice, guidance and supervision for performance of the following activities taking place in such Office.

(1) Solicitation of execution of Real Estate Syndication Contracts;

(2) Explanation of contents of Real Estate Syndication Contracts;

(3) Activities pursuant to the provisions of Article 28, Paragraph 1 hereof.

17.2 Real Estate Syndication Enterprise Operators shall, at each of their Offices and in accordance with the competent ministerial ordinance, prepare and maintain a register (hereinafter "Register of Operation Managers") of the person placed at each Office in accordance with provisions of the preceding Article 17, Paragraph 1 (hereinafter "Operation Manager"), including each person's name and any other matters designated by competent ministerial ordinance, and in the event an Enterprise Participant (including persons or juridical persons contemplating the execution of a Real Estate Transaction Contract) so requests, such Operator shall provide the Register of Operation Managers for inspection.

17.3 Real Estate Syndication Enterprise Operators shall not set up an Office in violation of Article 17, Paragraph 1 above, and in the event an Office comes to be in violation of Article 17, Paragraph 1, such Operator shall take necessary corrective measures to comply with Article 17, Paragraph 1 within two weeks of the date such Office first came to violate Article 17, Paragraph 1.

Article 18 (Regulation of Advertising)

18.1 Real Estate Syndication Enterprise Operators shall not advertise a Real Estate Syndication Enterprise with land still being developed or buildings under construction and not yet completed prior to disposition of the license necessary for such construction or development pursuant to Article 29, Paragraph 1 and Article 29, Paragraph 2 of the City Planning Law (1968, Law No. 100), prior to disposition of the written confirmation necessary for such construction or development pursuant to Article 6, Paragraph 1 of the Building Standards Law (1950, Law No. 201), and prior to disposition of any other license, etc. necessary under any laws or ordinances in accordance with relevant cabinet ordinance.

18.2 In the event a Real Estate Syndication Enterprise Operator intends to advertise matters regarding a Real Estate Syndication Enterprise, such Real Estate Syndication Enterprise Operator shall clearly indicate in such advertisement whether such Operator would be acting as an agent, intermediary or in its own capacity in the execution of Real Estate Syndication Contracts, and shall also clearly indicate the type of Real Estate Syndication Contract as classified in accordance with Article 2, Paragraph 3, Item 1 through Item 5 hereof.

18.3 In an advertisement about the operations of a Real Estate Syndication Enterprise, Real Estate Syndication Enterprise Operators shall not, with respect to the prospect for a return of profits and other matters set forth in the competent ministerial ordinance, make any representations which significantly deviate from fact nor make any representations which are likely to cause significant misunderstanding.

Article 19 (Limitation on Commencement of Business)

Real Estate Syndication Enterprise Operators shall not commence a Real Estate Syndication Enterprise with land still being developed or buildings under construction and not yet completed prior to disposition of the license necessary for such construction or development pursuant to Article 29, Paragraph 1 and Article 29, Paragraph 2 of the City Planning Law, prior to disposition of the written confirmation necessary for such construction or development pursuant to Article 6, Paragraph 1 of the Building Standards Law, and prior to disposition of any other license, etc. necessary under any laws or ordinances in accordance with relevant cabinet ordinance.

Article 20 (Prohibition against Unfair Solicitation, etc.)

20.1 In soliciting the execution of a Real Estate Syndication Contract, Real Estate Syndication Enterprise Operators shall not, with respect to significant matters contained in the Real Estate Syndication Contract which may influence the other party's judgment, intentionally withhold facts or relay false information.

20.2 In order to prevent the termination (including withdrawal from an association (*kumiai*), below the same) of a Real Estate Syndication

Contract, Real Estate Syndication Enterprise Operators shall not relay false information with respect to significant matters contained in such Contract which may influence an Enterprise Participant's judgment.

Article 21 (*Same*)

21.1 Real Estate Syndication Enterprise Operators, their agents, employees designated by cabinet ordinance and any other employees (in this Article 21, hereinafter "Real Estate Syndication Enterprise Operators, etc.") shall not, in soliciting the execution of a Real Estate Syndication Contract, affirmatively declare or do any act vis-à-vis any potential party which may be construed as an affirmative declaration that profit is certain to arise from such Contract.

21.2 Real Estate Syndication Enterprise Operators, etc. shall not continue soliciting a certain party to execute a certain Real Estate Syndication Contract after that party has indicated it will not execute such contract (which includes an indication to the Real Estate Syndication Enterprise Operators, etc. to cease with such solicitation).

21.3 Real Estate Syndication Enterprise Operators, etc. shall not do any act to intimidate or frustrate an Enterprise Participant's termination of a Real Estate Syndication Enterprise Contract.

21.4 In addition to the acts specified in Article 21, Paragraph 3 above, Real Estate Syndication Enterprise Operators, etc. shall not commit any act designated by competent ministerial ordinance as deficient in protecting the interests of Enterprise Participants or potential contract parties with respect to the solicitation of execution of a Real Estate Syndication Enterprise Contract or with respect to preventing the termination of a Real Estate Syndication Enterprise Contract.

Article 21-2 (*Mutatis Mutandis* Application of Financial Instruments and Exchange Law)

The provisions of Article 39 (except for Paragraph 5 and the proviso in Paragraph 3) and Article 40 of the Financial Instruments and Exchange Law (1948, Law No. 25, hereinafter "FIEL") apply *mutatis mutandis* to the execution of Real Estate Syndication Contracts by Real Estate Syndication Enterprise

Operators, including their agents or intermediaries. Therefore, "Financial Instruments Transaction Broker, etc." in FIEL Article 39, Paragraph 1, Article 39, Paragraph 2, each Item, Article 39, Paragraph 3 thereof and in all of FIEL Article 40 is replaced with "Real Estate Syndication Enterprise Operators", and the following sections are replaced with "execution of Real Estate Syndication Contracts": in FIEL Article 39, Paragraph 1, Item 1 "Sale and purchase transactions etc. in securities (except for transactions where buy back is mandatory and the buyback price is set forth in advance and other transactions exempted by cabinet ordinance) and derivative transactions" (hereinafter "Sale and Purchase Transactions in Securities, etc."), in FIEL Article 39, Paragraph 1, Item 2 and Article 39, Paragraph 1, Item 3, and in Article 39, Paragraph 2 "Sale and Purchase Transactions in Securities, etc.", and in FIEL Article 40, Paragraph 1 "Act in dealing in securities." "Securities and/or derivative transactions" (hereinafter "Securities, etc.") in FIEL Article 39, Paragraph 1, Item 1 and "Securities, etc." in FIEL Article 39, Paragraph 2 and Article 39, Paragraph 3, and in FIEL Article 40, Item 1 "Securities Transaction Contracts" is replaced with "Real Estate Syndication Enterprise Contracts." "Customer" in FIEL Article 39, Paragraph 1 and Article 39, Paragraph 3, FIEL Article 40, Paragraph 2, "Customer of Securities Transactions Broker etc." in Article 39, Paragraph 2, and "Investor" in FIEL Article 40, Item 2 are replaced with "Enterprise Participant." "Transaction in securities or derivatives" in FIEL Article 39, Paragraph 1, Item 1 is replaced with "execution of Real Estate Syndication Enterprise Contract." "cabinet ordinance" in FIEL Article 39, Paragraph 3 and FIEL Article 40, Item 2 is replaced with "competent ministerial ordinance", "hereinafter in this clause and the next clause" in FIEL Article 39, Paragraph 3 is replaced with "in the next Paragraph", and "Customer" and/or "Investor" in FIEL Article 40, Item 1 is replaced with "other party or Enterprise Participant."

Article 22 (Prohibition against Providing Monetary or other Loans, or the Mediation, etc. thereof)

In the course of soliciting the execution of a Real Estate Syndication Contract, Real Estate Syndication Enterprise Operators shall not, regarding a Real Estate Syndication Enterprise, provide any loans in cash or in the form of negotiable securities to any potential party, including acting for any third party as the agent, mediator or intermediary for loans in cash or negotiable securities for any potential party.

Article 23 (Execution of Agreements based on Real Estate Syndication Contract Standard Terms and Conditions)

Real Estate Syndication Enterprise Operators shall execute Real Estate Syndication Contracts based on the Real Estate Syndication Contract Standard Terms and Conditions used for their license under Article 3, Paragraph 1 hereunder and any changes thereto authorized under Article 9, Paragraph 1 hereof.

Article 24 (Delivery of Document prior to Execution of Agreement)

24.1 Prior to a Real Estate Syndication Contract coming into effect, Real Estate Syndication Enterprise Operators shall send and explain to the other potential party or parties a document containing matters regarding the contents of such Real Estate Syndication Contract and performance of such Contract as set forth in the competent ministerial ordinance.

24.2 Upon completion of drafting the document referred to in Article 24, Paragraph 1 above, Real Estate Syndication Enterprise Operators shall cause their relevant Operation Manager to sign and stamp such document.

Article 25 (Delivery of Document after Execution of Agreement)

25.1 Upon a Real Estate Syndication Contract coming into effect, Real Estate Syndication Enterprise Operators shall send without delay a document containing the following matters to the other party or parties to such Real Estate Syndication Contract.

(1) The type of Real Estate Syndication Contract classified in accordance with Article 2, Paragraph 3, Item 1 through Item 5 hereof;

(2) Information necessary to specify the Real Estate which is the object of the Real Estate Transaction under the Real Estate Syndication Contract and the details of such Real Estate Transaction;

(3) A description of the distribution of revenue and/or profit to Enterprise Participants;

(4) A description of the management of assets under such Real Estate Syndication Contract;

(5) The effective term of such Real Estate Syndication Contract;

(6) A description of liquidation procedures upon expiration of such Real Estate Syndication Contract;

(7) Provisions regarding the termination of such Real Estate Syndication Contract, if any; and

(8) Other matters set forth in the competent ministerial ordinance.

25.2 Upon completion of the drafting of the document referred to in Article 25, Paragraph 1 above, Real Estate Syndication Enterprise Operators shall cause their relevant Operation Manager to sign and stamp such document.

Article 26 (Termination in Writing)

26.1 Enterprise Participants may terminate in writing a signed Real Estate Syndication Contract after eight days have elapsed from the date of receiving the document referred to in Article 25, Paragraph 1 above.

26.2 Termination pursuant to Article 26, Paragraph 1 above is effective upon dispatch of the document indicating such termination.

26.3 In the event of termination of a Real Estate Syndication Contract by an Enterprise Participant in accordance with Article 26, Paragraph 1 above, Real Estate Syndication Enterprise Operators shall not demand payment of any penalty fees or any compensation for damages.

26.4 Any covenant in a Real Estate Syndication Contract in violation of Article 26, Paragraph 3 which is to the disadvantage of an Enterprise Participant is invalid.

Article 27 (Separate Management of Assets)

In accordance with the competent ministerial ordinance, Real Estate Syndication Enterprise Operators shall manage assets under a Real Estate Syndication Contract separately from their own assets and separately from all other assets received pursuant to any other Real Estate Syndication Contract.

Article 28 (Delivery of Report on Management of Assets)

28.1 Upon request by an Enterprise Participant, Real Estate Syndication Enterprise Operators shall provide an explanation regarding the management of assets under the applicable Real Estate Syndication Contract.

28.2 Real Estate Syndication Enterprise Operators shall send a written report to Enterprise Participants regularly and in accordance with the competent ministerial ordinance regarding the status of the management of assets under a Real Estate Syndication Contract.

28.3 Upon completion of the drafting of the report referred to in Article 28, Paragraph 2 above, Real Estate Syndication Enterprise Operators shall cause their relevant Operation Manager to sign and stamp such report.

Article 29 (Inspection of Documents)

Real Estate Syndication Enterprise Operators (herein and in Article 30 below limited only to actual parties to Real Estate Syndication Contracts) shall, in accordance with the competent ministerial ordinance, prepare and maintain in each Office documents regarding the status of the Real Estate Syndication Enterprise's operations and assets, and upon request from a relevant Enterprise Participant, shall allow inspection thereof.

Article 30 (Register of Enterprise Participants)

30.1 Upon execution of a Real Estate Syndication Contract, Real Estate Syndication Enterprise Operators shall, in accordance with the competent ministerial ordinance, prepare and maintain a register of names of Enterprise Participants (hereinafter "Register of Enterprise Participants") in Real Estate Syndication Contracts.

30.2 Upon request by an Enterprise Participant listed therein, Real Estate Syndication Enterprise Operators shall allow such Participant to inspect the Register of Enterprise Participants.

Article 31 (Duty of Confidentiality)

31.1 Absent justifiable cause to the contrary, Real Estate Syndication Enterprise Operators shall not disclose any secrets learned in the course of operating a Real Estate Syndication Enterprise, and shall not disclose any such secrets after operations of such Real Estate Syndication Enterprise have ceased.

31.2 Absent justifiable cause to the contrary, all agents, employees designated by cabinet ordinance and all other employees of Real Estate Syndication Enterprise Operators shall not disclose any secrets learned in the course of facilitating the operations of a Real Estate Syndication Enterprise, and shall not disclose any such secrets after their employment or engagement as an agent has ceased.

CHAPTER 4 SUPERVISION

Article 32 (Books of Account for Operations)

Real Estate Syndication Enterprise Operators shall prepare and maintain books of account regarding their operations in accordance with the competent ministerial ordinance.

Article 33 (Submission of Report on Operations)

Real Estate Syndication Enterprise Operators shall prepare a report on the operations of a Real Estate Syndication Enterprise in the form prescribed by competent ministerial ordinance every fiscal year for such Enterprise and shall submit such report within 3 months of the end of such fiscal year to the Prefectural Governor or competent Cabinet Minister which granted such Operator its license pursuant to Article 3, Paragraph 1 hereof.

Article 34 (Instructions)

34.1 The competent Cabinet Minister or Prefectural Governor may, in the event a Real Estate Syndication Enterprise Operator receiving a license therefrom under Article 3, Paragraph 1 hereof falls under any of the below Items, or in the event such Operator violates any of the provisions of this law, give necessary instructions to such Operator.

(1) In the event an Enterprise Participant has suffered damages or there is a significant likelihood that such Participant may suffer damages in connection with a Real Estate Syndication Enterprise's operations;

(2) In the event a Real Estate Syndication Enterprise Operator has acted against the principle of fairness, or there is a significant likelihood that such Operator will so act in connection with the operations of a Real Estate Syndication Enterprise;

(3) In the event there is a violation of another law or ordinance in connection with operations which is considered to be inappropriate for Real Estate Syndication Enterprise Operators.

34.2 In the event a Real Estate Syndication Enterprise Operator falls under one of the situations indicated in Article 34, Paragraph 1, Item (1) through Item (3) above, or in the event such Operator violates any of the other provisions in this law, any Prefectural Governor may give necessary instructions to such Operator who is carrying out business in the Governor's prefecture, even if the Operator is licensed under Article 3, Paragraph 1 by the Governor of another prefecture or the competent Cabinet Minister.

34.3 Upon giving instructions under the preceding Article 34, Paragraph 2, in case the Real Estate Syndication Enterprise Operator subject to such instructions has received its license under Article 3, Paragraph 1 from the competent Cabinet Minister, the Prefectural Governor shall report this matter without delay to the competent Cabinet Minister, and in case such Operator subject to such instructions has received its license under Article 3, Paragraph 1 from the Governor of another prefecture, the Prefectural Governor shall notify this matter without delay to the Governor of such other prefecture.

Article 35 (Order for Cessation of Operations)

35.1 The competent Cabinet Minister or Prefectural Governor may, in the event a Real Estate Syndication Enterprise Operator receiving a license therefrom under Article 3, Paragraph 1 falls under any of the below Items, order the cessation of operations of such Operator, in whole or in part, for a period of less than one year.

(1) The situation described in Article 34, Paragraph 1, Item 3 above;

(2) A violation of the following provisions hereof: Article 8, Paragraph 1, Article 9, Article 10, Article 15, Article 16, Paragraph 1, Article 17, Article 18, Paragraph 2 and Article 18, Paragraph 3, Article 19 through Article 21, Article 22 through Article 25, Articles 27 through Article 30, Article 31, Paragraph 1, Article 32, the last part of Article 37, Paragraph 1 (including *mutatis mutandis* application in Article 37, Paragraph 3), and Article 21-2 as subject to Article 39, Paragraph 1 and Article 40 of the FIEL ("*Mutatis Mutandis* Financial Instruments and Exchange Law", hereinafter "MMFIEL");

(3) Not complying with instructions received under Article 34, Paragraph 1 or Article 34, Paragraph 2 hereof;

(4) Violation of any disposition under any provision of this law by a Prefectural Governor or the competent Cabinet Minister;

(5) Committing any act with regard to the operations of a Real Estate Syndication Enterprise which is fraudulent or conspicuously unfair;

(6) One of the directors of a Real Estate Syndication Enterprise or an employee designated by cabinet ordinance of such Operator has committed a fraudulent or conspicuously unfair act within the five years preceding such order of cessation of operations.

35.2 Any Prefectural Governor may, with respect to a Real Estate Syndication Enterprise Operator carrying out business in such prefecture pursuant to a license under Article 3, Paragraph 1 from another Prefectural Governor or the competent Cabinet Minister, order the cessation of operations of such Operator, in whole or in part, for a period of less than one year.

35.3 The provisions of Article 34, Paragraph 3 shall apply *mutatis mutandis* to the above Article 35, Paragraph 2.

Article 36 (Revocation of License)

36.1 The competent Cabinet Minister or Prefectural Governor may revoke the license it has granted to any Real Estate Syndication Enterprise Operator under Article 3, Paragraph 1 hereof when such Operator falls under any of the below.

(1) Such Operator has come to fall under Article 6, Item 2, Item 3 (only with respect to the parts of foreign laws or ordinances corresponding to this law), Item 5 or Item 6 hereof;

(2) Such Operator has come to violate the conditions indicated in Article 7, Item 1 or Item 2 hereof;

(3) Such Operator received the license under Article 3, Paragraph 1 hereof in a fraudulent manner;

(4) Such Operator has violated any conditions to licensing pursuant to Article 4, Paragraph 1 hereof;

(5) Such Operator has violated any of Item (1) through Item (6) in Article 35, Paragraph 1 above and the circumstances of such violation are particularly severe, or such Operator has violated an order to cease operations under Article 35, Paragraph 1 or Article 35, Paragraph 2.

Article 37 (Order for Dismissal of Operation Manager)

37.1 The competent Cabinet Minister or Prefectural Governor may order a Real Estate Syndication Enterprise Operator with license therefrom under Article 3, Paragraph 1 hereof to dismiss a Operation Manager in the event such Operation Manager has committed a fraudulent or conspicuously unfair act in the course of operating the Real Estate Syndication Enterprise of such Operator. In such case, such Operator may not reemploy the dismissed person as its Operation Manager for a period of time determined by competent Cabinet Minister or Prefectural Governor within one year from the date of such order to dismiss.

37.2 A Prefectural Governor may order a Real Estate Syndication Enterprise Operator with license under Article 3, Paragraph 1 hereof from another Prefectural Governor or the competent Cabinet Minister to dismiss an Operation Manager in the event such Manager has committed an act indicated in Article 37, Paragraph 2 above in such Governor's prefecture.

37.3 The provisions of Article 34, Paragraph 3 and the second sentence of Article 37, Paragraph 1 shall apply *mutatis mutandis* to the above Article 37, Paragraph 2.

Article 38 (Public Announcement of Punitive Measures)

The competent Cabinet Minister or Prefectural Governor shall make a public announcement in case of a disposition under Article 35, Paragraph 1, Article 35, Paragraph 2 or any provisions of Article 36 hereof in accordance with the competent ministerial ordinance.

Article 39 (Guidance, etc.)

In order to further the sound development of real estate syndication enterprises and ensure their appropriate administration, the competent Cabinet Minister may give necessary guidance, advice and/or special recommendations to all Real Estate Syndication Enterprise Operators, and any Prefectural Governor may give necessary guidance, advice and/or special recommendations to any Real Estate Syndication Enterprise Operators carrying out a Real Estate Syndication Enterprise in such Governor's prefecture.

Article 40 (On-Site Inspections, etc.)

40.1 The competent Cabinet Minister may, with respect to all juridical persons which operate a Real Estate Syndication Enterprise, and Prefectural Governors may, with respect to all juridical persons which operate a Real Estate Syndication Enterprise in such Governor's prefecture, when deemed necessary to enforce this law, order the submission of information or a report regarding the operations of such Real Estate Syndication Enterprise or related assets, cause Cabinet Minister's or Governor's employee(s) to enter an Office or other premises for operations of such Real Estate Syndication Enterprise in order to inspect such operations, related assets, books of account, and any other matters, and question any parties relevant to the operations of such Real Estate Syndication Enterprise.

40.2 In the event of an on-site inspection in accordance with Article 40, Paragraph 1 above, the employee(s) of the competent Cabinet Minister or Prefectural Governor shall carry documents for identification purposes and shall present these to any relevant party upon request.

40.3 The authority for the on-site inspection referred to in Article 40, Paragraph 1 above shall not be construed to be an authorization to carry out a criminal search (*hanzai sousa*).

CHAPTER 5 ASSOCIATION OF REAL ESTATE SYNDICATION ENTERPRISES

Article 41 (Association of Real Estate Syndication Enterprises)

41.1 In order to protect the interests of Enterprise Participants and contribute to the sound development of real estate syndication enterprises, Real Estate Syndication Enterprise Operators may establish a juridical person pursuant to the provisions of Article 34 of the Civil Code (1954, Law No. 89) which uses in its name the words "Association of Real Estate Syndication Enterprises" and has Real Estate Syndication Enterprise Operators as its members.

41.2 The juridical person pursuant to the above Article 41, Paragraph 1 (hereinafter in this Chapter, the "Association") may carry out the following activities to achieve its purposes:

(1) With respect to the operations of its member Real Estate Syndication Enterprise Operators, give guidance, special recommendations, etc. to its members regarding compliance with the provisions of this law, the Real Estate Transactions Law, the Law concerning Regulation of Receipt of Investment Equity, Deposits and Interest, etc., and any other laws or ordinances;

(2) With respect to the operations of its member Real Estate Syndication Enterprise Operators, give necessary guidance, special

recommendations, etc. to its members regarding the appropriateness of the contents of its Real Estate Syndication Contracts and any other matters to protect the financial interests of Enterprise Participants;

(3) With respect to the operations of its member Real Estate Syndication Enterprise Operators, resolve complaints from Enterprise Participants, etc.;

(4) Any investigations or research necessary to ensure the appropriate and reasonable use of Real Estate and/or deter speculative dealings;

(5) Any other activities necessary to achieve the Association's purposes.

41.3 The Association shall provide a register of its members for public inspection.

Article 42 (Limitation on Use of Name)

42.1 Juridical persons which are not Associations shall not use the words "Association of Real Estate Syndication Enterprises" in their name.

42.2 Juridical persons which are not members of an Association shall not use the words "Member of Association of Real Estate Syndication Enterprises" in their name.

Article 43 (Resolution of Complaints)

43.1 The Association shall, in the event of a request from an Enterprise Participant or other person to resolve a complaint regarding the operations of a Real Estate Syndication Enterprise Operator, respond and provide necessary advice to the person making such request, investigate the factual circumstances of such complaint, notify the contents of such complaint to the relevant Association member, and demand the swift resolution thereof.

43.2 In the event it is necessary to resolve the complaint pursuant to the request in Article 43, Paragraph 1 above, the Association may demand written or oral explanations and the submission of documents from its members.

43.3 In the event of a demand pursuant to Article 43, Paragraph 2 above, a member shall not refuse such demand in the absence of a justifiable reason.

43.4 The Association shall inform its members of any requests pursuant to Article 43, Paragraph 1 above, the factual circumstances underlying the relevant complaint and details of the resolution thereof.

CHAPTER 6 MISCELLANEOUS PROVISIONS

Article 44 (Termination of Operations pursuant to Revocation, etc. of License)

In the event the license under Article 3, Paragraph 1 hereof loses its validity pursuant to the provisions of Article 11, Paragraph 2, or in the event such license is revoked pursuant to the provisions of Article 36, the formerly-licensed Real Estate Syndication Enterprise Operator or its general successor shall still be authorized to act as a Real Estate Syndication Enterprise Operator to the extent necessary to finish performance of operations under any existing Real Estate Syndication Contracts.

Article 45 (Technical Interpretation, etc. of the Law for Application with respect to Foreign Juridical Persons)

In the event a Real Estate Syndication Enterprise Operator is a foreign juridical person, or in the event the Real Estate for a Real Estate Syndication Enterprise is located in a foreign country, the provisions of this law for application with respect to such Operator and/or such Enterprise, and any other matters necessary in relation to the application of this law, are to be interpreted technically in accordance with the relevant cabinet ordinance.

Article 46 (Special Measures for Trust Companies, etc.)

46.1 The provisions of Article 3 through Article 10 and Article 36 hereof do not apply to a trust company which has received a license under Article 3 or Article 53, Paragraph 1 of the Trust Business Law (2004, Law No. 154) (except as designated by cabinet ordinance) and has submitted the notification required under Article 77, Paragraph 3 of the Real Estate Transactions Law (hereinafter "Specified Trust Company").

46.2 A Specified Trust Company which operates a Real Estate Syndication Enterprise is to be regarded as a Real Estate Syndication Enterprise Operator with license under Article 3, Paragraph 1 hereof from the relevant Cabinet Minister, except as provided in Article 46, Paragraph 1, and is subject to the provisions of this law. In this event, in Article 23 hereof "license under Article 3, Paragraph 1 hereunder and any changes thereto authorized under Article 9, Paragraph 1" is replaced with "notification under Article 46, Paragraph 3 and Article 46, Paragraph 4" and in Article 38 hereof "disposition under Article 36" is replaced with "an order for cessation of operations under the provisions of Article 46, Paragraph 5."

46.3 A Specified Trust Company which intends to operate a Real Estate Syndication Enterprise shall send a notification of this intention to the location designated by relevant ministerial ordinance with a copy of the Real Estate Syndication Contract Standard Terms and Conditions attached thereto.

46.4 A Specified Trust Company regarded as a Real Estate Syndication Enterprise Operator in accordance with Article 46, Paragraph 2 above shall, in the event of a change in any of the matters listed in the Register of Real Estate Syndication Enterprises under Article 12 hereof (except for matters listed in Article 5, Paragraph 1, Item 5), or in the event of an addition or amendment to its Real Estate Syndication Contract Standard Terms and Conditions, send a notification within 30 days of such change, addition or amendment to the competent Cabinet Minister in accordance with the relevant ministerial ordinance.

46.5 In the event a Specified Trust Company regarded as a Real Estate Syndication Enterprise Operator in accordance with Article 46, Paragraph 2 above comes to fall under any of the situations specified in Article 35, Paragraph 1, Item 1 through Item 6, and the circumstances thereof are deemed particularly severe, or in the event such Company violates an order to cease operations under Article 35, Paragraph 1 or Article 35, Paragraph 2 hereof, the competent Cabinet Minister may order such Company to cease all or part of its relevant operations for a period less than five years.

46.6 Any matters necessary for the application of this law with respect to financial institutions which concurrently operate a trust business, or with respect to a trust company designated by cabinet ordinance pursuant to Article 46, Paragraph 1 above, shall be set forth by cabinet ordinance.

Article 46-2 (Exemptions)

In the event a Real Estate Syndication Enterprise Operator is designated to be a juridical person with specialized knowledge and experience for investing in Real Estate equivalent to a bank or trust company in accordance with the competent ministerial ordinance, or in the event an Enterprise Participant or other potential party to a Real Estate Syndication Enterprise is a joint stock company with an amount of capital equal to or greater than the amount designated by competent ministerial ordinance, application of the provisions of Article 19 through Article 21, Article 22, Article 24 through Article 26, Article 28, Paragraph 2, Article 28, Paragraph 3 hereof and application of the provisions of Article 40 of the MMFIEL to such Real Estate Syndication Enterprise shall be exempted.

Article 47 (*Same*)

47.1 The provisions of Article 22 hereof do not apply in the event the potential party to a transaction is a licensed real estate broker under Article 2, Item 3 of the Real Estate Transactions Law (also below in Article 47, Paragraph 2 "Licensed Real Estate Broker").

47.2 The provisions of Article 26 hereof do not apply in the event an Enterprise Participant is a Licensed Real Estate Broker.

47.3 The provisions of this law do not apply to the national government nor to any local government agencies.

Article 48 (Non-Application of Real Estate Transactions Law)

The provisions of the Real Estate Transactions Law do not apply to Enterprise Participants who carry out Real Estate Transactions based on the contract defined in Article 2, Paragraph 3, Item 1 hereof nor to other Enterprise Participants as designated by cabinet ordinance.

Article 48-2 (Course for Applications, etc.)

The application to be submitted to the competent Cabinet Minister pursuant to Article 5, Paragraph 1, Article 8, Paragraph 1, Article 9, Paragraph 1 and Article 9, Paragraph 2, Article 10 and Article 11, Paragraph 1 hereof and any other relevant documents shall be sent via the Prefectural Governor with jurisdiction over the location of the main Office (regarding the above Articles, the main Office of the juridical person falling under any of the relevant Paragraphs or Items).

Article 48-3 (Division of Official Work)

The work to be performed by the prefectural governments pursuant to Article 12, Article 13 and the above Article 48-2 (with respect to work to be performed under Article 12 and Article 13, only such work concerning the preparation, listing and inspection of the Register of Real Estate Syndication Enterprises by a licensed Real Estate Syndication Enterprise Operator) is to be considered the first category of Item 1, legally delegated work within the meaning of the provision of Article 2, Paragraph 9, Item 1 of the Local Government Law (1947, Law No. 67).

Article 49 (Competent Cabinet Minister, etc.)

49.1 The competent Cabinet Minister shall be as follows.

(1) With respect to matters regarding a Real Estate Syndication Enterprise utilizing the Real Estate Syndication Contracts indicated in Article 2, Paragraph 3, Item 1 and Article 2, Paragraph 3, Item 2 above, and/or matters regarding a Real Estate Syndication Enterprise utilizing Real Estate Syndication Contracts indicated in Article 2, Paragraph 3, Item 4 above which correspond to or resemble the Real Estate Syndication Contracts indicated in Article 2, Paragraph 3, Item 1 and Article 2, Paragraph 3, Item 2 above as designated by competent cabinet ordinance, and where there is an intention in such Contracts to receive investments in monetary form and, at the

time of expiration of such Contracts, the investments will be returned in monetary form through the division of remaining assets or return of invested money and/or such other similar matters as set forth by competent cabinet ordinance; in this case the Prime Minister and the Minister of Land, Infrastructure, Transport, and Tourism shall have competency.

(2) With respect to all matters regarding Real Estate Syndication Enterprises not subject to Article 49, Paragraph 1, Item 1 above, the Minister of Land, Infrastructure, Transport, and Tourism shall have competency.

49.2 The ministerial ordinances applicable to this law are cabinet ordinances and ministerial ordinances from the Ministry of Land, Infrastructure, Transport, and Tourism.

49.3 The Prime Minister delegates all authority under this law to the director of the Financial Services Agency (except for matters established by cabinet ordinance).

49.4 With respect to the authorities delegated to the director of the Financial Services Agency pursuant to Article 49, Paragraph 3 above, and with respect to the authorities conferred on the Minister of Land, Infrastructure, Transport, and Tourism pursuant to this law, such authorities may be delegated in part to the heads of local regional bureaus (concerning the authorities delegated to the director of the Financial Services Agency, to the head of a local financial affairs bureau or to the head of a branch thereof) in accordance with the competent cabinet ordinance.

Article 49-2 (Submission of Materials to Finance Minister, etc.)

The Finance Minister may, with respect to the management of financial crises and the system for disposal of insolvent financial institutions under such Minister's jurisdiction, require the submission of necessary documents and an explanation from the Prime Minister in the event the Finance Minister deems it necessary for the design or planning of the system for Real Estate Syndication Enterprises.

Article 50 (Delegation to Competent Ministerial Ordinance)

Matters necessary for implementation of this law not set forth herein are to be established by competent ministerial ordinance.

Article 51 (Interim Measures)

In the event an order is established based on the provisions of this law, or in the event an order is amended or abolished, such order may establish any requisite interim measures to the extent reasonably necessary (including interim measures regarding potential penalties) for such order to be executed, amended or abolished.

CHAPTER 7 PENAL PROVISIONS

Article 52

In the event a person falls under any of the following, such person shall be subject to incarceration for a period not more than three years, a fine of not more than JPY three million, or both.

(1) Any person who operates a Real Estate Syndication Enterprise without the license under Article 3, Paragraph 1 hereof;

(2) Any person who procures a license under Article 3, Paragraph 1 hereof by fraudulent means;

(3) Any person who violates Article 15 hereof and allows another person or juridical person to operate a Real Estate Syndication Enterprise; or

(4) Any person who violates an order for cessation of operations under the provisions of Article 35, Paragraph 1, Article 35, Paragraph 2, or Article 46, Paragraph 5 hereof.

Article 52-2

In the event of a violation of Article 39, Paragraph 1 of the MMFIEL, any representative, agent, person designated by cabinet ordinance and/or other employee of the Real Estate Syndication Enterprise Operator which committed such act shall be subject to incarceration for a period of not more than three years, a fine of not more than JPY three million, or both.

Article 53

In the event a person falls under any of the following, such person shall be subject to incarceration for a period of not more than one year, a fine of not more than JPY one million, or both.

(1) Any person who violates any of the conditions to licensing under Article 4, Paragraph 1 hereof;

(2) Any person who, in violation of Article 9, Paragraph 1, changes its Type of Operations and/or changes or adds to the Real Estate Syndication Contract Standard Terms and Conditions in Article 5, Paragraph 2, Item 4 hereof;

(3) Any person who intentionally withholds facts or relays false information in violation of Article 20, Paragraph 1 hereof;

(4) Any person who relays false information in violation of Article 20, Paragraph 2;

(5) Any person who violates the provisions of Article 39, Paragraph 2 of the MMFIEL; or

(6) Any person who, in violation of Article 22 hereof, makes loans in monetary form or in the form of negotiable securities, including acting for any third party as the agent, mediator or intermediary for loans in cash or negotiable securities.

Article 53-2

With respect to Article 53, Item 5 above, any profits of the person committing such violation, including any financial profits of third parties with knowledge of such violation, shall be confiscated. In the event it is not possible for such profits to be confiscated in whole or in part, a corresponding penalty shall be levied.

Article 54

In the event a person makes any representations which significantly deviate from fact or are likely to cause significant misunderstanding in violation of Article 18, Paragraph 3 hereof, such person shall be subject to incarceration for a period not more than six months, a fine of not more than JPY500,000, or both.

Article 55

Any person who commits any of the following acts shall be subject to a fine of not more than JPY500,000.

(1) Any person who submits fraudulent information in the application specified in Article 5, Paragraph 1 hereof or in any of the documents referred to in Article 5, Paragraph 2, Item1 through Item 5 hereof;

(2) Any person who submits fraudulent information in the application referred to in Article 8, Paragraph 1 hereof;

(3) Any person who sets up an office and/or fails to take the necessary corrective measures in violation of Article 17, Paragraph 3 hereof;

(4) Any person who fails to send the relevant document or report in violation of Article 24, Paragraph 1, Article 25, Paragraph 1, or Article 28, Paragraph 2 hereof, and/or any person who sends the relevant document or report containing fraudulent information and/or lacking required information;

(5) Any person who sends the document under Article 24, Paragraph 2 to an applicant to a Real Estate Syndication Contract without the requisite stamp and signature;

(6) Any person who sends the document under Article 25, Paragraph 2 to a party to a Real Estate Syndication Contract without the requisite stamp and signature;

(7) Any person who sends the document under Article 28, Paragraph 3 to an Enterprise Participant without the requisite stamp and signature; or

(8) Any person who fails to terminate employment of the relevant Operation Manager in violation of an order under the Article 37, Paragraph 1 or Article 37, Paragraph 2 hereof, and/or a person who reemploys an Operation Manager in violation of Article 37, Paragraph 1 (including *mutatis mutandis* application of Article 37, Paragraph 3).

Article 56

Any person who commits any of the following acts shall be subject to a fine of not more than JPY300,000.

(1) Any person who violates Article 10 hereof and fails to send the requisite notification, or sends the requisite notification with fraudulent information;

(2) Any person who violates Article 16, Paragraph 1 hereof;

(3) Any person who violates Article 16, Paragraph 2 hereof and displays the placard indicated in Article 16, Paragraph 1 or any similar placard;

(4) Any person who fails to prepare and maintain a Register of Operation Managers in violation of Article 17, Paragraph 2 hereof, and/or any person who prepares and maintains such register without all of the requisite matters and/or containing fraudulent matters;

(5) Any person who executes a Real Estate Syndication Contract which is not based on the Real Estate Syndication Contract Standard Terms and Conditions in violation of Article 23 hereof;

(6) Any person who fails to prepare and maintain the requisite documents under Article 29 hereof or fails to allow an Enterprise Participant to inspect such documents upon request, and/or any person who prepares and maintains such documents containing fraudulent matters or allows an Enterprise Participant to inspect any such documents which contain fraudulent matters;

(7) Any person who fails to prepare or maintain a Register of Enterprise Participants in violation of Article 30 or fails to allow an Enterprise Participant to inspect such register upon request, and/or any person who prepares or maintains a Register of Enterprise Participants which contains fraudulent matters or allows an Enterprise Participant to inspect any such register containing fraudulent matters;

(8) Any person who fails to prepare or maintain the books of account in violation of Article 32 hereof, or any person preparing or maintaining such books of account containing fraudulent matters;

(9) Any person who fails to prepare or submit a report on operations in violation of Article 33 hereof, or any person preparing or submitting such report on operations containing fraudulent matters;

(10) Any person who fails to report or submit the requisite documents in violation of an order under Article 40, Paragraph 1 hereof, any person reporting fraudulently or submitting documents containing fraudulent information pursuant to such an order, or any person refusing, obstructing or evading entry for an inspection under Article 40, Paragraph 1 hereof;

(11) Any person who uses in its name the words "Member of Association of Real Estate Syndication Enterprises" in violation of Article 42, Paragraph 2 hereof;

(12) Any person operating a Real Estate Syndication Enterprise who fails to send the requisite notification, or sends the requisite notification containing fraudulent information, in violation of Article 46, Paragraph 3 hereof; or

(13) Any person who fails to submit the requisite notification in violation of Article 46, Paragraph 4 hereof, or any person submitting such notification containing fraudulent matters.

Article 57

57.1 In the event the representative of a juridical person (including public foundations and non-profit corporations with rules in place for determining representatives or managers, the same in Article 57, Paragraph 2 below) or any employees, persons designated by cabinet ordinance, or agents of such juridical person violate any of the following Articles with respect to the assets or operations of such juridical person, such juridical person shall be subject to the following fines (in addition to the fines levied on the individuals committing such violations).

(1) Article 52-2 — a fine of not more than JPY300 million;

(2) Article 53 (Item 5) — a fine of not more than JPY100 million;

(3) Article 52, Article 53 Item (1) through Item (4), Item (6), and Article 54, Article 55, and Article 56, the fines designated in the relevant Articles

57.2 In the event the above Article 57, Paragraph 1 applies to a public foundation or non-profit corporation, in accordance with the juridical person's rules for dispute proceedings, the representative or manager of such non-juridical person public foundation or non-profit corporation will represent such non-juridical person public foundation or non-profit corporation, and in such event the legal rules for criminal procedure where a juridical person is the defendant or accused will apply *mutatis mutandis*.

Article 58

Any person who fails to submit the requisite notification in violation of Article 11, Paragraph 1 hereof, and/or any person submitting such notification containing fraudulent matters, shall be subject to a fine of not more than JPY one million.

Article 59

Any person who uses in its name the words "Association of Real Estate Syndication Enterprise" in violation of Article 42, Paragraph 1 hereof shall be subject to a fine of not more than JPY100,000.

-END-

Main Sources

1. *Takuchi tatemono torihiki no chishiki*, Kokudokoutsuushou Fudousangyouka, 2009.
2. *Kiso kara manabu fudousanjitsumu to kin'yuushouhin torihikihou*, Tanabe Nobuyuki, 2008.
3. *Fudousanshoukenka kyoukai ninteimastaa youseikouza tekisuto (101-105)*, Fudousanshoukenka Kyoukai, 2012.
4. *Derujuntakken takkengyouhou, kenrikankei, houreijou no seigen, zei, sonota*, Toukyou Riigarumaindo, 2009.
5. *Tanpo to hoshou no kihon to jitsumu ga wakaruhon*, Kamijikkoku Tetsuro, 2006.
6. *Takuchitatemono torihiki shuninsha takkengyouhou, kakushuhourei, sonota dokodemo sokushuu handobukku*, Shinfuku Yasutaka, 2005.
7. *Shoukai kaishahou no riron to jitsumu (dainihan)*, Tanabe Mitsumasa *et al*, 2007.
8. *Fudousanshoukenka handobukku*, Fudousanshoukenka Kyoukai, 2012.
9. *Fudousan nyuumon*, Nihonfudousan Kenkyuujo, 2004.
10. *Fudousan no houritsu chishiki*, Kamano Kuniki, 2005.
11. *Keesu de wakaru jissen CRE kigyoufudousan senryaku*, Moridaira Souichirou, 2007.
12. *Saishin fudousanfuando ga yoku wakaruhon*, Wakimoto Kazuya, 2007.
13. *Fudousan kin'yuu bijinesu no subete*, Izumo Toyohiro, 2006.
14. *Fudousanshoukenka no subete*, Mitsubishi UFJ Shintaku Ginkou Fudousan Konsaruteingubu, 2006.
15. *Takuchi tatemono torihiki shuninsha koushuu tekisuto*, Fudousan Ryuutsuu Kindaika Sentaa, 2008.
16. *Touroku jitsumu koushuu tekisuto,* Kokudokoutsuushou Sougou Seisakukyoku Fudousangyouka, 2007.
17. *Handobukku Fudousantokuteikyoudoujigyouhou*, Matsubayashi Hisayuki, 1997.
18. *Fudousantokuteikyoudoujigyou no gyoumukanrisha no jitsumu*, Fudousan Shinjikeeshiyon Kyougikai, 2000.
19. *Fudousan toushihandan no kiso kouza*, Ishibashi Katsuyoshi, 2008.

20. *TMK (tokutei mokuteki kaisha) no houritsu jitsumu Q&A*, Tsuchiya Toshihiko, 2009.
21. *2006 Naniga nandemo goukaku takken (jou) kenrikankei*, Waseda Seminar, 2005.
22. *Fudousanshoukenka no jissen*, Satou Kazuo, 2005.
23. *Zukai tochitatemono no houritsu*, Miki Kunihiro, 2008.
24. *Kiso kara yoku wakaru fudousanshoukenka gaidobukku*, Kokudokoutsuushou Sougou Seisakukyoku Fudousangyouka, 2008.
25. *Kaihatsugata Fudousanshoukenka no chishiki to jissai*, Kokudokoutsuushou Sougou Seisakukyoku Fudousangyouka, 2007.
26. *Fudousan torihiki kankeihou no kaisetsu*, Tanuma Masaki, 2005.
27. *Fudousan toukihou no kaisetsu*, Tanaka Minoru, 2008.
28. *Shakuchishakuyahou no kaisetsu*, Kumata Hiroyuki, 2008.
29. *Shisan/saiken no ryuudouka/shoukenka*, Nishimura Tokiwa Houritsujimusho, 2006.
30. *Fudousan no chousa/bunseki/hyouka no jitsumu*, Fudousantoushibunseki Kenkyuujo, 2007.
31. *SPC & tokumei kumiai no houritsu/kaikeizeimu to hyouka*, Nagasawa Tooru, 2005.
32. *Atarashii ryuudouka/shoukenka uiikuru no kiso to jitsumu*, Fujise Yuuji, 2006.
33. *Fudousan jitsumuhyakka Q&A*, Sugimoto Yukio, 2008.
34. *Fudousan torihiki no jitsumu*, Chiba Takashi, 2007.

About the Author

Jeff Wynkoop is a US attorney (Washington), CPA (Delaware) and certified Japanese Real Estate Transaction Manager (*takken*). He first came to Japan in 1990, and has studied Japanese and Japanese history at universities in Tokyo and Osaka. In addition to his native English, he is fluent in Japanese and German.

www.ingramcontent.com/pod-product-compliance
Lightning Source LLC
LaVergne TN
LVHW052311200926
848481LV00002B/530
9780988217409